PERSONALITY AND ADJUSTMENT IN THE AGED

R. D. SAVAGE, L. B. GABER, P. G. BRITTON
N. BOLTON and A. COOPER

1977

ACADEMIC PRESS
LONDON · NEW YORK · SAN FRANCISCO
A Subsidiary of Harcourt Brace Jovanovich, Publishers

ACADEMIC PRESS INC. (LONDON) LTD.
24/28 Oval Road
London NW1

United States Edition published by
ACADEMIC PRESS INC.
1111 Fifth Avenue
New York, New York 10003

Library of Congress Catalog Card Number: 77-76848
ISBN: 0-12-619550-1

Printed in Great Britain by W & G Baird Limited
Antrim, Northern Ireland

List of Authors

N. BOLTON, *Senior Lecturer in Psychology, University of Durham, Durham, England.*

P. G. BRITTON, *Lecturer in Applied Psychology, University of Newcastle upon Tyne, England.*

A. COOPER, *Community Clinical Psychologist, Social Services Department, London Borough of Newham, London, England.*

L. B. GABER, *Chief Psychologist, Department of Psychiatry, Rambam University Hospital, Haifa, Israel, formerly Senior Research Associate in Applied Psychology, University of Newcastle upon Tyne, England.*

R. D. SAVAGE, *Professor of Psychology, Murdoch University, Perth, Western Australia, formerly Senior Lecturer in Applied Psychology, University of Newcastle upon Tyne, England.*

List of Authors

Preface

There is no doubt that we owe our greatest debt and that we wish to express our sincere gratitude to the old people of Newcastle upon Tyne who so willingly and patiently gave their time and co-operation to this investigation. We trust that, in the long run, the knowledge gained will justify their efforts by helping society to provide more suitable facilities and a better way of life for its elderly citizens.

The investigation would have been impossible without the financial assistance given to us in the form of research grants to Professor Sir Martin Roth from the Department of Health and Social Security and the Medical Research Council between 1963–73. During that period, the interdisciplinary group of workers in the field of old age within the Department of Psychological Medicine at the University of Newcastle upon Tyne, England, included a number of psychiatrists, social workers, psychologists and administrative personnel. We are grateful for the assistance given to us by these colleagues and, in particular, for the help rendered by Dr K. Bergmann, Dr G. Blessed, Mr B. Geraghty, Miss D. Pidwell, Miss E. M. Foster and Miss S. O. Allison.

Special mention, however, must be made of the interest and major contribution to the old age research of Dr D. W. K. Kay, now Professor of Psychological Medicine at the University of Tasmania and Deputy of the M.R.C. Unit in Newcastle upon Tyne during this period.

March 1977   THE AUTHORS

Contents

1

Personality and Adjustment

Introduction

The definition and measurement of personality, particularly in terms of normality and abnormality in old age, present numerous, complex problems. This is reflected in the variety of approaches to the study of ageing and personality. Psychologists such as Havighurst and his colleagues (1953–1963) have tried to define and measure successful ageing on the basis of a study of public opinion concerning the activities of older people. Roth and his associates in the psychiatric literature (1955, 1971) have stressed the natural history and classification of mental disorders in old age based on clinical practice and methodology. The identification of gross psychiatric abnormalities and organic diseases in the aged has been immensely improved (Birren, 1959; Roth, 1955; Slater and Roth, 1969). Some, but far from sufficient, attention has been paid by psychologists to providing limited systematic theoretical models and empirical, factual evidence on personality in the elderly in terms of either multivariate dimensional analysis of personality characteristics or, in terms of the psychodynamic approach and explanation of the aged person.

Over the past 25 years, however, increasing concern has been shown to ageing and old age in terms of psychological or behavioural development generally. There have been a number of comprehensive reviews of various aspects of old age including those by Kubo (1938); Lorge (1941, 1944, 1956); Miles (1942); Kaplan (1945, 1956); Anderson (1949); Donahue (1949); Granick (1950); Shock (1951); Grewel

(1953); Watson (1954); Welford (1964, 1968) and Savage (1972). "The Handbook of Ageing and the Individual", edited by Birren (1959), and Anderson's (1956) "Psychological Aspects of Ageing" may be regarded as the initial attempts to organise the inaccessible and complex literature in this area, and research workers are considerably indebted to the "Annual Reviews of Psychology", in particular chapters by Shock (1951), Lorge (1956), Birren (1960), Chown and Heron (1965), and Botwinick (1970). Books by Cowdray (1939), "Problems of Ageing", Tibbit's "Living through the Older Years" (1949), Welford's "Ageing and Human Skill" (1958), Botwinick, "Cognitive Processes in Maturity and Old Age" (1967), Post, "The Clinical Psychiatry of Later Life" (1965), Slater and Roth, "Clinical Psychiatry" (1969), and Savage et al. (1973) "Intellectual Functioning in the Aged", to name a few, will be found useful to readers interested in the details of particular areas of research into and knowledge about the aged.

Even so, this work on the aged—spurred on perhaps more by actual or potential economic necessity than ethical or academic virtue—has a considerable way to go before we can be at all happy about the situation. Much more needs to be known before psychology can be even moderately satisfied with the contribution it should and could make to improving the welfare of our aged citizens in both developed and underprivileged countries or sub-cultures within our societies. In particular, the academic investigator and the clinical practitioner will both be impressed more by what is not available about personality measurement and functioning in the aged than by what is known.

In our investigations of the aged at the University of Newcastle upon Tyne, we have been interested, therefore, in the application of the dimensional analysis of personality characteristics by British and American schools of multivariate analysis, alongside the study of self concept and adjustment.

It would, perhaps, prove helpful to our understanding of the aged and to the role of the Newcastle upon Tyne investigations to be reported here to present the reader with an overview of the situation as and when we began our studies in 1963, as well as to discuss where appropriate some of the work published whilst we were doing these investigations. This is the subject matter of Chapter 1.

Chapter 2 will set out the research methodology used in, or perhaps it would be better to say, emerging from the series of investigations.

Hindsight is perhaps painful in these situations, but, for the benefit of future research, we have recorded in that chapter exactly what happened. The influence of practical situations on theoretical requirements are only too obvious, but future investigations may well profit from our mistakes.

Chapter 3 deals with what can be classified as some personality characteristics of the Community Aged and their measurements. Data on some personality categories and dimensions in mentally ill aged and those needing special care are presented in Chapter 4. Finally, an approach to the analysis of the structure and types of personality in the aged and the implications of this work is discussed (Chapter 5).

This book then attempts to make some contribution to the measurement and understanding of personality in the aged for, as Professor P. B. Medawar (1955), in his address to a Ciba Foundation Colloquia on Ageing, stated "nothing is clearer evidence of the immaturity of gerontological science than the tentative and probationary character of its systems of definitions and measurements."

Personality Measurement

The problems of personality in the aged have been approached from a number of points of view. In reviewing previous work we shall concentrate upon four major bodies of literature—(i) personality measurement, (ii) adjustment, (iii) self concept and (iv) mental illness in the aged.

The identification, description, and presentation of adequate psychometric techniques for the measurement of personality in the aged has lagged behind that of cognitive assessment in the elderly. The development of more adequate personality assessment procedures by Cattell, Eysenck and others gives hope for the future, but one cannot help but be disappointed by the small amount of research so far with old people. It was felt, however, when planning this research that a *rapprochement* between the apparently antagonistic views on adjustment, personality and mental illness in old age may well come from a more thorough understanding of the characteristics of the aged in terms of the dimensions of personality or personality types identifiable from psychometric investigations.

Emotionality or neuroticism was one of the first most important personality characteristics of the elderly to receive the attention of investigators. Willoughby in 1938 concluded that neuroticism increased significantly between the sixth and eighth decades of life. He suggested that old age was one of the periods of greatest stress for both sexes, married or single, and noted the important, but often forgotten point, that the diagnostic significance of a particular behaviour or scores on test items may vary significantly with age. However, even now, few methods of measuring personality have any, let alone satisfactory, normative data for the elderly. The personality theorists have given little or no attention to changes in old age or even to adequately describing old age personality until very recently. Watson, in a review of the situation in 1954, suggested that research of personality in the elderly was in a naturalistic, exploratory stage rather than at a theoretically or experimentally based level.

The developmental changes accompanying increasing age were mentioned rather briefly by Rorschach (1942), who commented that "the older individual loses the capacity for introversion and becomes coartated or constricted". He described further influences of age as an increase in stereotype and a decrease in the freedom of associations, and claimed that the protocols of normal subjects 70 to 80 years of age closely resembled those of cases of dementia simplex.

A study by Klopfer (1946) reported the results of individual examinations of 50 people over 60 years of age, 30 of whom were institutionalised and 20 of whom lived outside an institution. Their capacity for making use of inner resources seemed diminished, and emotional responsiveness tended either to be egocentric and labile or highly restricted. The ability to establish satisfactory relationships with others was considerably reduced. Klopfer also mentioned that, while there were some differences between his institutionalised and non-institutionalised samples, the patterns suggested more similarities than differences between the two groups.

Another Rorschach study was reported by Prados and Fried (1947) who examined 35 persons ranging in age from 50 to 80 years and reported results in terms of trends for the three decades. By this division, they hoped to learn something about the evolution of changes in personality structure. Their findings were similar to those of Klopfer, except for their observation of greater productivity and more frequent use of both movement and colour. They suggested that with increasing age, impoverishment of the creative intellectual faculties occurred, with the oldest subjects resigned to this deficit, but the younger groups still showing some anxiety about it. They also stated that the capacity for emotional responsiveness and control over instinctual demands diminished with age, resulting in a return to some of the primitive manifestations of early childhood.

Davidson and Kruglov (1952), who were concerned only with institutionalised subjects, administered the Rorschach to 46 men and women, ranging in age from 61 to 91. Means of the various scoring categories were reported for the total group and for the younger and older subgroups. In addition, the authors scored all the protocols on the 17 Davidson adjustment signs which had been established on younger groups. The personality characteristics of this elderly group were listed as decreased productivity and drive, faulty perception of reality, bizarre thought processes, and decreased capacity for creative and original thinking. Emotional responsiveness was diminished, and general adjustment was less adequate than that found in younger subjects, with the women showing better adjustment than the men. The outstanding formal attributes of the records upon which these interpretations were based included low numbers of responses, over-emphasis of form responses, relatively few movement responses, extreme paucity of responses to colour, and a limited range of interests. However, their conclusion that the group showed less adequate adjustment than younger groups may be open to question, as in their sample the average number of adjustment signs was 8 out of 17, while in younger samples it has been found to be 9, a difference of only one point. Caldwell's (1954) paper presents similar results for 47 women aged 61 to 92 with a mean IQ of 85. She comments:

"A comparison of the similarity in test protocols as reported by the various investigators provides one method of evaluating the Rorschach for use in personality research with the aged. That is, the fact that different samples have yielded roughly comparable quantitative results indicates that whatever is being measured appears with a fairly respectable degree of consistency. One can say little, however, of the quantitative accuracy of the data in terms of evaluating personality in the aged. Furthermore, the titles of the three studies reviewed, namely, 'Personality Patterns of Old Age', 'Personality Structure of the Older Age Groups', and 'Personality Characteristics of the Institutionalised Aged', respectively, clearly illustrate how Rorschach findings are assumed to be synonymous with personality characteristics. It is significant to note that none of the studies stated as its explicit purpose the establishment of norms for older groups, although it is highly probable that this was implicit in all of them. Logically, it would seem that this should come first."

Light and Amick (1956) presented a paper on Rorschach responses in normal aged, and follow-up studies have been published by Ames (1960*a*, *b*) and Vinson (1961). Both suggested that personality changes with age in the aged. Sixty-one elderly subjects aged 70 to 102 were retested by Ames after a four- to five-year period. A restriction in the number of responses, decreased variety of content, less use of colour, but increased F and M type responses were reported. Vinson's work showed that 20 geriatric patients without organic brain damage became more stimulus bound, but still had adequate emotional adjustment after one year.

The conclusions given in all the studies, as well as the meaning implied in the titles, have reflected this willing transposition of the assumed rationale of the Rorschach scoring categories for younger into the older age groups. Implicit in all the investigations is the fact that more credit has been given to the integrity of the test than to the integrity of the subjects. That is, the assumption is made that the rationale of the test variables does not change with age and, since different profiles are found at different age levels, these must represent change within the individual. This may well be true, but in view of the lack of conclusive evidence, it seems that one should more parsimoniously assume that either is equally plausible.

The Thematic Apperception Test (Murray, 1943) (TAT) has also been used on the aged in an effort to describe and understand their personality. A series of studies from the Kansas City project followed up the work of Peck (1956), Peck and Berkowitz (1959), and others who had not found statistically significant age differences in the analysis of ratings of flexibility, collection, mental flexibility, ego transcendence, body transcendences, body satisfaction or sexual integration from six TAT cards with 40- to 64-year-olds. Neugarten (1965) argued that the same information from the TAT given by a 40- or a 70-year-old may have a very different meaning. She investigated 131 working and middle-class men and women 40 to 70 years of age. The older person felt that the world was more complex and dangerous, and that he or she was passively manipulated by it. The elderly felt that they were no longer in control of the situation; ego qualities were contracted and turned inward. Sex differences were also seen. A further study by Gutmann and co-workers (1959) using four standard TAT cards on over 60-year-olds suggested that these men had resolved many conflicts, stories were conforming, friendly, and mild. Aggression was ascribed only to the external world.

In their 1960 study, Rosen and Neugarten looked at the hypothesis that four dimensions of ego functioning diminish in effectiveness with age. The Thematic Apperception Test was used on 144 subjects aged 40 to 71 years divided by age, sex, and social class; the older subjects showed fewer extra characteristics in their stories, used less conflict, less strong emotion, and described less vigorous activities. Neugarten (1963) concluded that personality does change significantly with age to give way to passive mastery of the situation in 60- to 70-year-olds and that important sex differences remain. Lakin and Eisdorfer (1960) showed a similar pattern of personality in the aged with the Reitman stick figures and Dean (1962), in her questionnaire investigation of 200 aged men, 50 to 95, also commented on the decrease in emotional responsiveness, anger, and imitation with age. However, the studies of aged on the MMPI, 16PF, and MPI to be discussed in detail later suggest that average or normative levels of emotionality, anxiety, and the like are increased in old age. It is possible that the average levels of emotionality are high, though they may not show themselves in the same type of emotional behaviour as seen at younger age levels.

Recent years have seen the introduction of psychometric personality questionnaires into research on old age personality measurement. This work is still in its infancy, for the practical and financial difficulties in this area of investigation are considerable. Indeed, the available data are far from adequate. The Minnesota Multiphasic Personality Inventory has been used in most of the investigations and has highlighted the need for caution when applying tests to the aged that have not been specifically standardised on the appropriate populations. Application of this large inventory, which measures several basic psychopathological aspects of personality, (*see* Chapter 2) to old people is in itself a somewhat difficult task and no doubt accounts for the limited extent of publication in this area, though one has the impression that the MMPI enjoys extensive clinical use, particularly in the USA.

Hathaway and McKinley (1951) reported that on D and Pt scales the mean of their 56- to 65-year-old male sample of 13 deviated from the mean of the general population standardisation group. MMPI T

re presented by Calden and Hokanson (1959) on 15 TB
ged 60 to 69 along with these for younger age groups. They
significant elevation of Hs, D and Si scaled scores in the old
le and stressed the need for age-related normative data.

Several investigations have been interested in personality changes
with age on the MMPI (Brozek, 1955; Aaronson, 1958, 1960, 1964;
Calden and Hokanson, 1959; Coppinger *et al.* 1963; Edwards and
Wine, 1963; Hardyck, 1964), but have presented only limited normative data on samples beyond 65 years of age. The study by Brozek
used men falling into two age groups; students 17 to 25 years, and
business and professional men 45 to 55. He chose these age groups, as
he believed it was necessary to study personality throughout the life
span, rather than gross differences between young and very old.

On most of the scales the older group answered a somewhat larger
number of items in the diagnostic direction. The older men scored
more highly on the "neurotic triad" scales Hs (hyperchondriasis),
D (depression) and Hy (hysteria), and also on the Pa (paranoia) scale.
The younger men scored higher than the older men on three scales:
Pt (psychasthenia), Sc (schizophrenia) and Ma (mania). These results
are expressed in terms of number of items scored in the diagnostic
direction.

Mean scores for the Hy and Si (social introversion) scales were
computed for each age group. The younger men showed somewhat
lower mean scores on both scales, but the difference reached significance only for the Introversion Scale. These results were compared
with the norms for the general adult population, and the differences
were not regarded as significant.

Brozek concluded that the obtained differences between younger
and older men were not sufficient to warrant a consideration of age in
setting up norms for clinical use. He seemed to prefer, however, a more
"psychologic" than "psychometric" analysis of the data. Items which
distinguished between the young and older men at a five per cent level
of significance were assigned to "personality areas" on the basis of
inspection and subjective judgement. These areas were as follows:
health (16 items), interests (16 items), attitudes to sex (8 items), work
(6 items), religious attitudes (7 items), emotional adjustment (32
items), self-confidence (12 items), compulsive-obsessive tendencies
(12 items), norms of conduct (17 items) and social attitudes (17 items).
It was felt that there were too many items here, and that factor analysis

might be used to unravel the relationship between items and isolate the main dimensions by which a parsimonious description of personality might be obtained. Some factor analytic studies of the MMPI have, indeed, been carried out, and will be described later, insofar as they have implications for personality in the aged.

In 1964, Hardyck reported a study of female subjects which was devised in a manner such as to make its findings comparable with those Brozek (1955) obtained with male subjects. Hardyck used college and adult female subjects comparable to Brozek's, and found 93 items which discriminated between these groups at the ten per cent level. The items were easily classified into the personality areas used by Brozek. Although the degree of item overlap between the present 93 and Brozek's 141 items was not large, an examination of content revealed characterisations very similar to those of Brozek's personality areas. The similarities between Hardyck's older females and Brozek's older males far outweighed the differences; the same finding applied to comparison of the younger subjects.

On the clinical scales, Hardyck's female older group scored significantly higher than the young group on the Hs and Hy scales and significantly lower on the F and Ma scales.

Calden and Hokanson (1959) investigated personality among 160 male tuberculosis patients ranging in age from 20 to 69, as part of a wider study of TB patients. The MMPI was administered during the first month of hospitalisation. All clinical and validity scales, as well as the Taylor Anxiety Scale, were examined by means of analysis of variance between groups defined in terms of age decades. Scales which manifested significant change with age were the Hs, D and Si scales. Change was in the direction of an increase with age. Again the trend is toward increasing preoccupation with oneself, both physically and mentally, as age increases.

Calden and Hokanson did not find the elevations on certain scales among the younger men that were found in Brozek's (1955) younger group. But Calden and Hokanson did regard the elevations on the scales among the older men to be of an order such as to warrant the development of appropriate norms for different age groups.

Canter *et al.* (1962) felt, however, that Calden and Hokanson's sample could not truly be regarded as a "normal" one. Canter and co-workers drew samples for each age decade group between 20 and 70 from employed males. The form of the MMPI used excluded Scale

Si. No subject had a known psychiatric disorder. Unfortunately, too few Ss were obtained for the 60–69 group and those that were, were combined with the 50–59 group.

Analysis of variance was carried out and a trend toward an increase on the D scale with age was examined. The median D scorers for the different age groups did not, however, differ significantly. Similarly, median tests for significance of differences on all the MMPI scales between the youngest and the oldest groups yielded negative results. Nor were there any significant differences found between the three-digit high codes of profiles in each age group. The D scale did, however, appear to occur somewhat more frequently among the first three-digit codes of the two oldest groups, and it seemed to displace the Pd scale after age 40. Thus there did appear to be a trend toward greater concern with failing self among older adults.

Using the Cornell Medical Index and a Morale Loss Index, Canter *et al.* (1962) examined the question of vulnerability to depression. They showed that when CMI level was high there was only a tendency toward increase in Hs and D scores; but a significant increase in scores on these scales was found when Morale Loss scores were high. These tendencies operated regardless of age.

Canter *et al.* (1962) felt that the contribution of age to the vulnerability to depression was not clear. Calden and Hokanson (1959) had shown that age appeared to accentuate the trend among persons subject to disease. The present results suggested that age does not contribute to elevations on the scales when disease is absent.

Canter *et al.* (1962) concluded that their results could not be regarded as supporting the call for age corrections for MMPI score norms. The elevations on the Hs and D scales appeared to be related to illness, or attitudes to health. Since older adults are more likely to be subject to ill-health, such elevations are perhaps not surprising.

The work of Aaronson (1958; 1960; 1964) on an MMPI ageing index also highlights the need for information about personality in old age. The first full-scale attempt to present normative data on the aged was by Swenson (1961) who reported on the validity and basic clinical scales of the MMPI from the records of 95 subjects of both sexes, aged over 60. He also criticised the representativeness of Calden and Hokanson's (1959) sample, noting that it included only 15 subjects over 60 years of age. Swenson described an MMPI study of 95 subjects over 60 years. Subjects came from three separate sources; Golden Age Clubs, homes for the aged, and places of employment. No subject with a known mental disorder intense enough to be accorded a psychiatric diagnosis was included. The subjects from the homes for the aged were generally physically incapacitated. Swenson found that the Hs, D, Hy and Si scales were the most frequently occurring high point scales for both sexes. The Pd and Ma scales were conspicuous by their absence as high points, although the original normative data for the MMPI showed them to appear relatively frequently among normal adults. Comparison of the normative group and the geriatric sample indicated greater statistical abnormality in the latter.

There were sex differences in pattern; high points for the males were Hy, D, Hs and Si, with Hy occurring most frequently; while for the females the scales are reversed in rank with Si being the most frequent high point. It was concluded that the typical profile for his sample of non-hospitalised aged is a neurotic one, with an absence of psychotic or behaviour disorder tendencies. Thus his findings are essentially comparable with those already cited.

Kornetsky (1963) adminstered the MMPI to 43 aged males and found significant elevations on the D and Mf scales. This tendency for a rise in D scale score with advancing age had also been reported by Canter et al. (1962).

Since our Newcastle upon Tyne studies of the aged began, a number of other people have entered the arena. In 1967, after our investigations had begun, Postema and Schell conducted a study of in-patients in a psychiatric hospital in order to compare them with Swenson's normal sample. Postema and Schell used male subjects; an older sample of average age 68·2 years and a young sample of average age 34·7 years. The two groups were comparable in terms of psychiatric diagnoses. The MMPI data were analysed in terms of a Neurotic Index, consisting of the neurotic triad scales Hs, D and Hy; and a Psychotic Index composed of scales Pa, Pt, Sc and Ma. The indices were derived by calculating average T scores on the three and four scales respectively.

The results were compared with data derived from Swenson's (1961) sample. Swenson's normal old and the present psychiatric old samples showed significantly higher mean scores on the Neurotic than on the Psychotic Index. Among the young subjects, the difference between the indices was in keeping with a chance occurrence.

The normal subjects scored significantly lower on both indices than the two psychiatric groups. The young psychiatric subjects scored significantly higher on the Psychotic Index than did the old psychiatric subjects. When all three samples were compared with the MMPI standardisation group it was clear that—except for the normal sample on the Psychotic Index—all three samples were higher on both indices to a significant degree.

Postema and Schell's (1967) results therefore confirm earlier findings that older people inclined to a greater neuroticism than young people. This appears to be the case among psychiatric patients just as among normal persons.

Earlier, Aaronson (1960) had demonstrated personality differences with age among an abnormal—psychiatric—population, using an index based on the relative distributions of peaks on the MMPI scales of Hs, D, Pd, Pt and Sc. The index has a mid-point of 50 and varies inversely with age. It is known as the Aging Index. (AgI). Sixty-six persons ranging in age from 16 to 65 completed a valid MMPI, and the AgI was computed for each profile. It was correlated with age at the time of taking the test.

The mean index value was 79 and it correlated -0.5 with age, which was significant beyond the one per cent level. Since 26 of the cases had schizophrenic or psychopathic diagnoses and were thought likely to weight on the scales suggestive of youth, they were removed from the sample. The correlation between the index and age for these two groups combined was not significant, but increased to -0.79. Even when further cases were removed, leaving a sample of 23 cases only, the correlation was still -0.67.

Consideration of the component scales of the index revealed that younger patients showed elevations on the Pd, Pt and Sc scales, while older patients were characterised by elevations on Hs and D. It was hypothesised that the index reflected a transition from concern with control over impulses which might impinge on society, to concern with one's physical and mental health. Thus the ageing index may be conceived of as a measure of "psychological age". It will be noted that the index utilises scores on scales composing Postema and Schell's (1967) Psychotic and Neurotic Indices.

In 1964, Aaronson reported the use of the AgI to study the question of whether ageing might exert its effects upon aspects of personality common to all, or whether its implications are specific to individuals. Correlations between the AgI and chronological age were computed for 98 persons with varied diagnoses and who ranged in age between

15 and 65 years. The ten MMPI clinical scales and a number of derived scales were also correlated with age. The only variable which correlated significantly with age was the AgI. When the six diagnostic groups were combined into a total group, the only variable which was favoured by such a combination was the AgI.

Aaronson felt that the fact that the AgI maintained a high relationship with age under heterogeneous conditions, lends support to the hypothesis that ageing affects personality in a manner common to all. Since the index seems to reflect increasing self-preoccupation, Aaronson regarded his findings as upholding the predictions of disengagement theory. We may recall, however, the distinction drawn by Neugarten (1964) between intrapsychic and socio-adaptational aspects of personality, and their differential response to ageing. It does not seem clear which aspect Aaronson's index is tapping.

It was again a psychiatric population from which Gynther and Shimkunas (1966) drew their sample of 420 subjects ranging from 14 to 76 years. They were primarily interested in the relationship between age and intelligence, as it might affect MMPI responses. Intelligence was measured in terms of the Wechsler Scale.

Product-moment correlations between age, IQ, education, and MMPI scales were examined for any differences attributable to sex. The only significant difference between male and female subjects was in the correlations between age and the Pd scale, but since 36 correlations were considered one might be expected by chance to differ significantly with sex. Thus the sexes were combined for subsequent analyses.

The only MMPI scale responsive to the effects of both age and intelligence was the F scale. Scales significantly influenced by age alone were the Pd, Ma, Pa and Sc scales. The scores on these scales decrease with age; a result consistent with the findings of other studies.

Mf scale results indicated that the admission of "feminine" interests was positively related to intelligence and education in both sexes, while L scores were negatively related to the same.

Partial and multiple correlations were obtained in order to assess the relative and combined contributions of age and IQ to scale scores. The two variables again appeared to have relatively independent effects.

Gynther and Shimkunas noted that when profiles were coded, older patients obtained more peak scores on the Hs, D, Hy and Pt scales than the younger patients, whereas these latter showed an over-representation of peaks on the Pd, Pa, Sc and Ma scales. These findings are again consistent with those of earlier studies. However, in the age-scale correlations, elevations on the Hs, D, Hy and Pt scales had not been found with increasing age.

Directing their attention to the D scale results, Gynther and Shimkunas carried out a number of tests of the validity of their finding that D scale scores did not change with age. They concluded that this was a valid result, and explained it in terms of peak scores appearing higher due to age-linked decreases on other scales, rather than because scores had, in fact, been elevated.

Thus, although the results of this study are essentially comparable with findings already cited, Gynther and Shimkunas offer an alternative explanation.

An interesting study has recently been reported by Uecker (1969) on the comparability of two methods of administering the MMPI to brain-damaged geriatric patients. The two methods of card form and oral presentation, given to 30 highly selected elderly male patients with a diagnosis of chronic brain syndrome, did not result in any significant scale differences. However, the test-retest reliability was very low, correlations ranging from $0 \cdot 43$ to $0 \cdot 70$ and the author concluded that the use of the MMPI on elderly brain-damaged patients was not justified. It might be interesting to add here that an attempt by Britton and Savage to administer the Cattell (1970) 16PF scale to 20 elderly people living in the community, but diagnosed "organic" was even less successful; only 6 were able to complete the inventory, even though it was read to them.

There are, however, other considerations to be taken into account when assessing the value of the MMPI as an instrument for assessing old age personality. What is the structure of personality it measures?

We noted earlier that Brozek (1955) had commented that factor analysis of the MMPI might be useful in isolating the main dimensions by which a parsimonious description of personality might be achieved. Indeed, in 1959 Kassebaum, Couch and Slater reported the results of a factor analytic study of the MMPI as used with 160 college students. Thirty-two MMPI scales were administered, thus including 19 non-clinical scales. Thurstone's centroid method was utilised, with rotation to simple orthogonal structure. Two main factors were elicited. The first, accounting for 39 per cent of the total variance, was named Ego Weakness. Scales Pt and Sc loaded highly and positively on Factor I.

The second factor, accounting for 10 per cent of the variance, had a high positive loading on Si and a negative loading on Ma, and was identified as Introversion-extraversion. A third factor accounted for 5 per cent of the total variance, and loaded highly on Hy—and, indeed, on the whole neurotic triad. Its interpretation was not clear, however, and it was tentatively named Tender-minded Sensitivity.

Two further factors were elicited. These were defined as the vectors lying midway between the primary references axes, and since they might be conceived of as the combinations of the primary factors, they were termed "fusion factors". Fusion factor A was defined as Social Withdrawal versus Social Participation—Si and D loaded positively upon it. Fusion factor B, on which Ma loaded positively, was interpreted as Impulsivity versus Intellectual Control.

Kassebaum et al. (1959) suggested that the two primary factors might be likely to emerge from any factor analysis of the personality sphere.

In 1964, Slater and Scarr published the findings of a study conducted on 211 subjects of mean age 65·9 years. The subjects were drawn from a population of high socio-economic status. Analysis was accomplished by the centroid method with rotation to orthogonal structure in order to facilitate comparison with the Kassebaum et al. (1959) study.

Four factors were extracted for both male and female subjects, but since there was close similarity between the two sets of factors, the results for male subjects only are reported here. Factor I was identified as Ego Weakness and accounted for 32 per cent of the variance. Factor III, covering 15 per cent of the variance, was an Extraversion-Introversion factor. Factor IV showed some resemblance to Kassebaum et al. (1959) third factor of sensitivity. Factor II also showed similarities with the sensitivity factor, and with the sensitivity factor identified by Fisher, in an unpublished study (1957). Slater and Scarr's Factor II, however, also loaded on all the main components of Fisher's Factor V, which was a general pathological factor. Slater and Scarr hypothesised that this Factor II reflected a general lack of integration and they labelled it as "Dissociated Personality". It accounted for 8 per cent of the variance.

Comparing the two studies, Slater and Scarr concluded that structural changes in personality did not appear to occur with age, so far as the dimensions of Ego Weakness and Introversion are concerned.

Fusion factors were extracted. Two fusion factors A and B, to associate primary factors I and II, seemed only plausible. Fusion factors C and D, associating Factors I and III, seemed valid.

Slater and Scarr (1964) then turned their attention to age-related changes in level on personality dimensions, noting that Brozek (1955) alone had investigated the commonly hypothesised increase in introversion by means of an MMPI study. Slater and Scarr used male subjects only for this analysis. They applied t-tests to all common scales, and then used the pooling-square technique to examine the loadings of scales which consistently discriminated between the present sample and a number of samples of younger men. In this manner, the location of an ageing vector was determined. The ageing vector was located not, as had been expected, on the Extraversion-Introversion dimension, but on Fusion Factor C. This fusion factor united Factors I and III in a manner such as to create a dimension of Impulsivity versus Intellectual Control, comparable to Kassebaum's Fusion factor B. The younger men clustered toward the Impulsivity pole and the older men toward the Control pole of the dimension.

To test whether these differences in level applied to individuals or to the populations, Slater and Scarr conducted a pilot study of the "Quick and the Dead". Eight pairs of subjects were located; in each pair one subject was deceased whereas the other had lived at least one year longer since the administration of the MMPI. They carried out t-tests of the differences between test-score means on all four primary factors. Differences between the pair members occurred on Factors I, where the deceased scored higher, and II, where they scored lower, suggesting that Fusion factor C would, indeed, express most parsimoniously the differences between the two samples.

A general pathological factor had emerged from an analysis by Coppinger, Bortner and Saucer (1963) in a study of patients suffering from either physical or psychiatric illness and ranging from 26 to 69 years of age. A battery of measures was used which included the MMPI. Nine factors were extracted, only two of which showed age-relatedness. One was a factor of sensory alertness. Another was termed "Deviations in behavioural controls" and loaded on the Ma, Pt, Pa and Sc scales, and appeared to reflect the garrulousness and uncertainty of control over behaviour found among the older subjects.

The factorial studies of the MMPI by Kassebaum and associates (1959) have provided a basis for comparison of structure across a wide age range. With the use of factor-analytic procedures that facilitated comparison of results, a basic similarity of structure was found between young and old samples. The major factors of "ego weakness *vs* ego strength" and "introversion *vs* extraversion" appeared in both analyses. However, in the aged, a factor of "dissociated personality", with a strong somatic emphasis was interpolated between the above factors. This finding is of interest in the context of personality change with age suggested by Birren (1964). Successful personality adaptation in old age is thought to depend on a relationship between stable, long-term components of personality, rather than on those components that are more sensitive to the ageing processes. In old age a somatic emphasis might be expected in the latter, reflecting physiological change. This could be evident in MMPI factor-analyses as a factor similar to the "dissociated personality" identified by Slater and Scarr (1964). However, the aged sample used by Slater and Scarr, although obtained from a non-hospitalised, normal population, was biased towards subjects of high socio-economic status and was thus not wholly representative.

Social introversion may represent a dimension of personality where psychological and social factors are closely interrelated. We have seen that no conclusive evidence has emerged as to whether or not this characteristic is more often present in older people, despite the commonly accepted assumption that this is the case. Perhaps one of the earliest studies of the effect of age upon this dimension was conducted by Gray in 1947, with a questionnaire designed specifically to tap Jung's personality traits. Gray used one thousand subjects, ranging from 10 to 80 years in age. He found, among other trends, a definite decrease in extraversion with age.

A more intensive examination of the question was performed by Craik in 1964. Craik used the Heron Inventory, a two-part personality measure giving scores on the two dimensions of emotional adjustment and sociability. A preliminary study had indicated age differences in the relationship of these two dimensions, despite the fact that they were held to be independent by Heron.

Accordingly, Craik examined the responses of a larger sample of 240 men ranging from 20 to 79 years of age. Correlations between adjustment and sociability were computed for each decade group and then for 5-year groups. A consistent pattern emerged, whereby the two dimensions were strongly positively associated among the youngest subjects, but the association decreased with age until there was a negligible relationship among those over 60 years of age. This tendency for the relationship to decline with age was found to be statistically significant. However, no age trend was found among the same number of female subjects.

Thus the results for the male sample were scrutinised. The trend could not be accounted for in terms of non-verbal intelligence, nor by age-related differences in item response or reliability. Nor did the proportions of well- or poorly-adjusted subjects change with age group. What was found was that among the youngest subjects the greatest maladjustment was associated with unsociability, whereas among older subjects the tendency was for maladjustment to be related to sociability. Much the same trend existed for the female subjects, but there was no such markedness of difference between young and old.

Craik (1964) was obliged to conclude that his study left the issue open to question, but he did feel that his results raised the possibility of personality change with age, and also highlighted the need for caution in using tests standardised on younger groups.

Cameron (1967) noted the fact that some theorists, especially the adjustment theorists, have regarded the characteristics of introversion and egocentricity as co-existent. Cumming and Henry (1961), for example, tend to make this assumption. Cameron used the Eysenck Personality Inventory (1963) to measure introversion, and his own technique of consciousness sampling to assess egocentricity among three aged samples (over 59 years) and a young sample (18–40 years). The aged subjects were drawn from their own homes, co-operative apartments, and a hospital.

Those aged females who were residing in their own homes were clearly more introverted than their younger counterparts. Aged females residing in co-operative apartments were as extraverted as the young subjects. Hospitalised female subjects were more introverted than all but the aged females living in their own homes.

Male subjects falling into the same groups exhibited no such trends. They showed no differences with regard to egocentricity also. Among the females, the young group were the least egocentric, and less so than the young males. The hospitalised aged females were less egocentric than their male counterparts, but on the whole the aged females evidenced only a slight tendency toward greater other-centredness than the males.

Thus both dimensions do appear to increase with age among the female subjects. The finding does not apply to male subjects. As with Craik's (1964) results, the differences by sex—in the opposite direction, incidentally—leave the issue undecided. Moreover, Cameron found that the females residing in the co-operative apartments were at the same time the most extraverted aged group.

The paucity of studies on the aged with Cattell's and Eysenck's well-developed measures of personality assessment is of some considerable concern. Lynn in 1964 discussed the implications of Eysenck's theory of personality and age. He argues that the behaviour of older persons is like that of extraverts on a number of laboratory tests, but that their behaviour patterns are like those of introverts.

When we began our investigations of the elderly in 1963, no normative data on the Eysenckian or Cattellian approaches to the measurement of personality were available. Byrd (1959) had suggested that anxiety increased with age on Cattell's measure. The subjects were of both sexes, living in the community at various levels of socio-economic status. The median age was 75. Byrd assessed his data in relation to Cattell's findings that a high level of anxiety obtains in adolescence, declines rapidly until the 40's and then more slowly up to the sixth decade (Cattell, 1957).

The scores on five of the six primary factors loading on Anxiety were indicative of an increase with age over 65 years. Factor Q3, the controlling aspect of anxiety, manifested no change. Thus Byrd concluded that the maturational course of anxiety reverses in old age. Older people appear to experience what might be regarded as a "second adolescence" which is, however, more controlled than the original.

Sealy (1965) used the 16PF on several thousand Americans aged between 16 to 70, but separate data for the aged are not available. It was suggested, however, that men and women become more depressed and gloomy (F), more adventurous and outgoing (H), more unconventional (M) and more tough-minded (I) with age. Sex differences also emerged—the women became less dominant (E), the men more radical. Sealey also described interesting pre- and post-four-year-old patterns of change.

Four years later, in 1969, Goodwin and Schaie reiterated the comment that there was a paucity of studies of personality changes with age. They attributed this to the fact that questionnaires do not lend themselves to studies where participation is voluntary and set themselves that task of discovering whether information otherwise collected might yield scores in terms of Cattell's primary factors.

Schaie and Strother (1968) had devised a 75-item rigidity-flexibility questionnaire which contained many masking items. Data had been collected for over a thousand subjects, covering the age range 21 to 75 years, who constituted a stratified random sample. Since the sample was so representative, and the data had been obtained at one point in time, an attempt was made to retrieve the variance on other personality dimensions which might be contained in the questionnaire.

The rigidity questionnaire was administered to 271 college students, who also completed Form B of the 16PF. The questionnaire items were regressed on all 16 personality factors, and regression equations computed for 13 factors for which the multiple correlations between questionnaire items and factor scores exceeded 0.50. Thus scores on the 13 factors could be indirectly obtained for the larger sample to whom the 75-item questionnaire had earlier been administered.

The factors which showed an increase over the age span were self-sufficiency (Q_2), self-sentiment (Q_3) and guilt-proneness (O). This last showed a significant sex difference, with women scoring higher on self-sufficiency. Factors E (Dominance) and Q_4 (Ergic tension) showed decreases with age. Men tended to score higher on Dominance than women, but the scores of the two sexes tend to converge with increasing age.

Three factors manifested a curvilinear U-shaped trend, declining over the middle years, followed by an increase and then a further decline after age 65. These factors were A (warm vs aloof), H (adventurous vs shy) and L (suspicious vs secure). The results for factor H differ from those reported by Sealy and Cattell at the British Social Psychology Conference in 1965; they had found an increase on factor H through age 55.

No significant differences with age appeared on factors C (ego-strength, G (super-ego strength), I (tender vs toughmindedness), M (autia vs praxemia) or F (surgency). Again, differences are to be found from Sealy and Cattell's findings; they reported age-related increases on factors C, G and M, and a decrease on F.

Goodwin and Schaie's (1969) results on the second-order factors of Introversion and Anxiety are in agreement with those of Sealy and Cattell (1965), the trends being toward increasing introversion and decreasing anxiety with increasing age.

Cattell, *et al.* (1970) report results so far available from the work of Sealy and Cattell on age norms.

The corrections may be applied to raw scores before entering the norms. They are, however, more directly relevant to research than to clinical work, since if the correction is not greater than $0 \cdot 5$ of a raw unit, it will not alter the sten score.

As may be seen in the table, not all corrections apply throughout the life span. Those trends which do appear to continue into the later years are as follows: a decrease on Factor F (surgency) for both sexes; an increase on Factor M (autia) for men only; a slight increase on Factor Q (radicalism) for males only; and a slight increase on Q_3 (integration) for both sexes.

The more general tendency is for the age of 35 years to be point of inflexion. It is reported that research is presently being directed toward the task of separating the changes due to age and those differences between age groups which derive from subjects growing up in different historical epochs.

Meanwhile, Fozard and Nuttall (1971) have studied age differences in 16PF scores with a view to comparing their results with those already described. They further wished to study the effects of socio-economic status. Forms A and B of the 16PF were administered to over one thousand subjects who were participants in a longitudinal study of healthy ageing. The subjects fell into six age groups; the youngest being 28–35 and the oldest 56–83 (median age 59). A multiple analysis of variance with these six levels of age and four levels of SES was performed on the 16PF scores.

Results indicated that although there were differences by age and SES, these were independent; there were no interactional effects. Statistically significant differences with SES were found for six scales. Higher scores were associated with higher SES on Factors A (warm *vs* aloof), H (adventurousness) and Q_1 (radicalism), and with lower SES on Factors C (ego strength), L(suspicious *vs* trusting) and Q_4 (tension). The largest SES effect was associated with Factor B. These observed effects appeared to be consistent with descriptions of occupational differences in scores described by Cattell *et al.* (1970).

Age exerted a statistically significant effect upon Factors I (tough *vs* tender-minded), Q_2 (self-sufficiency) and Q_3 (self-sentiment), all of which showed higher scores with increasing age, and also Factor F (surgency) which showed a decrease.

The results on Factor Q_3 agree with those already cited of Goodwin and Schaie (1969) and Cattell *et al.* (1970). The higher Factor I scores are inconsistent with findings of both these studies. The increase on Q_3 is consistent with the findings of Goodwin and Schaie (1969) but Cattell *et al.* (1970) suggest no age correction for this factor. The decline on Factor F was not reported by Goodwin and Schaie (1969) but does agree with Cattell *et al.* (1970).

Statistically significant effects of both age and SES were found on Factors B (intelligence) E (dominance), G (superego Strength) and N (shrewdness). Factor B scores were lower among those of older age and lower SES, as might perhaps be expected. Factor E scores tend to the "submissiveness" pole among the same group. This is consistent with observations of Cattell *et al.* (1970) about occupational differences in scores on this factor. The age differences on Factor E agree with both sets of earlier data. Factor G scores increase with increasing age and higher SES; both trends agree with those described by Cattell *et al.* (1970), while disagreeing with those reported by Goodwin and Schaie (1969). The increases on Factor N with advancing age and higher SES are again consistent with the findings of Cattell *et al.* (1970).

The results of the 16PF studies are not only characterised by their scarcity but also by their lack of specificity. Byrd (1959), using a group of persons aged over 65 years, was able to show that what seemed likely to be a linear trend, might, in fact, show a reversal in advanced age. Thus the reporting of gross age-related changes may not be particularly helpful in the prediction of personality function in later old age. We await, hopefully and with interest, more data on the aged.

Mental Illness

By 1963 the identification of mental illness in old age, increasingly important to modern society and particularly relevant to the understanding of personality in the aged, had made some significant steps. A number of studies over the previous two decades had illuminated the nature and size of this problem on an international basis in terms of both diagnostic categories and treatment procedures. Recently, the World Health Organization has been increasingly active in this field as well as several national bodies in supporting research and international conferences.

Early clinical diagnoses of old age psychiatric disorders were effectively dominated by the accounts of senile psychosis and dementia (Kraepelin, 1909–1913; and Bleuler, 1943). The scientific advances necessary to tackle the problems of mental illness in the aged more realistically are a product of the twentieth century, but readers will find remarkably full accounts of the ageing phenomenon in Burdach (1890–1926) and Burstein (1949) who summarise the early literature in this area. Historically the work of Rothschild (1937, 1942) is an important landmark in our understanding of the aged. He recognised that factors other than degenerative changes in the brain, such as the influence of personality and environment, played a role in mental disturbances in old age, even though these were still included under the general heading of senile and arteriosclerotic psychoses. Pathological studies by Grunthal (1927) and Gellerstedt (1933) established that the changes in the brains of senile dements could also be found in the brains of normal old people and pointed to the need to clarify the relationship between clinical and pathological phenomena.

In practice, however, the term "senile psychosis" continued to be applied until quite recently to a wide range of syndromes with onset in old age. Many patients were considered to be suffering from illness or abnormality due to senility and to have a poor prognosis. They tended to be segregated in wards of mental hospitals set aside for the aged. The presence of hypertension, peripheral arteriosclerosis, or minor neurological changes, all of which are common in the aged, appeared to confirm the brain-damage aetiology of their illness. This was an era of pessimism and therapeutic nihilism as far as the elderly were concerned.

The increasing numerical importance of mental disorder among the aged, the burden on the community, and the threat to the hospital services, in modern civilised society stimulated an interest in the problems of the aged in the 1945 period (Pollock, 1945; Kaplan, 1945; Lewis, 1946). Studies by Semrad and McKeon (1941) and Williams et al. (1942) showed that in mental patients over the age of 70 committed to hospital for the first time, most had long histories of personality and financial difficulties with the breakdown of their home environments as a major precipitating cause. On investigating comparable groups of arteriosclerotic and senile dements, they concluded that personality factors were insignificant in the former. Clow (1940), however, reported contradictory results. He stressed that psychotics with cerebral arteriosclerosis had abnormal anxiety and tension in their adult lives, narrow interest ranges, and sexual mal-adjustment. At this time, several short-term follow-up studies of elderly patients showed that those with predominantly depressive symptomatology had a relatively good outcome compared with those with "organic brain syndromes" (Post, 1951; Clow and Allen, 1951). Moreover, favourable responses were reported in depressed patients after ECT, even in the very old (Evans, 1943; Mayer-Gross, 1945; Feldman *et al.* 1946), and further served to demarcate the functional from the organic states. This acceptance of functional as well as organically based mental illness in the aged was of paramount importance. It allowed new perspectives for the diagnosis and treatment, especially as it was paralleled by an increased availability of pharmacological agents. It also highlights the need for more detailed analysis of the structure or dimensions of personality in the aged—normal and abnormal.

Epidemiology

The prevalence of psychiatric disorders in the elderly has been investigated in a number of community surveys, general practice studies, and by means of hospital statistics. The World Health Organisation (1959) pointed out that first and second or more admissions of old people into mental hospitals is taking place at an increasing rate in many countries. In the USA between 1904 and 1950, the number of persons over 60 multiplied by four, yet the number of first admissions to mental hospitals increased nine times. Figures presented by the Registrar General (1964) for England and Wales show a similar progressive rise. The number of people over 65 increased by 1 per cent between 1951-60, but first admission rates rose by over 35 per cent. About 50 per cent of aged in mental hospitals had been there many years, the other 50 per cent were late onset admissions (Kidd and Smith, 1966). The relative incidence of various mental disorders in old age is indicated by these hospital admission rates, but the picture is incomplete as far as the total incidence and distribution is concerned. In this respect population surveys are extremely important and since the pioneer work of Sheldon (1948) several population surveys have appeared (Bremer, 1951; Hobson and Pemberton, 1955; Essen-Möller, 1956; Gruenberg, 1961; Primrose, 1962; Kay *et al.*, 1962; 1964*a,b*; Watts and Watts, 1952; Miller, 1963; Nielsen, 1963; Williamson *et al.*, 1964;

Table 1. Mental illness in the Aged: Estimated incidence for the main psychiatric disorders per 1,000 population aged 65 years or over (*modified from* Slater and Roth, 1969, p. 541)

	Institutional cases per 1,000	Cases living at home per 1,000	Total incidence per 1,000
Senile and arteriosclerotic dementia	6·8	38·8	45·6
Other severe brain syndromes	0·8	9·7	10·5
Organic syndromes, mild cases	5·3	51·8	57·1
Organics, all cases	12·9	100·3	113·2
Manic-depressive disorder	0·7	12·9	13·6
Schizophrenia, chronic	(0·2)*	9·7⎫	10·8
Paraphrenia, late onset	0·9	0·0⎭	
Character disorders, including paranoid states	0·5	35·6	36·1
Psychoses, all forms	2·3	58·2	50·5
Neuroses and allied disorders (Moderate/severe forms)	1·9	87·4	89·3
All disorders	17·1	245·9	263·0

*Long-stay mental hospital schizophrenics not included

Garside *et al.*, 1965; Parsons, 1965). These writers' estimates of the prevalence of the main psychiatric disorders and less disabling mental illness of old age diverge to some extent owing to differences in diagnostic criteria. Table 1 modified from Slater and Roth (1969), represents a summary of the estimated prevalence rates for the main psychiatric disorders of the 65 plus age group per 1,000 of that population.

The investigations suggested that between 20 and 30 per cent of persons over 60 exhibit psychiatric symptoms or psychological deviations. Some 10 per cent showed conditions consistent with pathological brain damage, of which about half were seriously disabling. Psychotic disorders were diagnosed in 5 to 7 per cent of the population, severe depressive and paranoid illness to 2 per cent, and neurotic classification in about 10 per cent, but a further 10 to 15 per cent of minor neurotic symptomatology are noted (Gruenberg, 1961; Kay *et al.*, 1964a,b; 1966; Nielsen, 1963; Parsons, 1965). Functional, particularly affective disorders predominate up to the age of 70, thereafter psycho-organic states increasingly account for the rising psychiatric morbidity. However, even beyond 85, some 70 per cent of community residents are free from severe forms of mental deterioration (Gruenberg, 1961). Successful suicides in both sexes tend to increase with age, though the attempted suicide incidence decreases and probably half of them are associated with depression and/or physical illness (O'Neal *et al.* 1956; Stengel and Cook, 1961; Capstick, 1960; Sainsbury, 1962). However, it is important to keep things in perspective and remember that the overwhelming majority of elderly people pass through a normal aged period without recognisable or diagnosed mental illness. Minor emotional and cognitive adjustment problems are common and increase between 60 and 90 years of age, but for serious old age mental disorders the main risk found is between 60 and 80 (Kay, personal communication, 1969).

General practice studies have also made a vital contribution to the understanding of old age mental disorders. Kessell (1960) and Kessell and Shepherd (1962) suggested that minor psychiatric illness tends to remain unrecognised by general practitioners and this was confirmed in further investigations by Williamson *et al.* (1964). Shepherd *et al.* (1966) pointed out that family doctors were aware of about 50 per cent of the psychiatric disorders in their elderly patients and that very few of the milder cases were receiving any form of treatment or support. As Post has suggested, this shows that elderly psychiatric patients tend to be sent for specialist care only late in their illness, with requests for in-patient care rather than curative treatment. Nevertheless, it is now fair to say that a great deal can be done to treat successfully functional mental illness in the elderly and to alleviate the burden of those suffering from organic pathologically based senile disorders (Post, 1951, 1962*a,b*, 1965, 1966*a,b*, 1968; Slater and Roth, 1969). Every effort must be made to identify and diagnose the potential recipient and thus improve the general quality of life in old age.

MODERN CLASSIFICATION

Indeed, the classification of mental illness in the aged has undergone fundamental changes over the years, and the taxonomy proposed by Roth and his colleagues has now been generally accepted (Roth and Morrissey, 1952; Roth, 1955; Slater and Roth, 1969; Kay *et al.* 1964*a,b*; Post, 1965, 1967). Roth's classification is based on symptomatological rather than aetiological considerations. However, the groups of patients so defined have been found to differ from each other not only in prognosis and cause of death (Kay, 1959; Post, 1962a) but also on several psychological measurement techniques (Hopkins and Roth, 1953; Roth and Hopkins, 1953); in association with somatic illness (Kay and Roth, 1955); in their EEG's, genetically (Kay, 1959; Larsson and Sjorgren, 1954), and in the postmortem findings (Corsellis, 1962). Within the "organic" groups, the neuropathological studies of Corsellis confirmed the clinical differentiation into senile, arteriosclerotic and acute confusional psychoses; and within the functional groups, the course of illness (Kay, 1962) and the response to different forms of treatment (Post, 1962a) are in accord with the clinical separation into affective and paranoid psychoses. More recent work by Roth et al. (1967) and Blessed et al. (1968)—coincidental with the psychological studies of personality reported here—has developed the analysis of the relationships between neuropathological and mental illness phenomena in the aged.

The general classification for old age mental disorders from Roth (1955) and subsequently in Slater and Roth (1969) "Clinical Psychiatry" (Chapter 10) divided psychiatric features into five categories:

1. Affective disorder

2. Late paraphrenia

3. Acute or sub-acute delirious state

4. Senile dementia

5. Arteriosclerotic psychosis

The affective disorders have been sub-classified into neurotic and endogenous depressions, and neurotic disorders as such have since been found to be prevalent among the aged. Late onset depression appears to have less genetic loading than early onset depression, and significantly more late onset manic depressives experience clear physical or social stress compared with that for early onset (Stendstedt, 1959; Kay, 1959; Post, 1962a; Chesser, 1965). Persons developing depression late in life also have more robust previous personalities than those with previous depressive episodes (Roth, 1955; Chesser, 1965). Several diagnostic subcategories of depression are presented by Slater and Roth (1969) viz. a typical depression, pseudo-demented depression, depression with clouding of consciousness, physical illness and depression, "reactive" depressions and organic depression. Attacks of mania or hypomania are also noted as constituting 5 to 10 per cent of the affectedi visorders in old age.

Early reports suggested that the success of treatment for depression in old age is limited, but there seems no doubt that some alleviation of the situation is possible (Post, 1962a). Indeed, recent studies discussed by Post (1968) support the view that depression in old age responds very well to modern methods of treatment and that depressives do not develop *de novo* senile dementia or arteriosclerotic dementia any more frequently than the elderly population as a whole.

Mild or moderate neurotic disorders are possibly much more frequent in the aged than they were thought to be, probably 10 to 15 per cent of the elderly population (Kay *et al.* 1964*a,b*; Bergmann, 1966). The severe neurotic disorders in the elderly tend to be present in those with a longstanding predisposition to respond adversely to various kinds of stress, who tend to be less sociable, moody and have an anxious concern about their health (Vispo, 1962; Garside *et al.* 1965; Bergmann, 1966). Both Post (1967) and Slater and Roth (1969) also stress that anxiety is usually associated with some degree of depression. Physical health emerges clearly as a causative factor in late onset neurotic disorders. In other recurrent old age neurotics, marriage is usually late or not at all: the divorce or separation incidence is high in this group, and a portion had suffered breakdown in middle age. To quote Slater and Roth (1969) in "Mental Disease in the Aged", p. 578: 'Viewed in retrospect, the lives of many of those who breakdown in old age, look rather like a protracted game of chess in the early stages of which some powerful figures have been eliminated from the game thus restricting the possibilities of effective action and survival for the remainder.'

When obsessions, phobias, or hypochondriasis occur for the first time in late life, they are usually much less permanently incapacitating and tend to be associated with introversion. Hysterical conversion symptoms rarely, if ever, present in old age and when they do are indicative of functional psychosis or organic disease rather than being of neurotic origin (Post, 1965; Slater and Roth, 1969). On the other hand, McDonald (1965) in a general practice survey concluded that neurotic symptoms were not the forerunners of dementia.

Treatment of neurosis tends to concentrate on the use of anti-depressant and minor tranquillising drugs and advice or help to family. Psychotherapy is considered difficult for financial and theoretical reasons and as well as for other practical considerations (Post, 1965), though general supportive therapy is helpful. One must generally suggest that a great deal more work into functional disorders in the aged would be most profitable to the health and life satisfaction of that aged population.

Late Paraphrenia

The symptoms of schizophrenia in the aged have been known for some considerable time and were described by Bleuler in a review article in 1943. Early clinical practice tended to regard these disorders as of organic origin, but Roth (1955) drew attention to a group of patients whose first illness occurred in senescence, in whom the most prominent features of the illness were paranoid delusions and hallucinations often with unclear schizophrenic features, and who tended to be diagnosed as suffering from senile or arteriosclerotic psychoses. He called this condition *late paraphrenia*. Unlike early schizophrenia, it is mainly confined to women, about 8 to 9 per cent of female first admissions over the age of 65. According to Slater and Roth (1969) personality deterioration does not appear to accompany late paraphrenia, except after such long periods of observation that senile degenerative changes are a more likely explanation than a schizophrenic process and the disease does not run in families to the extent that schizophrenia appears to do (Kay, 1959). This view of the reduced significance of genetic factors in elderly schizoid type illness, was confirmed by Post (1966*b*) in a review of the literature in this area and by Herbert and Jacobson (1967).

It has been suggested that there are many elderly ill of this type in the community tolerated as eccentrics (Macmillan and Shaw, 1966). This condition does, however, seem very responsive to treatment by the pharmacological agents used therapeutically on younger age group schizophrenics (Post, 1966*a*; Slater and Roth, 1969). Roth (1963) maintains that the circumstances surrounding breakdown and the features of the illness in paraphrenia are in some ways more reminiscent of the course of events in neurotic illness (except presumably its late onset) than of that associated with schizophrenia in early life.

Senile Dementia

Senile dementia is the most common mental disorder in the

associated with degenerative diseases of the nervous system and the disorganisation of all aspects of personality (Larsson *et al.* 1963; Kay *et al.* 1964*a*,*b*). Simchowicz (1910) regarded senile dementia as an accentuation of the normal processes of ageing. This view was obviously implicit in Wechsler's (1944; 1958) concept of intelligence and its decline in normal and abnormal aged. However, the psychometric evidence, much of which was discussed earlier, suggests that there may be qualitative as well as quantitative differences between the cognitive functioning of senile dements and normal aged persons (Botwinick and Birren, 1951*b*; Savage, 1970*b*). Clinical evidence by Kral (1962) and Kay *et al.* (1966) supports this view.

It has long been suspected that hereditary factors are important in the development of senile dementia (Meggendorfer, 1926; Kallmann, 1948; 1951) and this appears to be supported by the work of Larsson *et al.* (1963) who found a higher incidence of senile dementia in families of dements than in the comparable general aged population. A link between senile organic psychoses and neuropathology has been established by the work of Corsellis (1962), Roth *et al.* (1967), and Blessed *et al.* (1968) and it is also of interest to note that the survival period for "uncomplicated senile dements" is shorter than for those whose dementia is coloured with loosely knit paranoid delusions or depressive symptoms (Kay, 1962). Presumably the pure senile dements have a more organic pathological basis to their disorder. It would certainly appear that the occurrence of senile plaques and associated neuropathological changes are correlated with changes in psychological performance. All the pathological changes described in senile dementia —argentophil plaques, neurofibrillary changes, and granulovacuolar degeneration—have been found in normal old subjects at death. Neuro-fibrillary change is often confined to the hyppocampal region (Geller-stedt, 1933; Tomlinson *et al.* 1968) and this has potential importance in view of the role of the limbic system in memory functioning.

The independence of arteriosclerotic and senile dementia has been discussed by both clinical and pathological investigators. Corsellis (1962) showed that the processes were distinct to a large extent neuro-pathologically; 45 per cent of his cases were due to cerebrovascular disease, 34 per cent showed changes associated with senile dementia, and 21 per cent of the patients had both disease processes. Clinically, arteriosclerotic psychosis is frequently associated with hypertension and follows a number of cerebrovascular accidents. Intellectual impairment and other symptoms show marked fluctuation in the course of the illness and total disintegration, as seen in senile dementia, does not show until very late in the illness. Prognosis in arteriosclerotic dementia is better than for senile dementia, but even so within two years of diagnosis, mortality is 70 per cent (Roth, 1955).

Psychodynamic factors operating in patients with chronic brain syndromes may result in difficulties in coping with the organically based difficulties (Katz *et al.* 1961). Several investigators have also reported that additional brain damage results from circulatory inefficiency (Albert, 1964; Mueller, 1967). The early hope of Rothschild (1937; 1942) that ability to compensate for cerebral deterioration might be more important than actual anatomical changes in chronic brain syndromes cannot, unfortunately, now be accepted, nor can the implicit socio-medical therapeutic possibilities. Treatment of associated symptoms of depression, anxiety, paranoid episodes and the like, along with adequate social-environmental conditions will probably result in the main improvements in life for these patients.

ACUTE CONFUSIONAL OR DELIRIOUS STATES

These are probably the most frequent, yet least understood conditions in old age, occurring and seen by general practitioner and specialist alike during both physical and mental illnesses. The principal causes of delirium in old age are cardiac failure, chronic and acute respiratory disease, anaemias, malignant disease, alcoholism, overdosage of drugs, vitamin and nutritional deficiency, surgical operations, dehydration, and electrolyte disturbances. Patients are usually incoherent, hyperactive, and levels of awareness fluctuate. A considerable need for research into behaviour functioning associated with pre- and post-acute and chronic delirious states is evident as they appear to be the least understood of the five major categories of old age outlined by Roth (1955) and his colleagues.

In general, psychiatric classification of disorders in the aged has taken considerable strides over the past 20 years, even though more refinement in diagnostic techniques and treatment methods is necessary and will undoubtedly follow. We regret that the same could not be said for psychometric and experimental psychological research in the area of personality functioning in the aged. A dearth of investigations of real value was only too evident in the early 1960s.

Since we began our investigations of personality in the aged, a number of important developments in the psychiatric aspects of the aged have been published which bear mention at this point. Despite the major contributions to classification by Sir Martin Roth and his colleagues, a number of writers have commented upon the fact that psychiatric practitioners have found themselves somewhat daunted by the problems which diagnosis and treatment of mental illness in the aged present. Macmillan (1969) has gone so far as to say that the pessimistic outlook on senile breakdown has lead to "therapeutic nihilism" (p. 109). He fears that the concentration of research upon organic factors may have diverted attention from emotional and functional conditions which may more readily respond to prompt treatment. Speaking as a member of a service in which hospital and community resources were closely combined, he posits that emotional factors may be of primary etiological importance in psychogeriatrics. He claims that loneliness is found to be a component in every case of senile breakdown. Loneliness may be actual, in which case isolation leads to deterioration through restriction of interests with the development of apathy and loss of initiative. On the other hand, the old person living within a family setting may suffer from psychological loneliness. The burden which the family has to carry may lead to interpersonal tension and rejection of the elderly member. This rejection is likely to lead to adverse effects upon the old person, to the development of resentment, apathetic acceptance, or depression. In both these cases, prevention of senile breakdown may be brought about by early intervention. Community resources may be brought to bear on the problem, alleviating the distress of both the aged person and his relatives. If emotional tensions are effectively relieved, the kind of deterioration necessitating full-time hospital care may be avoided. The emotional withdrawal and apathy may be generally reversed in the early stages; senile breakdown tends to be irreversible.

Oberleder (1969) expresses similar thoughts about breakdown in the elderly. Like Macmillan, she feels that an emphasis upon organic aspects has led to a pessimistic view of the chances of recovery in the aged. Moreover, she holds that symptoms common to all psychiatric patients may take on a different significance when the individual is over 60. Early symptoms may be regarded as "natural" in the light of the patient's age; the consequence is that such a person does not come to medical attention until he is in an emergency state of breakdown.

Oberleder suggests that anxiety may underline most "senility". Memory loss and confusion may represent ways of tuning oneself out of an unbearable situation; incontinence may be an effective means of vengeance or crying for help. While a proportion of patients will be subject to irreversible organic deterioration, many may be exhibiting transitory reactions to stress which are treatable and reversible. While suggesting practical approaches to treatment, Oberleder also calls for a change in expectations for the elderly. It is the expectation of senility rather than its reality against which we must marshal our efforts.

Oberleder (1969) makes the point that elderly persons under stress will choose age-appropriate symptoms. Payne, Gibson and Pittard (1969) come to a similar conclusion in their examination of the etiology of senile psychosis. They regard the transition from adult to aged status as a question of choice. When a person may no longer regard himself as non-aged, he may do one of four things. He may accept that he must now move to the aged status, he may commit suicide, he may encourage the possibility of death or he may succumb to a psychotic state to avoid decision-making and its consequences. If this last choice is made, the individual is likely to exhibit a psychotic pattern identical to that of organic psychotics similar in age and subculture. The writers urge that detailed investigation of "senility" be carried out in order to clarify the nature of the relationship between organic and behavioural factors. Meanwhile, therapy aimed at widening the environment of the aged may prevent a good many of them from retreating into senility as a defence against a relatively featureless world.

Friedman and Strachan (1972) also comment upon a defence mechanism among the elderly against frustration and anxiety. They found a high degree of pessimism among persons over 65, whether or not they had been psychiatrically ill. Noting that functional disorders do not appear to show an increase with age, they suggest that low expectations and pessimism may represent a premium-free insurance policy for mental health in old age. They do not comment upon the possibility of such pessimism leading to organiform deterioration.

One point which clearly emerges from these studies is that diagnosis of psychiatric disturbance in the elderly is by no means an easy task. McDonald (1968) points to the fact that there are few, if any symptoms which are pathognomic of one particular condition. In many cases a diagnostic label is virtually useless in indicating treatment. A diagnostic multifactorial formulation, involving both physical and psychiatric aspects, is much to be preferred.

Clausen (1968) makes a similar observation about the multiplicity of factors involved in disturbances of aged persons. He, however, draws attention also to the importance of social factors, noting that the relative independence of the physiological, psychological and social spheres no longer obtains in old age. The assessment made by a psychiatrist focusses upon symptoms and deficits: it is not aimed at the areas where functioning is good. The implications of such a bias are even more crucial for a person who is, in fact, less severely ill. We need a series of standardised measures upon cognitive, intrapsychic and interpersonal dimensions. Standardised languages referring to such dimensions are likely to provide a broader and less clinical description than the nomenclature of symptomology.

Gaitz and Baer (1970) make reference to a report by the Gerontological Society in America which was concerned with the problems of assessment of the aged. The report commented upon the lack of agreement among those working with the elderly upon the relative importance of different aspects of their functioning. There had been hopes that progress might be made toward development of a single assessment tool for the aged, which had been unrealised owing to this disagreement. Gaitz and Baer are of the opinion that the relative importance of different aspects cannot be assessed in a valid way until a multifunctional assessment of any individual patient has been conducted.

This was carried out with 100 patients over 60 years of age, the ultimate goal being comprehensive care of the patient. Medical, psychiatric, psychological, nursing and social work staff were involved in the project. They all made investigations of patients' functional capacity. It was shown that, with each addition of information from a different source, the estimate of functional capacity came closer to the patient's actual status. Gaitz and Baer point out, however, that the multifunctional model does not merely involve the collection of multiple evaluations. More important is the synthesis of the findings; the different staffs must meet to weigh and balance their results. Moreover, for efficient utilisation of available services, their conclusions must be couched in concise terms and transmitted to all relevant agencies. Since these are likely to be diverse, the information must be presented in a manner understandable by all. Sharing of information is vital to effective comprehensive care.

Gaitz and Baer (1970) believe that a single assessment tool for the aged cannot be developed in terms of a prior judgment of the relative importance of different aspects; it must be founded on empiricism. They feel that the development of such a tool might best be promoted in the context of a project such as they have described.

A step toward the development of such a measure has been made by Gurel, Linn and Linn (1972) who themselves represent something of a multidisciplinary team. They comment upon the proliferation of instruments for assessment of the general population of psychiatrically ill, but the scarcity of measures designed for geriatric patients. They made it their aim to construct a measure specifically for geriatric patients, which would also cover a broad range of functions (rather than narrowly psychiatric ones); Gurel *et al.* again stress the need for a multifunctional approach to the aged where there is a complex interplay of psyche and soma. They further regarded as important the need for a design which would promote maximum reporting of overt behaviour, rather than judgements made about it. Their instrument was developed from two earlier scales and applied to 845 male patients of mean age 66 years. Half of these had medical complaints; in the other half the problems were predominantly psychiatric. Principal factor analysis of the instrument yielded ten first order factors. Gurel *et al.* (1972) were able to show that there was a high degree of uniformity in dimensionality of the scale for the medical and psychiatric sub-samples. Several of the first order factors, although conceptually separable, showed intercorrelations. This was thought to be due to the fact that certain characteristics were often found together in the same subject. Second order factors were elicited which suggested three remarkably clear-cut second order dimensions: physical infirmity; psychological deterioration and psychological agitation. The first order factor of self-care dependency loaded significantly upon both physical infirmity and psychological deterioration; a finding which confirmed the utility of a multifunctional approach. The scale was validated successfully against a number of external criteria, and the authors believe that it holds considerable promise as an assessment of behavioural disorders in the disabled aged. It should be noted, however, that social factors are not explicitly recognised in this scale.

A group of workers who have illustrated especially clearly the value of a multifunctional approach are Brody, Kleban, Lawton and Silverman (1971). They directed their attention toward the factors involved in the handicaps exhibited by institutionalised women whose clinical signs and test scores pointed strongly to a diagnosis of chronic brain syndrome. They were able to show the existence of social influences by effecting an improvement in family relationships of these aged women. They founded their beliefs that treatment should involve all possible aspects upon two points. The first is that there is no one-to-one relationship between the degree of organic impairment and the overall level of the individual's functioning. Thus, the behaviour and capacities of the mentally impaired aged have a range of possible variations. Secondly, the level of functioning is influenced by a variety of psychological, physical, social and cultural factors. Actual destruction of nervous tissue constitutes but one component contributing to the observed level of performance. Thus, Brody *et al.* (1971) subscribe to the notion of "excess disability" of Kahn *et al.* (1958). This concept is used to describe the discrepancy which may exist between an individual's functional incapacity and that which may be warranted by the actual impairment. Brody *et al.* made the assumption that excess disabilities could be attributed to treatable physical, social or psychological factors. A highly individualised multidisciplinary treatment regime was instituted, whereby excess disabilities in a variety of spheres of functioning were identified and successfully ameliorated. Brody and co-workers concluded that they had illustrated "the responsiveness, accessibility and potential for improvement of those for whom the designation 'senile' too often signals assignment to a category as 'untreatables' " (p. 131). This study is not, of course, the first among attempts to rehabilitate severely and chronically ill aged patients. Donahue (1962) for example, reported the success of a regime centred upon craft and socio-recreational training used with long-term aged patients. What is significant about the work of Brody *et al.* (1971) is the fact that they were able to demonstrate the existence of treatable disabilities which were in excess of that warranted by the organic handicap. This was shown by the finding that amelioration in the areas designated as excess disabilities did not generalise to all areas of functioning. Thus, improvements could be attributed to the specific treatments, and not merely to the increased overall attention to the patients. Moreover, improved health status was not a prerequisite for improvement in the target areas, which suggests that the pessimistic view that we must wait for advances in medical science before being able to offer any real help to the elderly is a mistaken one.

In the course of this brief discussion, evidence has been presented to illustrate the development of a new optimism with regard to treatment of psychiatric disturbance in the elderly. It has been suggested that many symptoms displayed by the aged need not be taken as indicating the onset of an inevitable process of deterioration, and the views of Oberleder (1969) have been described with reference to this topic. In 1970, Oberleder reported the application of "crisis therapy" to twelve patients of over 60 years of age who had been admitted to a state mental hospital with diagnoses of senile psychosis or arteriosclerosis with psychosis. The treatment consisted of brief psychotherapy involving family and other significant persons. Pharmacological approaches were not excluded. The therapy is applied at a time when the individual may be maximally influenced—when he is in a crisis. Hospitalisation without strict treatment goals at such a time may have the effect of exacerbating disorganisation and regression. Crisis therapy, on the other hand, is aimed at "catching the individual off guard" and turning reduced resistance to good effect by encouraging free expression of feelings, and unblocking repressed material. In such a manner, all twelve patients recovered to a degree sufficient to allow discharge from hospital. It is significant that Oberleder describes such an approach as being specifically geared to persons for whom long-term psychotherapy is not suitable, especially the aged and those from low socio-economic groups.

Unfortunately the evidence suggests that this sort of therapy tends not to be available to the majority of mentally disturbed aged. It seems likely that institutionalisation is the most predictable outcome when an elderly person finds himself in a crisis situation. We have already seen that Brody and her colleagues (1971) were able to achieve successful improvements in the functioning of elderly institutionalised women. Earlier, Brody and Gummer (1967) had examined factors which influence the families of elderly people in their decision as to whether to hand the care of their aging relatives over to an institution. They compared two groups of aged individuals, all of whom had had at least one screening interview at a home for Jewish aged: one group consisted of those who applied for places after interview, while the second was composed of non-applicants. Thirty-five variables were used for purposes of comparison and only three of these showed significant differences between the two groups. Among applicants and their families there appeared to be more than one reason for application; this was the case for twice as many applicants as non-applicants.

Further, attitudes of the elderly and other members of the family were favourable toward admission among applicants. It was suggested that these attitudes were not unrelated to the clustering of assaults upon the family. Attitudes may, of course, be related to other factors such as the personality of the aged member, the family's structure, quality of relationships and tolerance for stress.

What was striking was the fact that the group which was destined for institutionalisation was not in any way unique. Especially, its members did not differ significantly from the comparative group in terms of health or functional capacity. Brody and Gummer concede that they cannot comment upon the fate of the non-applicant members. Nevertheless, they feel justified in noting that the applicant group appeared to be characterised not so much by their incapacities as by the fact that the family crises precipitating application appeared to be particularly chaotic. Brody and Gummer do not regard the institution as necessarily being unacceptable, but they do feel that earlier case-finding might enable orderly planning to be substituted for admission from a crisis situation.

The assumption that aged disturbed persons require hospital treatment was, however, questioned by Dobson and Patterson (1961). Their work was prompted by the fact that hospitals for war veterans were becoming overloaded, and had adopted a policy of transferring some of their patients to nursing homes. Dobson and Patterson investigated two groups of veterans, one in hospital and the other in nursing home care. The subjects were assessed, prior to the transferral of the nursing home group, on behavioural and need for nursing care scales. The groups selected were comparable in terms of age, diagnosis and initial ratings. These ratings were repeated after a lapse of twelve months. It was found that these chronic geriatric patients made as adequate an adjustment to nursing homes as to the hospital. Furthermore, most of the nursing home patients preferred the free and home-like atmosphere than that of the hospital. A more specific comparison was made of schizophrenic and chronic brain syndrome patients in hospital and nursing homes. The severity of behavioural disturbance of the schizophrenic patients was not reflected in the good adjustment these persons made to nursing home care. CBS patients, on the other hand, did seem to require the services of the hospital.

Nevertheless, Dobson and Patterson had been able to show that, for their samples at least, hospital care was not necessarily required for all cases of geriatric disturbance, not even for those likely to be most disturbed: the schizophrenics.

Markson, Kwoh, Cumming and Cumming (1971), using larger and broader samples, obtained results which raised questions about the suitability of either hospital or nursing home care for many elderly persons. They compared two groups: one was of applicants to a state mental hospital, where there was a policy of screening patients for suitability for admission: the other consisted of persons admitted without screening to another hospital. The subjects were comparable in all relevant aspects and were of median age 75 years. They were followed up and assessed in terms of their symptom patterns, competence in personal care and unmet needs.

Of those persons rejected at screening, 40 per cent were found in their own homes. Twenty per cent of these showed moderate to severe symptom patterns and a similar proportion were unable to bathe themselves without assistance. These persons thus had unmet needs, but this still left sixty per cent who had none. On the other hand, nearly half the patients who were in hospital were thought fit to return to the community, while a further quarter to a third were thought more suited to nursing home care. Meanwhile, of those who were found in nursing homes, one quarter were judged as not requiring the special services provided.

Markson and her colleagues regard the conclusion from this and other studies as "inescapable"; namely, that a very mixed group of elderly persons is referred to psychiatric facilities, but, for most of them, mental hospitalisation is not the treatment of choice. Moreover, the most common alternative—the nursing home—may be similarly unsuitable. Markson et al. (1971) believe that two kinds of psychiatric service are most frequently needed and infrequently available: crisis resolution and continuing support. The provision of such services could prevent a large number of elderly persons ever requiring hospitalisation.

We have already looked at Oberleder's (1970) report of the successful application of "Crisis Therapy", to problems encountered by the elderly patients. Oberleder's work was done with patients who had been admitted to hospital with diagnoses of psychosis. Millard (1968), in examining the role of the clinician in the community, looks more closely at the views of Caplan, who was the original proponent of the concept of crisis intervention as a valuable preventative approach. Caplan (1964) saw the provision of measures to allow crisis intervention as constituting primary prevention. Such measures would be oriented towards the not-yet sick, and would cover a wide range. They might thus be brought to bear upon a potentially critical situation in such a manner that the absolute incidence of psychiatric breakdown might be reduced, and admission to hospital be obviated.

The kind of services which are presently available as alternatives to hospitalisation are those such as out-patient clinics, day-care clinics, hostels and so on. Not only are they still scarce, but they are not aimed at primary prevention. They function to minimise the duration and extent of psychiatric disturbance—Caplan's secondary prevention—and to reduce the impairment of function in the individual in his family and in society at large—tertiary prevention. The task of primary prevention is one which has proven difficult for psychiatric agents. In part this is due, says Millard, to a lack of a coherent body of directly relevant knowledge to guide the clinician in his attempts to practise community psychiatry. A further problem lies in difficulties of integration of clinical and local authority services. Central to both these problems is the concept of flexibility. The clinician must be able to adopt an experimental approach, involving the use of unconventional and imaginative techniques. The structure of services must be sufficiently flexible to permit this.

The need for integration of services to provide care while the individual is still in the community is stressed by Macmillan (1969). His views on the distinct possibilities of preventing senile breakdown have been outlined above. Integration may take the form of joint domiciliary visits by hospital specialist, social worker and general practitioner. In such a manner, assessment of all the factors in the individual's environment is possible. Day centres constitute a vital prophylactic measure by catering for "at risk" individuals rather than those who have already succumbed. Voluntary neighbourhood groups can perform extremely valuable functions in this respect—a point which Millard (1968) also stressed. Such groups are particularly well-positioned to ascertain potential breakdown situations. Short-term admissions will always be necessary in some cases; if these can be made to an assessment unit, misplacement may be obviated to a large extent. Macmillan found that unspecified and untreated medical conditions were frequently found in persons admitted to such a unit. Treatment of the medical complaint permitted a return to the home in many such cases.

Psychiatric day hospitals constitute a vital bridging measure in the system of services available to the aged patient, by providing the opportunity for detailed investigation while maintaining the individual in the community. Hospitalisation may be avoided altogether. On the other hand, a day hospital may provide a bridge for the patient who is discharged from full-time care; allowing him to be eased back into the community with less risk of relapse.

Millard (1968) and Macmillan (1969) are British gerontologists. Kobrynski (1968), writing in Canada, makes virtually identical comments upon the need for an integrated service for the elderly, among whom social, economic, psychological and health factors are more closely related than in any other group. Kobrynski also comments upon the origins of the day hospital. The first to be introduced was a psychiatric unit in Montreal in 1946; the first geriatric day hospital was opened in Oxford in 1952.

Goldstein, Sevriuk and Graver (1968) report the establishment of a psychogeriatric day hospital in Montreal. They quote a survey of psychiatric day hospitals which showed that in 1964 no unit specifically designed for psychogeriatric patients could be found in North America. Criteria for admission to their unit included the absence of gross psychosis, proper orientation to place and person, and the ability to accept the rules and routines of the unit. Otherwise, they felt that most types of psychiatric illnesses could be accommodated. While acute psychotic states were thought not to be amenable to this type of approach, less disturbed chronic psychotics—who might otherwise be obliged to remain in full-time care—were accepted. Of 50 patients accepted during the first year, 29 remained at the end of the year. Of those who had dropped out, three were too disturbed to adapt to the unit, three had falsely hoped that day unit attendance might speed up full-time admission, a further five were convinced the program could not help them, five were discharged to clinical agencies in view of deteriorating physical health and five were transferred to more intensive psychiatric care. The authors felt that this degree of drop-out reflected their inexperience in formulating a suitable admission policy.

An examination of the patients benefitting from the day care suggested to the authors that they were succeeding in a number of aims. They felt that they were obviating the need for full-time admission not only of isolated elderly, but also of those individuals who were creating extremely stressful situations for their families. They were further providing the means by which in-patients might be discharged earlier and with less risk of relapse.

What Goldstein and his colleagues did not achieve, however, were any discharges due to improvement. This, they felt, was primarily due to patient dependence upon the unit. The authors felt that this may have been caused, to some extent, by over-generous allocation of attendance. They intended to reduce initial attendances to a minimum. They also hoped to make discharge easier by first transferring dependence to more suitable agencies. Groups of patients were to attend "Golden Age" and other day centres, the cohesion of the group providing the support necessary for this transition.

Goldstein and his co-workers found that patients with confusional states, generally deriving from chronic brain syndromes, did not integrate well into the unit. They did not feel that this excluded the possibility of day care for such patients, but that it suggested that units catering specifically for them were indicated.

Bower (1969) describes the development of a psychogeriatric day centre in Melbourne, Australia. In the absence of financial resources, this unit had to be funded privately. Unqualified staff were used to good effect. Psychotherapy was, at the time of writing, undeveloped and treatment appeared to be based on chemotherapy and stimulation. No sitting room exists in the unit, since activity, in a wide variety of forms, is the goal. A diagnostic breakdown of 122 patients attending in one year showed that a near-complete spectrum of mental illness in the aged was represented. As in the case of Goldstein's unit, a minimum of efficient functioning was a pre-requisite. With this qualification, Bower feels that persons with both functional and organic disorders were amenable to the day care approach and he commented upon the surprising degree to which persons with these disorders were able to mix.

The rationale for the day hospital is founded on the belief that there is no reason why elderly persons, given the appropriate assistance, should not continue to function effectively in the community. The day hospital may thus be seen as an important factor in the development of a new attitude to the potential of the aged individual. The existence of such institutions bears witness to the increased optimism in the field of gerontology, and their success functions to promote it further. Shock (1968), in an article entitled "Age with a Future", regards a re-definition of the role of the elderly as vital. Elderly people, he states, must not be seen simply as a group for whom special services must be provided, but as participants in community life. Older people may themselves be capable of providing services for their less able peers; this area warrants further research. An indication of the possibilities in this direction is given by Rybak *et al.* (1968) who report a foster-grandparent program. Eighty persons over 60 years of age participated in the program which was geared to the stimulation of mentally-retarded children. An informal scale of psycho-social needs satisfaction, administered before and after participation, produced results which indicated that the elderly persons were functioning at a significantly more positive level as a result of their participation.

Every study referred to in this discussion reflects the process of re-definition of the role of the aged. Implicit in them all is the notion that we have for too long underestimated the chances of enabling elderly people to be community participants rather than mere on-lookers—or, at worst, refugees. It seems that this pessimism is now distinctly on the wane, and that the emergence of new attitudes is gaining momentum. Evidence that this is the case may be found in the fact that theoretical studies of the process have been made.

Baizerman and Ellison (1971) have proposed that the use of the term "senility" has had important implications for the fate of the person so labelled. The label structures the perception of an individual by others and allows a shift from the status of person to that of patient. By so doing, it absolves that person's family from any guilt they might otherwise feel about their allowing him to be removed from the community. Baizerman and Ellison suggest that viewing senility as a social role would shift the emphasis back to the family and enable us to study the processes which result in an individual being deprived of his "person" status. Role analysis might follow a number of lines. For example, the concept of role discontinuity might be used to examine the effect upon the family's structure if its elderly member refuses to "act his age". The concept of role conflict might be applied to explain the results of sons and daughters of elderly parents holding differential expectations.

The authors regard the development of such an approach as particularly important in view of the increasing trend toward returning elderly patients to the community. If the social system is at present geared to socialising the aged out of it, what happens when the elderly member's absence is only temporary? A treatment ideology involving return to the home may cause many intra-familial stresses. We need to be aware of this possibility and its derivation. Lipscomb (1971), describing the work of a psychiatric centre which returns the majority of its patients to the community, stresses the extreme importance of attitudes cultivated at the time of referral. It is vital, he says, that the persons referring the patient are left in no doubt that they are expected to receive him back when the disturbance is resolved. One wonders about the efficacy of such a measure if it were not related to a detailed examination of the family structure and the patient's place in it. Such an investigation is not explicitly described.

Response to Psychiatric Care

It may be of interest to readers to close this section with a brief look at the response to psychiatric care which the elderly have made. Kleemeier (1961) explored the parameters which operate to make use of time effective in institutions for the aged. He suggested that the use of time by any individual is a function of that person's energy, behavioural repertoire, and the milieu in which he finds himself. Kleemeier points out that an institution staffed by persons younger than its inmates must take especial care to examine the dynamics of time use. Older people are likely to have less energy and narrower repertoires than younger adults, and the tendency too often is for staff members to take the responsible roles. Many old people will gladly take the opportunity to avoid responsibility, while others who have the necessary resources are likely to become frustrated and opt out. Neither of these outcomes is beneficial to the patient. The outcome is a function of the individual plus the institution, and it is the responsibility of the staff of the institution to be aware of their contributions, functional and dysfunctional, to this outcome. Davis (1968) makes this very point in relation to the role of the nurse in geriatric care, and makes comments very similar to those expressed by Coser (1956). Davis notes that over-co-operative patients may be relinquishing their independence too early, while the resentful patient may be hanging on, in the only way he knows, to some measure of self-determination. Davis cautions that the nurse whose uppermost values are authority and efficiency may help cure the ailment but leave the total organism a social or psychological cripple.

These authors have not only outlined the unfortunate aspects of hospitalisation, but have indicated the kind of individual who may best be able to avoid the less desirable consequences; namely the unsubmissive one.

Turner, Tobin and Lieberman (1972) have made a specific study of personality traits as predictors of institutional adaptation among the aged. They examined 84 subjects of mean age 78 years residing in a Jewish home. The subjects were ambulatory, had no major illnesses and showed no signs of brain deterioration. They were assessed on a previously devised set of dimensions of personality not less than three months prior to admission and again twelve months after admission. The subjects were divided into two groups: one survivor group where there was no change or positive change and a vulnerable group which manifested negative change and/or death within one year.

Factor analysis of the personality dimensions was carried out. The factor which discriminated most clearly between the two groups was characterised in terms of a near-combative attitude. The survivor group were aggressive, active and narcissistic; the vulnerable group were characterised by a bland stance and little interest in status striving. These findings were supported by factorial analysis of a 100-item personality Q-sort results, which again indicated one significant discriminating factor. Again, the intact group were characterised in terms of controlling, manipulative, hostile and assertive traits. This work may be related to the study by Garside et al. (1965) which outlined a factor structure for physical and psychiatric symptoms in the Newcastle upon Tyne Community Aged, full details of which are presented in the papers of Kay et al. (1964a,b), and from which the present Newcastle upon Tyne Community Aged I were selected.

More recently, Kleban, Brody and Lawton (1971) reported an investigation into personality as it affected response to a treatment program applied to institutionalised mentally-impaired women. (This program is described in greater detail in the following section). The personalities of the women were assessed by means of a specially devised 50-item rating scale completed by a number of their relatives. Assessments were made of personality in middle life and for the present. The mean scores given by all relatives were used to represent a subject's score. Fifty-nine patients were rated on a 7-point scale of improvement after one year. Principal component analyses were performed on the 50 items for personality in the middle years and at the present.

The factor which was most powerful in predicting improvement was characterised by aggression. Aggression was related to improvement not only among patients in the treatment program, but also among controls, who apparently had the ambition necessary to find ways to improve themselves. The treatment program appeared to provide a focus and direction for the aggressive individuals and they thus showed greater improvement than their peers and controls.

There was considerable concordance between the middle years and current age personality factors. This not only lends support to the theory of continuity of personality with age; it also illustrates the potential for improvement which remains despite extreme old age, impairment and institutionalisation.

In 1972, Kleban and Brody reported a study designed to check the validity of these findings. In order to remove any possible bias existing among relatives' ratings, the ratings were repeated by social workers, who were unaware of the previous results. Again, the aggression factor emerged as one which was a powerful predictor of improvement. The factor was, however, differently characterised by the social workers, who focussed upon control aspects. Thus, those rated highly on this factor were poorly controlled and negativistic, and did not improve. It seems that the form of aggressiveness which is predictive of improvement involves assertiveness without negativism. This is not to say that the assertive patient may not be the traditionally regarded "difficult" patient.

Kleban et al. (1971) point to the implications of these findings for management. They note that a good deal of staff time and energy may be devoted to coping with the chronic crises which "difficult" patients tend to precipitate. Yet, these patients are the very ones who best respond to individualised treatment programs. How much better spent would the time and energy be if it were directed to such programs than to sorting out crises. Benefits would accrue not only to the patient, whose energies would be directed toward improvement rather than self-defeating aims, but also to the atmosphere of the environment in which the rest of the patients reside. Thus, Kleban et al. illustrate the way in which the interaction between individual and the institution is a two-way process. A study of personality among recipients of treatment has implications not only for they themselves, but also for the structure and function of treatment agencies. This provides an illustration of the very real contribution which studies of personality among the aged may make toward provision of appropriate services for elderly people.

*

Self Concept

Gordon Allport (1961) posed what seems to be a facile question, yet very pertinent to this study: "Does psychological science need the concept of self?". He proceeds in answering this important question and points out that the self concept is an essential feature of personality.

It seems that through the years the central objection to the self has been that the concept seems "question begging". It somehow seems extremely easy, and sometimes exceedingly desirable, to assign certain functions which are not wholly understood to a mysterious central agency, and then to declare that "it" performs in such a way as to unify the personality and maintain its integrity. Allport points out that for more than two generations psychologists have tried every conceivable way of accounting for integration, organisation and striving of the human person without having recourse to the postulate of a self.

In recent years, however, the tide has turned and many psychologists have begun to embrace what once would have been considered heresy. They have reintroduced self and ego and have employed ancillary concepts such as self-image, self-actualisation, phenomenal-self and many other hyphenated elaborations which to experimental positivism still have a slight flavour of scientific obscenity. There is a large body of literature now growing up in which "self" is the central concept.

The self-concept theory of personality maintains that the self-concept, or the way in which an individual views himself, is a primary directional factor in the individual's personality, and is instrumental in determining the individual's level of adjustment. The concept an individual has of his own self-worth governs his basic motivations and levels of aspiration. Raimy (1943) is usually given credit for the first formal statement of this view although related lines of thinking have been noted in earlier writing which have been mentioned in the last section.

Raimy (1943) emphasised that what a person believes about himself is a generally accepted factor in the social comprehension of others. Peculiar or "different" behaviour can frequently be understood by cliches such as "he has an inferiority complex" or "she is conceited". Here we are referring to a description of himself which the person referred to has apparently accepted and acts upon. This is often useful in understanding others, even when ignorant of the historical development of the self-belief. In Raimy's work, the Self-Concept theory postulates that a person's notion of himself is an involved complex and *significant* factor in his behaviour. He further maintains that one can build a systematic theory of personality organisation which neglects neither historical nor physiological events yet depends essentially on the data of immediate experience. The person in his biological, social and historical setting is the concrete object of self-perception. The Self-Concept is the more or less organised perceptual object resulting from present and past observation. Self-perception is a process which is more than activation of internal or distance receptors. There is in self-perception an organisation which involves memorial and situational factors as well as the sense data themselves. To over-simplify Raimy's (1943) theoretical position, one can say that we perceive ourselves just as we perceive a chair or another person. *What* we perceive in ourselves (the Self-Concept) may have only partial correspondence with what other people perceive in us or so-called objective personality. Yet, as always, we behave in accordance with our own perceptions even though the opinions of others or the urgencies of our biological make-up interact to influence our perceptions of ourselves. Our general behaviour, then, is to a large extent, regulated and organised by what we perceive ourselves to be, just as behaviour towards a chair is regulated by our perception of a given chair.

Raimy has defined this perceived self as a complex organisation of perceptions of greater or lesser degree of importance to the individual and defining his relationships to the world as he sees it. According to Raimy it can be seen as a map which each person consults in order to understand himself, especially during moments of crisis or choice. The approval, disapproval or ambivalence he "feels" for the self-concept or some of its sub-systems is related to his personal adjustment. A heavy weighting of disapproval or ambivalence suggests a maladjusted individual, since maladjustment in a psychological sense inevitably implies distress or disturbance in connection with oneself. When successful personality reorganisation takes place in a maladjusted individual we may also expect a shift from self-disapproval to a positive or self-approving balance. The adjusted individual may dislike or disapprove of certain aspects of the self-concept but in general he finds himself to be attractive and desirable. Raimy went on to show that at the conclusion of non-directive counselling the "successful" cases show a vast predominance of self-approval: the "unsuccessful" case showed a predominance of self-disapproval and ambivalence.

Lecky (1945) puts forward his theory in terms of "self-consistency". He conceives the mind or personality as an organisation of ideas which are felt to be consistent with one another.

The concept of the self as an underlying order that exists in the ceaselessly changing flow of experience is found in Carl Rogers's (1951) work. In fact, he is one of the leading exponents of this idea. He sees the organisational principle with which he identifies the self not only in the area of conscious perception—although he sometimes speaks of the self in that limiting way—but, as Hall and Lindzey (1957) point out, Rogers more often includes the unconscious, or, in Freudian terms, preconscious experiences and everything else that is going on in an organisation at any given moment.

Rogers (1951) and his school have contributed much to the knowledge of the self as it appears in self-perception. According to his definition, "the self-concept, or self-structure, may be thought of as an organisational configuration of perceptions of the self which are admissible to awareness. It is composed of such elements as the perceptions of one's characteristics and abilities; the percepts and concepts of the self in relation to others and the environment; the value qualities that are perceived are associated with experiences and defects; the goals and ideas which are perceived as having positive or negative valence". This means that Rogers thinks of our self-concept as pertaining to perception of ourselves, perception and concepts of our relationships with others, and to values, goals and ideals.

According to Rogers (1950) the self is related to behaviour in a significant way, in that all behaviour which is perceived as being in the realm of conscious control is consistent with the concept of self. Consequently, when the concept of self is change, alteration in behaviour is a predictable concomitant. The new behaviour will be consistent with the new structure of self.

In the light of our present study it is worth taking special note that Combs (1949) states that "it seems to be self-concept which the individual perceives to be threatened rather than his self that appears to others".

Perhaps the question "Who am I?" (which seems so important to many), would be less important if an individual did not experience anxiety and threat whenever he lacks a set of ready definitions (concerning his self-concept). Investigations (for example Erikson, 1959) often single out adolescence as the time when problems of adjustment and identity are most acute. But what about old age? Old age is typically a time in which "old labels" of self-concept are no longer applicable. One's earlier way of defining himself in relation to his body, his role in life, his family and social life and his personal worth may become inappropriate. This, of course, may cause maladjustment which would impede "successful ageing".

Earlier studies attempting to assess self-concept have used various methods. Rogers and Dymond (1954), investigating psychotherapy and personality changes in relation to self-concept employed Q-sort techniques, while Hanlon, Hofstaetter and O'Connor (1954) in their study of the "congruence and ideal self in relation to personality adjustment" used modified Q-sort. Probing the subject of the stability of self-concept as a personality dimension, Brownfair (1952) found checklists useful. Checklists were also employed by Fiedler, Dodge, Jones and Hutchins (1958), Sarbin and Rosenberg (1955) as measures to estimate the self-concept, and Hess and Bradshaw (1970). Zimmer (1954) in his study on self-acceptance and its relation to conflict, and Rubenstein and Lorr (1956) comparing terminators and drop-outs in out-patient psychotherapy, used rating scales extensively. Rentz and White (1967) among other techniques, used the semantic differential in their inquiry into various dimensions of self-concept. Several investigations employed the Draw-A-Person techniques to assess self-image (Lehner and Gunderson, 1953; Lehner and Silver, 1948; Geidt and Lehner, 1951).

Finally, we would like to mention some recent work on the cognitive approach to problems in the ageing. Although not going along with Thomas's view that this represents a decisively "new look" in psychogerontology, it does seem interesting and may well relate to self-concept work which we are to present later in this book.

Thomas (1970) reports the development of a "new look" in psychogerentology, whose major premise is that:

> "It is not the main task for theories of ageing to explain why normal persons change into some kind of partial mental deficiency, even if they do not suffer from an organic disease." (Thomas, 1970, p. 2.)

Only very recently, claims Thomas, has the stereotypic view of gerontology as a study of decline been questioned. He does not deny that processes of impairment occur, but calls for movement away from regarding these processes as central to theory building. Thomas wishes to demonstrate the value of a cognitive theory of the ageing personality not as a substitute for other theories, but as an integrative approach.

Thomas defines cognitive personality theory as research upon the individual's manner of perceiving the world about him. Cognitive theory owes its origin to workers such as Kelly, Rogers and Snygg and Combs, as well as to more evidently cognitive theorists as Witkin (1954; see original article for references). Thus, schemata, perspectives, constructs and concepts are the reference points for this approach to human ageing. The terms may not be closely defined; perception, for example, is used in a global sense. Thomas feels that this looseness may be the major reason why cognitive theory has not found general favour in the personality area. Nevertheless, he feels that this approach is of value, especially as an integrative mechanism, and formulates postulates by way of illustrating how it might function (Thomas, 1970).

In our particular studies, the Continuous Self-Concept Scale developed by Fitts (1955) was employed. The Scale is three-dimensional with each statement classified along (1) a positive-negative continuum (2) internal categoric continuum and (3) external categoric continuum. The 90 items, which constitute the main body of this scale, are divided into 45 positive and 45 negative statements about the self. Details of these are presented in Chapter 2, pages 82–86.

Although quite extensive, the literature reviewed here on the aged still suffers from the fact that much of the work was on ageing rather than on the aged. It is one of the main purposes of the present book to demonstrate some of the applications of both the methods of measuring personality relevant here, and the theoretical and practical implications of such work in the elderly themselves.

Kuypers (1972) has similarly focussed upon adaptation to ageing insofar as it is mediated by the individual's own perception of the process. Kuypers adopted the concepts of internal and external loci of control. "Internals" may be defined as people who have a belief in their own power to control their destiny, while "externals" do not subscribe to such a belief. Sixty-four subjects of mean age 68 years were assessed in terms of locus of control, ego functioning, personality and intellectual function. It was found that there were clear differences between those experiencing internal and external loci of control. Internals showed greater activity, differentiation, complexity and adaptability, while externals were characterised by closed, defensive and non-adaptive modes of reacting to their environment. Kuypers believes that the concept of locus of control may be of great use in explaining differential reactions to ageing; it is equally capable of accounting for successful and unsuccessful adaptation.

The concepts involved in the cognitive approach all reflect individuality. In so doing, they obviate the necessity for categorisation, allow for variability and permit explanation of continuity. It may be remembered that Neugarten (1964) proposed that it is an ability to synthesise and reorganise experience which appears to account for the fact that most older people contrive to maintain a characteristic mode of response to age-related changes and losses.

The fact that the ageing personality shrinks—loses ego-energy—does not seem to be in dispute. The physiological facts would make it unlikely for no changes in level of personality functioning to occur. What does appear to be as yet unproven is the case for change in structure of personality with age. The weight of evidence appears to fall upon the likelihood of an individual reacting to encroaching age in a manner which is, and has been characteristic to him. Groups of such individuals may exhibit similarities in their own ways of dealing with the challenges of increasing years: but adequate explanation of the relevance of socio-cultural, psychical, economic and other relevant variables to any one individual must, it would seem, start from the standpoint of his own personal contribution to the situation—from the standpoint of personality, in fact.

Adjustment

Finally, adjustment, a major concept in the development of practical measurement devices and in elucidating theoretical problems related to ageing, must be considered. Though much of the work covers the age range 40 to 65, some studies have investigated older samples. Conkey (1933) stressed three factors relating to good adjustment in old age. Most important was (1) strong and varied interests or activities, followed by (2) economic independence or security, and (3) freedom from physical handicaps. She also pointed out that good adjustment in old age is largely a product of good adjustment prior to old age. The better adjusted also wished more frequently to relive their lives. These conclusions were reinforced by the subsequent investigations of Morgan (1937), Landis (1942) and Lawton (1943). In view of the stress laid on interests and activities in relation to adjustment, one might ask how stable or changing these are over age. Strong (1943) suggested that age and the experience that goes with age change an adult man's interests very little. Kuhlen (1945), on the other hand, notes that while the 25- and 65-year-old may be essentially alike in interests, the age differences that do exist in the correlational data are extremely important in the understanding of the older as compared with the younger man. One might have the same interests, but does one have the same ability or opportunity to enjoy them at 65 plus?

Since the 1940s, considerable emphasis has been placed on the development of methods of extracting quantitative scores for "adjustment" from subjects at various age levels. Cavan and colleagues (1949) reported the use of the Adult Activity Schedule. This Inventory "Your Attitudes and Activities" consists of some statements which are checked, others answered by "yes" or "no", while others have a four- or five-point intensity distribution. Categories covered in the inventory include health, family, friends, leisure, and recreation clubs and organisations, employment history, financial security, early life, and attitudes. The inventory was despatched to a total of 8,441 individuals geographically distributed over the entire United States. This sample was a fairly close representation of the population of the United States aged 60 years and over, with the exception that a much smaller representation of rural farm subjects was obtained. Subscores for the following categories were calculated: leisure activities (including organisations), religious activities, intimate contacts (friends and family), health, and security. The authors devoted considerable attention to the reliability and validity of the inventory and conclude that although improvements could be made, both reliability and validity are high enough to warrant the use of the scale. For instance, the correlation between ratings of adjustment made by two to five judges and scores on the schedule, range from $0 \cdot 53$ to $0 \cdot 78$. In the sample studies, increasing age was associated with reduced activity as shown by attendance at meetings and in fewer number of hobbies and plans for the future. There was also an increase in physical handicaps, illness, and nervousness, and a decrease in feeling of satisfaction with health. Religious activities and dependence upon religion increased with age, whereas feelings of happiness, usefulness, zest, and interest in life decreased. In general, the older subjects responded with lower median attitude scores indicating *poorer adjustment*. An increased feeling of economic security, despite a lower amount of income, was reported by many of the respondents. Sex differences in adjustment were also apparent; for instance, women reported more physical handicaps, nervous and neurotic symptoms, and accidents than men. Women had more religious activity and more favourable attitudes toward religion than did men, but were less happy than men.

A number of other studies have compared adjustment scores on the above questionnaire between specified groups of older people. Havighurst and Shanas (1950) obtained data on 28 members of the Fossils Club, a retired men's club in Washington, D.C., composed of former professional or administrative people. Responses were obtained from 30 per cent of the total membership of the club with a mean age of 73 years. This group of subjects showed much better adjustment to old age than that observed in the general population. The important factors seem to be economic security, relatively late retirement, and congenial housing and living arrangements. Other studies on retired Y.M.C.A. secretaries and public-school teachers have shown a wide range in adjustment patterns (Britton, 1949). Older people living in institutions were found by Pan (1950) to have lower adjustment scores on this inventory than those living in the community. All these studies suffer from methodological difficulties, such as lack of control for educational background, socio-economic status, cultural pattern of the community, and home influences. *They have, however, served to focus attention on the many variables involved in the adequate social adjustment of older people* and in defining what one may consider abnormal.

Fried (1949) found that inactivity in elderly people was six times greater among the lower economic groups than in the higher. The elderly people interviewed complained of inactivity and indicated preference for doing something. A desire for continued activity has important social implications and indicates the need for re-education both in individuals and in the community with respect to attitudes toward older people. It also seems evident that our educational system has not succeeded in giving individuals inner resources for continued expansion of interests and activities throughout life, particularly in the latter decades.

The interrelationships between "social" and "personal" adjustment evident in the earlier work continues to provide a need for more detailed analysis in this area. Moberg (1953) reported that those old people who had formerly been leaders in the church were better adjusted than those who had never held leadership positions, but that there was no difference between church members and non-church members in personal adjustment to old age. Older people must adapt to many new life demands, such as retirement, death of family and friends, changes in standards and styles of living, as well as to personal, psychological, and biological changes. These important changes are largely initiated by forces beyond the individual's control. It would also appear that individual differences in social roles determine many features of adjustment in old age (Phillips, 1957; Beckman et al. 1958; Pappas and Silver, 1958). Empirically there appears to be a significant correlation between the number of social roles and adjustment: activity and interpersonal contact may be prophylactic for many problems of later life (Shepard, 1955; Havighurst, 1957; 1959). The onset of illness in late life does have marked effects on personal and social adjustment (Mack, 1953; Kahn et al. 1958), but there is also considerable evidence that persons lacking successful adjustment in early or middle life continue to do so in old age (Shepard, 1955; Slater and Roth, 1969).

The measurement of *personal adjustment in terms of happiness* as well as social activity has also attracted considerable attention, though the reports offer conflicting results. Early studies by Morgan (1937) and Landis (1942), based on interview material, concluded that most people of advanced age considered the happiest period of their lives to have been that between 25 and 45 years. Kuhlen (1948), on the other hand, in a study of 300 adults between the aged of 20 and 80, reported that happiness ratings tended to increase up to the twenties and thirties and to decrease thereafter. The primary sources of unhappiness were bereavement and poor health. Though most of the foregoing subjects reported higher degrees of happiness at early ages, it is important to note that only 3 per cent of the aged people (two-thirds being 70 or over) interviewed by Gardner (1948) reported that they were unhappy. Furthermore, wide individual differences in happiness ratings were found by Lawton (1943). One should remember, however, that happiness is almost certainly a multi-dimensional quality that requires precise definition, and dependence on retrospective information about happiness in previous decades of life is hazardous. There is also considerable evidence that happiness and successful adjustment, both personal and social, in old age are intimately bound up with physical and mental health. Lebo (1953) and Mack (1953) found that happiness in old age depended on health and minimal financial support. Happy old people were more alert and flexible than those who were unhappy. Interestingly, the ill did not see themselves as different from normal, and the hopefully ill were better adjusted.

There are obviously many difficulties in assessing and defining "adjustment" or "successful aging" as it is undoubtedly a multi-dimensional concept both in terms of definition and aetiology. However, the work of Havighurst (1949; 1950; 1953; 1963) and his colleagues gives many useful indications of the nature and for the measurement of old age adjustment. To quote Havighurst (1963):

"The practical purpose of gerontology is to help people live better in their later years. However, we do not have general agreement on what good living in later years is. We agree on some of the determining conditions of good living, such as health, economic security, presence of friends and family, but there is disagreement on the actual signs of good living in the feelings and behaviour of a person as he grows older. Some believe that good living in old age consists of maintaining actvity and involvement as in middle age, others believe that good living for elderly people is just the opposite—a retirement to a rocking chair and decrease of activity as the years pass by. Thus, the definition of successful ageing may appear to require a value judgement on which people are bound to disagree."

As he also points out, it should be possible to develop an instrument to measure the various aspects of success in ageing or in old age. Havighurst and Albrecht published a scale in 1953 based on a study of public opinion concerning the activities of older people.

Cavan et al. (1949) and Havighurst's own work mentioned earlier (1953; 1957) and later developments have concentrated on the definition of successful ageing in terms of social competence. Several measures recognise the inner and outer aspects of successful ageing, in particular the Chicago Attitude Inventory (Cavan et al. 1949) Havighurst and Albrecht, 1953; Havighurst, 1957). Scores are a combination of attitudes about activities in several areas and inner feelings of happiness independent, to some extent, of outward behaviour.

This area has been extended by the work of Bernice Neugarten in 50- to 80-year-olds in Kansas City study. The research group began by examining measures of adjustment morale used by other investigators. After extensive interview assessment, they produced an operational definition of life satisfaction in five components: (1) zest *vs* apathy (2) resolution and fortitude (3) goodness of fit between desired and achieved goals (4) positive self-concept and (5) mood tone. Each component can be rated on a five point scale (Neurgarten *et al.* 1961; Havighurst, 1963) and the ratings can be added to get a life satisfaction rating ranging from 5 to 25.

Two forms of self-report instruments are now available from the work of this research team (Havighurst, 1963): (1) *Life Satisfaction Index A—* an attitude inventory of 20 items which correlates 0·58 with the interview scale, N = 90, mean 12·4, S.D. 4·4: (2) *Life Satisfaction Index B—* consists of six open-ended and six check list items scored 0, 1 or 2 which correlates 0·71 with the rating scale, N = 92, mean 15·1, S.D. 4·7. A and B correlates 0·73, total mean 27·6, S.D. 6·7.

These procedures for measuring life satisfaction all depend on inner definitions of successful ageing. They can be used to study the effects of social and economic conditions on people, to assess their life satisfaction. The definition of successful ageing as satisfaction with present and past life does not favour either of the apparently rival, though one might add not mutually exclusive, activity and disengagement theories.

The activity theory is favoured by most of the practical workers in gerontology. They believe that people should maintain the activities and attitudes of middle age as long as possible and then find substitutes for the activities they must give up—for work when they are forced to retire, for clubs and associations, for friends and loved ones whom they lose by death. Disengagement theory is based on the observation that as people grow older they generally curtail the activities of middle age. As stated by Cumming and McCaffrey (1960):

"This theory starts from the commonsense observation that in America, the old person is less involved in the life around him than when he was younger and proceeds without making assumptions about the desirability of this fact. Ageing in the modal person is thought of in this theory as a mutual withdrawal or disengagement which takes place between the ageing person and others in the social systems to which he belongs. He may withdraw more markedly from some classes of people and remain relatively close to others. This withdrawal may be accompanied at the outset by increased preoccupation with himself. When the ageing process is complete, the equilibrium which existed in middle life between the individual and his society has given way to a new equilibrium characterised by a greater distance and an altered type of relationship. In a previous report, we have presented data which suggest that one of the early stages of disengagement occurs when the ageing individual withdraws emotional investment from the environment. We have thought of the inner process as being an ego change in which object cathexis is reduced; this results in an appearance of self-centredness, and an orientation to others which betrays less sense of mutual obligation. This is accompanied by a somewhat freer and more expressive manner. The fully disengaged person can be thought of as having transferred much of his cathexis to his own inner life; his memories, his fantasies, his image of himself as someone who was something, and did accomplish things."

There is no doubt that disengagement does take place with ageing, but proponents of the activity theory regard this as a result of society's withdrawal from the ageing person against his will and desire. However, the disengagement theory stated by Cumming and co-workers (1960) regards disengagement as a natural process the ageing person accepts and desires. They speak of disengagement as being "primary intrinsic, and secondarily responsive."

Cumming et al. (1960) have stated and tested three hypotheses about the process of disengagement:

1. Rate of interaction and variety of interaction will lessen with age.

2. Changes in amount, and variety, of interaction will be accompanied by concomitant changes in perception of the size of the life space.

3. A change in the quality of interaction will accompany decrease in the social life space, from absorption with others to absorption with self, and from evaluative to carefree.

One might suggest, however, that unless the process of disengagement is so thoroughly intrinsic that there is no stopping or delaying it, there is a considerable margin of social and individual choice between activity and disengagement, and within this area it would be useful to test the two theories to find out how they are related to life satisfaction.

Life satisfaction may be positively related to activity for some people and to disengagement for others. A person with an active, achieving, and outward-directed way of life style will be best satisfied to continue this into old age with only slight dimunition. Other people with a passive dependent, home-centred way of life will be best satisfied with disengagement. Cumming and McCaffrey (1960) suggested this when they said that there may be "important non-modal groups of the die-with-your-boots-on school. We do not yet know who they are, except that there is evidence that academics do not disengage, in the sense that we are using it here, to the same degree that, for example, skilled workmen or clerical workers do". Reichard et al. (1962) in a study of working-class men found three types of successful agers, one active, one passive, and one mature, who almost certainly would be differentiated if their activity-disengagement processes were studied. Indeed, disengagement itself refers primarily to the weakening of the bonds that tie the individual to his social environment. It may result in rocking-chair inaction, but it may also result in a carefree attitude combined with assertiveness and activity.

They believed that their subjects' personality characteristics had probably changed little throughout their lives—they examined past histories, and thus their work included the concept of life-span. Their personality typology can be used to explain differential response to ageing; the rocking-chair and the armoured men are equally well-adjusted, but the basis of their adjustment is diametrically opposed. The rocking-chair men derive their satisfaction from taking things easy, armoured man depends on maintaining activity. As a review article by Jones (1961) pointed out there are individual life styles (active, passive, social asocial, etc.), environmental pressures (economic, social, familial, etc.), and, last but not least, biological deteriorations and disabilities, to be taken into account when defining normal and abnormal, successful or unsuccessful ageing.

Because of the ways in which pressures and personality interact, it seems likely that we shall learn most about the aged by a thorough analysis of the components or the structure of aged personality and continuous longitudinal investigations.

Lemon et al. (1972) and others place the origin of the activity theory of ageing in the publication of Havighurst and Albrecht's study in 1953. They, as described earlier, found that activity was positively related to adjustment and stated that:

"The American formula for happiness in old age might be summed up in the phrase 'Keep active'. And yet there are a minority of people who are content with a very passive quiet life. Their 'rocking-chair' philosophy appears to fit their own personal needs so well that they are happy where the majority of older people would be unhappy" (p. 55).

One factor which has been more extensively and fruitfully studied is health and morale in adjustment. Sex differences in adaptation to ill-health have already been described and they illustrate the fact that physical disability may have a differential impact. Kutner *et al.* (1956) found that persons of higher socio-economic status tended to judge themselves as being in better health than those of lower socio-economic status, regardless of actual health status. Mack (1953) found a number of factors which appeared to modify the relationship between actual health and morale. Nevertheless, the conclusion most generally drawn is that health, whether objectively or subjectively perceived, is significantly related to morale. Tissue (1971) found that congruity between life-space and readiness to disengage (disengagement potential) was paramount in determining morale. The exception was where poor health obtained; morale was consistently low here, regardless of the congruity variable. Lowenthal (1968) found that interaction with a "confidant" was important for morale, but pointed out that this relationship did not appear to mitigage the effects of physical impairment upon morale. Fowler and McCalla (1969) found that health was the variable which accounted for the decline of morale with age. Messer (1967) set out to examine the effect of environment upon morale, but found that race and health were more powerful explanatory variables. Gubrium (1971) sought the opinion of the elderly as to those factors significant for life satisfaction in old age: his findings show that the elderly do, in fact, agree with the researchers in their designation of health as a significant variable.

Psychiatric health does not appear to operate in the same manner as physical health. Menotti (1967) failed to show a cumulative effect between the ageing process and mental illness. Feifel (1954) examined attitudes toward ageing among psychiatric patients in their thirties. He found no differences between this sample and a student sample in attitude toward ageing. Lowenthal (1964) found no relationship between psychiatric health and age-linked isolation. She found that good physical health and absence of intellectual deterioration were predictive of social interaction; isolation appeared to be a consequence of ill-health. Gilberstadt (1968) utilised measures of social adjustment, intellectual functioning and psychomotor skills. He concluded that assessment of social adjustment increases in relevance with age, and this adjustment may be dependent upon favourable environmental conditions. He pointed out that, if intellectual deficit is marked, however, the prognosis for social adjustment is poor. Thus, it would seem that organic deterioration may be classified as physical illness; with this exception made, psychiatric health does not appear to be relevant to morale in the elderly. Lowenthal (1968) makes this distinction when she discusses physical illness in the context of age-linked stress, and refers to psychiatric illness as deriving from inner conflict or failure.

A further variable which is generally regarded as significant in the study of the elderly is social class. Lowenthal (1964) found that socio-economic status was associated with isolation and psychiatric disturbance, and pointed out that such findings were consistent with sociological analyses of incidence of psychiatric illness. She did not find, however, any relationship between change of formal role status and morale.

Gubrium's (1971) study of the opinions of the elderly with regard to factors important to life satisfaction showed that they do attribute considerable importance to income. Fowler and McCalla (1969) found an association between income and morale, but only up to a certain level of yearly income. This would seem to suggest that a minimum level of income is required, but that money *per se* cannot compensate for the disadvantages of ageing. Mack (1953) did find a tendency for persons of higher social class to show better adjustment to chronic illness, and Kutner *et al.* (1956) also found higher morale among those of higher socio-economic status regardless of health status. In fact, Kutner and colleagues found no significant difference in morale between those in poor health of higher socio-economic status and those of good health of lower socio-economic status.

These complex interrelationships between inner satisfaction with life and outer behaviour in society need careful investigation in the elderly. We can thank workers for their efforts, but wish for considerably more *evidence* on large representative samples of the aged and hope for longitudinal studies to help unravel the confusions in this area which are not only theoretically fascinating to psychologists, but of *vital* practical importance to a society with an increasing aged population. The effect of retirement, for example, shows interesting variations between classes, across cultures and within economic conditions. In Great Britain 70 per cent of men compulsorily retired at 65 would have continued working if it had been possible, though only 25 per cent actually tried to find work (Clark, 1959). On the other hand, in America, where pensions are less generally available, Gordon (1960) found men tended to retire only when ill-health forced the issue. Furthermore, forced retirement will differentially affect those who have enjoyed rather than those who have tolerated or disliked their work. The evidence from Emerson (1959), Thompson *et al.* (1960) and Heron (1963) suggested that there is a "retirement impact" that varies with occupational class. When and under what conditions one might ask does the "retirement impact" become abnormal?

Some recent studies have cast doubt on the necessity of a polarised activity *vs* disengagement approach to understanding life satisfaction or abnormality in old age. What are successful or unsuccessful, normal or abnormal aged types? An interview project by Buhler (1951) named four groups of older people: (1) those who want to rest and relax; (2) those who wish to be active; (3) those dissatisfied with the past but resigned; (4) those who have led meaningless lives and are now frustrated, guilty and regretful. On the other hand, Reichard *et al.* (1962) in their book "Ageing and Personality" suggested three types of "successful" agers; one active, one passive and one mature (ego-integrated). There were two unsuccessful types: extra-punitive and self-rejective. "Life satisfaction", "activity" and "disengagement" would obviously mean different things for each of these groups.

A very important and recent publication by Britton and Britton (1972) reported a 9-year study of personality and adjustment in 146 subjects of over 65 years. They used a comprehensive selection of measures: the Chicago Activity and Attitude Inventories; the Cavan Adjustment Rating Scale; the Personal Relations and Sociability Scales from the Guilford-Zimmerman Temperament Survey; three TAT cards to measure attitudes to ageing self; an Opinion Conformity Scale based on a survey of community expectations for the elderly; a Reputation Rating whereby community adults named persons whom they thought were coping well or not in everyday life; a Community Rating on five dimensions; and an Interviewer's Rating based on observation of the subject during interview.

Change was examined in terms of the correlation of each of these measures with the longitudinal trend score (LTS). The LTS provided a global measure of change or stability over three assessments. Britton and Britton found that the tendency was for a decline on all measures, but the finding which received greatest emphasis was that of variability. Moreover, those persons exhibiting positive and negative change could seldom be distinguished in terms of a good number of social, health and economic characteristics.

Britton and Britton concluded that their study highlighted the complexity, diversity and variability of behaviour among the aged. They claim that there is a tendency to search for regularity, reflected in—or perhaps caused by—current measuring instruments and experimental techniques. They feel that this tendency has led psychologists to ignore the potential flexibility of the aged. They conclude by calling, as did the Chicago workers, for societal recognition of the need to provide for the aged an environment wherein they might exercise this flexibility whose root is in the personality system.

2

Research Methodology

Methodological problems of investigating the aged, particularly those associated with sampling and measurement, have been discussed at length by a number of investigators, including Schaie and Strother (1968) and Savage et al. (1973). The selection of participants in research on the aged presents a variety of problems. It is evident that a serious disadvantage of much of the psychological data on the aged has been the rather limited or biased sampling procedures employed. Studies have frequently used "volunteer" or "captive" populations from residential homes, old people's clubs, etc., so that the generality of their results may be questioned (Doppelt and Wallace, 1955; Heron and Chown, 1967). Consequently, in order to reduce the difficulties of understanding and interpretation of the data presented here, the sampling procedures as they were carried out at each chronological stage of the investigations, will be explicitly recorded. Hindsight showed up some of the warts, but in general the populations used were as free as practicably possible at the time from any bias known to us. It might be added that by their very nature aged samples are survivor populations, and though this raises problems, this might be more profitably looked upon as a reality or fact of life which influences the normative characteristics of the Aged than a sampling anomaly or imperfection.

The choice of personality characteristics and methods of measuring them also presents problems. These will be discussed and the reasons for our choice—later to be proved right or wrong—will be outlined. One cannot, for example, assume that all personality dimensions are evident and measureable at all ages. Even within the descriptions or models of personality and its development presented by Cattell and his colleagues, certain dimensions evolve, or have varied importance, at different ages (Cattell, 1965). Factors D, phlegmatic *vs* excitable, and J, vigorous *vs* doubting, do not appear in the adult forms of measurement (16PF), whilst Q_2 group dependent *vs* self-sufficient, is not seen in the CPQ or ESPQ, that is roughly below the age of twelve. Q_3, self conflict, is not assessed in the early school age range; L, trusting *vs* suspicious, practical *vs* imaginative characteristics, M and Q_1, conservative *vs* experimenting, only appear in those over the age of 16. Forthright *vs* shrewd (N) is absent for the 12–16 year old in the High School Personality Questionnaire.

We will, in effect, try to give future researchers and practitioners, as well as ourselves, all the information necessary or at least possible to evaluate accurately our findings to improve future research in this area. Each aged sample population used and the methods of investigation of personality employed will now be presented.

The Aged Sample Populations

Over the past 15 years, there have been numerous publications in books, psychological and psychiatric journals on the multi-disciplinary work with the aged in Newcastle upon Tyne by staff from the University Department of Psychological Medicine. For the convenience of readers a full bibliographic list is presented in an appendix of this book. In order to identify clearly the sample populations used by Dr. R. D. Savage and his clinical psychology colleagues, the specific designations were given to each sample used in their psychological investigations between 1963 and 1974. These were:

(1) Newcastle upon Tyne Community Aged I   (1964)
(2) Newcastle upon Tyne Community Aged II   (1965)
(3) Newcastle upon Tyne Hospital Aged III   (1964)
(4) Newcastle upon Tyne Combined Aged IV   (1969)
(5) Newcastle upon Tyne Community Aged V   (1971)
(6) Newcastle upon Tyne Institutions Aged VI   (1973)

Work on personality measurement and functioning was carried out on all but Community Aged II and the Combined Aged IV, the details of which are available in "Intellectual Functioning in the Aged", Savage *et al.* 1973, published by Methuen & Co. Ltd. A full description of the samples used in the personality studies will be presented here so that the populations and the parameters measured need only be briefly referred to in the chapters dealing with the major outcomes of the investigations.

COMMUNITY AGED I (1964)

One of the most important features of any selection and investigation of the aged is that the sample population should be as representative as possible of the total population. Many of the investigations reported in the literature have used easily available captive populations. These have often been drawn from sources such as "old persons" clubs and may have consisted of "volunteers" with very dubious motivation. Obviously, these factors seriously affect the generality of any conclusions which have been drawn.

In an effort to obtain as representative a sample of the aged in the community as possible, some initial personality investigations were carried out on the aged living in their own homes in the city of Newcastle upon Tyne, England, which had a population of about 350,000. The sample was part of that previously and conveniently used for the study of mental illness in the aged by Professor Sir Martin Roth and Dr. David Kay of the Department of Psychological Medicine, University of Newcastle upon Tyne, full details of which appear in Kay (1962); Kay *et al.* (1964*a,b* and 1966).

As it is impossible to obtain detailed and reliable lists of the elderly directly in the U.K., the electoral roles for the city were used as a basis for identification of persons over the age of 65. Electoral Wards were then identified which were representative of the City in terms of certain demographic variables, namely: (1) Mean rateable value; (2) Estimate of overcrowding in accommodation; (3) Criminal offence rate; (4) Infant mortality; (5) Mobility of population and (6) Incidence of mental illness. The details of the five wards chosen as representative of the City as a whole were, to quote Kay, Beamish and Roth (1964*a,b*):

> "(1) *Byker*. A stable working class district with poor housing, overcrowding, static population and with crime and infant mortality rates in the intermediate ranges. Demolition and rehousing had not begun in this area at the material time. Our

field investigations showed that families tended to live in close proximity to each other: there were also more children per person than in the other wards.

(2) *Dene.* A suburban type, middle-class residential area with good housing standards and no overcrowding. The population is static and the crime and infant mortality rates low.

(3) *Jesmond.* A residential area with the highest standard of housing, as judged by rateable value in Newcastle upon Tyne. Overcrowding and crime rate is negligible and infant mortality low, but the population is mobile. Jesmond contains many small hotels and boarding houses and a relatively high proportion of people living alone.

(4) *St. Nicholas.* The central area: commercial and working classes; there is a considerable degree of overcrowding and crime; mobility is high and infant mortality is far above average. The area includes markets and quayside areas and the old town.

(5) *Stephenson.* This area is heterogeneous, in the process of demolition. It includes some once valuable properties, now falling into decay, as well as slum areas. Overcrowding, crime, infant mortality and population mobility are all the highest recorded in Newcastle."

Some 1,780 individuals were randomly selected from the electoral lists and asked by letter whether they were aged 65 or over. Those who did not reply were visited individually and only 23 proved impossible to trace. The eventual result of this process and co-operation by the population, as well as of our Medical, Social and Administrative colleagues, was a sample of 309 persons aged over 65.

Our final sample of 100 for the Community Aged I used in the personality investigations represented every third person in this group, except where assessment proved impossible due to factors such as death, absolute refusal or sensory inadequacy. In this case a matched subject from those remaining with the same age, sex, psychiatric diagnosis and Electoral Ward as the original random one was substituted. The sample eventually assessed is shown in Table 2. The diagnoses represent the psychiatric state at the time of our investigation and were made in 1964 by, or under the supervision of, Dr. D. W. K. Kay, an internationally accepted expert in psychogeriatric research. The diagnostic categories used by Dr. Kay and his colleagues may be briefly described as follows:

(1) *Normal.* No signs of any functional or organic psychiatric disorder, or any form of clinically recognisable mental illness.

(2) *Functional disorders* group included neurotic, reactive and endogenous depressive categories of psychiatric diagnosis.

(3) *The organic group* consisted of aged people living in the community with senile and/or arteriosclerotic dementia, clinically recognisable, but for a variety of reasons not requiring hospitalisation.

Table 2. Newcastle upon Tyne Aged
Personality and Adjustment Study Samples

Sample	Total	Age		Sex			Diagnosis
		Mean	S.D.	Male	Female	N	
Community Aged							
I	83	74·8	3·7	27	56		
				16	27	43	Normal
				10	28	38	Functional
				1	1	2	Organics
Hospital Aged III	144	71·5	8·1	77	67		
				16	13	29	Normal
				22	20	42	Affectives
				16	15	31	Schizophrenics
				23	19	42	Organics
Community Aged							
V	82	79·6	5·2	26	56	82	Normal Community
Institutions VI(a)	57	67·0	3·1	25	32		
				9	10	19	Affectives
				8	12	20	Thought disordered Schizophrenic
				8	10	18	Schizophrenics
Institutions Aged							
VI(b)	42	74·5	3·6	17	25		
				7	7	14	Home
				3	11	14	Residential Care
				7	7	14	Psychiatric Hospital
Institutions Aged							
VI(c)	20	74·9	3·2	5	15	20	Mixed—*see* Text

HOSPITAL AGED III (1964)

The personality measurement of mentally ill patients presented quite different sampling problems. The major consideration in selecting this sample was to obtain groups which would represent the "types" of mental disorders seen in the aged. Consequently, it was decided to test patients representing some of the major diagnostic categories of psychiatric illness in old age, internationally recognised at the time and published by Professor Sir Martin Roth (Roth, 1955; Slater and Roth, 1969). Our sample consisted of 144 elderly subjects divided into a normal and three mentally ill groups and designated Hospital Aged III:

(2) Schizophrenia—late recurrent—and paraphrenia.

(3) Affective disorders—late onset.

(4) Senile and arteriosclerotic dementia.

This Hospital Aged III Sample is described in Table 2 in terms of illness, age and sex. The normals showed no signs of any form of clinically recognisable mental illness. The late onset schizophrenic and paraphrenic group of patients were those whose first illness occurred in senescence, in whom the most prominent features of the illness were paranoid delusions and hallucinations often with unclear schizophrenic features. The affective disorders were also of late onset and included neurotic disorders as well as reactive and endogenous depressive patients. Late onset depression appears to have less genetic loading than early onset depression, and significantly more late onset manic depressives experience clear physical or social stress compared with that for early onset (Stendstedt, 1959; Kay, 1959; Post, 1962a; Chesser, 1965).

The senile and arteriosclerotic dementias were fairly classical, though not severe at this point in terms of degeneration of the nervous system and the disorganisation of personality. The independence of arteriosclerotic and senile dementia has been discussed by both clinical and pathological investigators. Corsellis (1962) showed that the processes were distinct to a large extent neuropathologically; 45 per cent of his cases were due to cerebrovascular disease, 34 per cent showed changes associated with senile dementia, and 21 per cent of the patients had both disease processes. Clinically, arteriosclerotic psychosis is frequently associated with hypertension and follows a number of cerebrovascular accidents. Intellectual impairment and other symptoms show marked fluctuation in the course of the illness and total disintegration, as seen in senile dementia, does not show until very late in the illness. Prognosis in arteriosclerotic dementia is better than for senile dementia, but even so within two years of diagnosis, mortality is 70 per cent (Roth, 1955).

Members of the patient groups were randomly selected from a list of all patients over the age of 60 who had been admitted into St. Nicholas Hospital, Gosforth, since 1959, and recent intake to the Newcastle General Hospital. We are extremely grateful particularly to Dr. G. Blessed for the considerable effort and expertise in selecting these patients for us. They were diagnosed as part of a carefully designed research investigation on aged psychiatric disorders, some of which work has been published (Roth et al. 1967; Blessed et al. 1968; Tomlinson et al. 1968).

The normal elderly were randomly selected from those in the Newcastle upon Tyne Community Aged Survey (Kay, Beamish and Roth, 1964a,b) who had received a diagnosis of "psychiatrically normal," i.e. they were in effect positively normal. They were selected from three electoral wards—two working class and one middle class district. Virtually all of the normal group were co-operative; only three of the 32 contacted refused. This was probably due to the fact that every effort had to be made to secure the voluntary co-operation of these elderly people by fully explaining the whole nature and purpose of our investigations to them; they were then free to co-operate or refuse. The hospitalized patients with functional mental illnesses were also remarkably co-operative: only two schizophrenic and two patients with affective disorders declined to complete the personality investigations. On the other hand, there were 11 incompleted records obtained from patients with senile dementia. Some of the more demented patients were unable to score on any of the WAIS subtests and their low cognitive functioning made personality measurement impossible. Others who became agitated and distressed were unable or refused to complete the investigations. Finally, three of these patients died after inclusion in the sample but before the investigations of personality were completed. These three records are excluded from the data presented.

COMMUNITY AGED V (1971)

The Community Aged V sample of 82 subjects is also a cohort from a larger, randomly selected population of old people living at home originally described by Kay, Beamish and Roth (1962, 1964a) and Savage et al. (1973). The population from which this group was drawn in 1971 lived within six representative electoral wards of Newcastle upon Tyne, England, chosen to give an accurate cross sample of the population with regard to variables such as age, distribution, socio-economic status, as for Community Aged I and II.

Once again, cyclostyled letters had been sent out. Three thousand two hundred and ninety-four persons were contacted at random from published electoral registers for the city, bearing in mind the total population of each ward. The aim of this letter, which enclosed a stamped envelope and form, was to ascertain whether the recipient was 65 years or over. There were 2,399 replies to the initial letters. The balance of 895 was then sent to the local Executive Council, who were able to confirm the age of 590 persons. A social worker then visited the remaining 305 people to ascertain their age. A total Aged population sample of 494 was eventually identified. These subjects had been seen initially in 1964/5 by the social worker and by a psychiatrist, were again seen by a psychiatrist in 1967/8, and were known to be on the most recent Newcastle Electoral Register published in February 1972 (compiled October 1971).

It was felt that this overall sample represented as thorough a selection from the community aged as could be obtained in 1971 in the light of the absence of a register of all citizens over 65. In essence, this, as well as any aged sample, is a survivor population—the ramifications of which will be discussed in a later section. It is quite important to note again, however, that the subjects in no way "volunteered" for inclusion in the sample, even though at least a minimum degree of co-operation was exhibited.

The Community Aged V elderly Newcastle upon Tyne citizens initially consisted of 116 from the 494 identified. Of these, 17 were unco-operative: 11 refused at the beginning due to "health reasons" or were untestable and 6 refused to participate in the second assessment interview. In addition to this, 9 subjects died before they were seen by the interviewer and 6 were untraceable. Eighty-two subjects took part in the study. Consequently, the final Community Aged V cohort for this study comprised 82 community residents whose mean age was 79·6 with an S.D. of 5·2 years. Of this sample. 26 were men and 56 were women, their mean ages being 78·2, S.D. = 4·3 and 80·00, S.D. = 5·4 years respectively. Further details are given in Table 2.

INSTITUTIONS AGED VI (1973)

The Institutions Aged VI sample consists of three sub-samples investigated in 1968, 1971 and 1973. They represented various institutions: (a) hospital; (b) local authority nursing home; (c) day centre hospital care.

The first sub-sample was drawn from a mental illness hospital and represented affective, schizophrenic and thought-disorder schizophrenic patients. The nursing home sample was drawn from local authority institutions for care of the elderly in the Newcastle upon Tyne area, with some normal population and hospitalised patients for comparison purposes. The latest sample in 1973 was drawn from the Brighton Psychogeriatric Day Clinic in the Newcastle upon Tyne General Hospital.

(a) This was a purely hospital sample drawn from the Cherry Knowle Psychiatric Hospital. Each patient was carefully diagnosed by a consultant psychiatrist as suffering from an affective disorder or schizophrenia or thought-disordered schizophrenia. The sample consisted of 57 adult psychiatric patients, 19 of these being affectives, 20 thought-disordered schizophrenics and the remaining 18 being schizophrenics showing no signs of thought disorder. The three groups were matched for age and intelligence. (All were aged between 60–79, mean age for the total group being 67.)

Of the 19 affectives, 9 were male, 10 female. (Diagnosis was made by the consultant psychiatrists of the hospital in question and recorded in the case notes). Five of the affectives group were diagnosed as suffering from reactive depression, one as an agitated depressive, three as involutional depressives, one as manic depressive and the remaining nine simply diagnosed as depressives.

The 20 thought-disordered schizophrenics comprised 8 males and 12 females. Basis of this diagnosis was the opinion of the consultant psychiatrist and the emergence during the testing session of any of the clinical signs of thought disorder given by Mayer-Gross, Slater and Roth (1969). These are:

(i) Inconsequential following of side issues (thoughts being directed by alliteration, analogy, clang association, symbolic meaning, condensation).

(ii) Clinging to unimportant detail.

(iii) Thought blocking.

(iv) Pressure of thoughts.

(v) Emptiness and vagueness of thoughts.

Nine of this group were diagnosed as paranoid schizophrenics, one as a simple schizophrenic, the others simply as schizophrenics.

The 18 remaining patients were schizophrenics who showed no signs of thought disorder. Of these, 8 were male, 10 female—7 being diagnosed as paranoid schizophrenics the others having no differential diagnosis within the general schizophrenic classification.

It should be noted that only those patients who were thought capable by the psychiatrist of completing the Cattell 16PF were included in the sample. This perhaps accounts for the absence of hebephrenic or catatonic schizophrenics. (It also appeared that such diagnoses were rare in this particular hospital). Some 20 patients were rejected by the author on completion of some of the items in one or other of the personality tests, because of very poor co-operation, but most often because of their seeming inability to answer the questions in anything but a random fashion (e.g. one woman answered "yes" to every question in the first half of the EPI).

(b) The sample consisted of 42:

Fourteen S's (7 males, 7 females) residing in their own homes, mean age 72·29 years.

Fourteen residents (3 males, 11 females) of a council home for the aged, mean age 82·24 years, mean length of institutionalisation (in this particular institution) 17·3 months (range 3–24 months).

Fourteen psychiatric inpatients (7 males, 7 females) mean age 69·7 years in two large general psychiatric hospitals. Their diagnoses were as follows: 6 chronic schizophrenia, 3 psychotic depression, 2 G.P.1., 1 arteriosclerotic dementia, 1 chronic alcoholic, 1 neurotic depression. Mean length of hospitalisation was 15·5 years, range 19 months–50 years.

Subjects were in the main from working-class background, and the majority had received only elementary education.

All subjects, except two men and one woman in the old age home sample, completed both 16PF and LSI-A and B.

The sample was selected in the sense that it was necessary to rely on voluntary participation in the study. It might, therefore, be expected that the sample would be biased in favour of better-adjusted old people. However, a number of subjects were prepared to co-operate who expressed strong feelings of dissatisfaction and depression.

Age and type of residence were not correlated. Significantly $(r = 0 \cdot 1667)$.

(c) One population from which the sample was drawn consisted of persons attending the Brighton Psychogeriatric Day Clinic in Newcastle upon Tyne General Hospital, the University of Newcastle upon Tyne. The clinic was established not only to provide a service, but also with provision for research into the problems of catering for the needs of the aged psychiatric patient. We are grateful to Dr. K. Bergmann for his co-operation with this study.

Readers can obtain further details of the Unit from Bergmann (1972). For example, potential recipients of these services are referred from a number of sources; general practitioners, local authority staff, psychiatrists, geriatricians, and other medical staff. Patients may be accepted directly; or they may initially be assessed by a unit psychiatrist on an out-patient, ward consultation or domiciliary basis. The main criterion for entry is that the aged patient should present at a stage in his or her disorder which is sufficiently early to allow some intervention to be potentially effective. Thus patients with a wide variety of disturbances are considered; persons manifesting organic dysfunction are not excluded, but the degree and duration of impairment may be a decisive factor.

The unit functions appear to provide what Caplan (1964) designated secondary and tertiary prevention. The duration and extent of psychiatric morbidity may be minimised (secondary prevention), and the ill-effects of the aged person's disorder upon his functioning in the community may be alleviated (tertiary prevention).

Once accepted, a new patient attends the unit daily for two weeks, thus permitting extensive investigations into all aspects of his disorder. This culminated in the devising of a diagnostic formulation, and a corresponding treatment program by a multi-disciplinary team. The diagnostic formulation is compiled on the basis of what may be termed hierarchical diagnoses (Bergmann, 1974). At the top of the hierarchy is the organic brain syndrome. This term refers not only to brain damage; it must also imply some global impairment of higher cortical function. If OBS is present, in either acute or chronic form then, this constitutes the primary diagnoses. Next to be considered is the possibility of a functional psychosis, followed by that of a neurotic reaction, and lastly that of a personality disorder. This system helps overcome the difficulties of attempting to apply a unitary diagnosis in a context where there may be a complex interplay of factors in any given patient.

Minimum criteria were set for admission to the sample. The patients should be over 65 years of age; they should freely and willingly co-operate in the project; and their disturbances should reflect predominantly a functional condition. A small number of subjects with primary diagnoses of organic dysfunction, accompanied by depression, were admitted. Dementia was not, however, diagnosed in any of these cases. No patient who was approached declined to participate in the study.

Twenty-eight patients received the initial assessment, whereby a brief life history was obtained, and the measure of adjustment was administered. The more taxing personality assessment was not considered feasible for 8 of these cases. Four subjects were considerably deaf; 2 were overly anxious; 1 ceased to attend the unit; and 1 patient was exceptionally garrulous. Thus 28 cases were available for the analyses of adjustment; 20 were available for the analyses relating to personality, and to personality and adjustment.

The sample of 28 subjects showed an age range of 67 to 85 years. The mean age of the sample was 74·9 years. The majority of the subjects—22 of 28—were female.

The diagnostic composition of the sample was heavily weighted toward depression. Seven subjects had a primary diagnosis of reactive depression; 6 of atypical depression, 3 of endogenous depression; 1 of manic depression; and 4 subjects had primary diagnoses referring to an organic dysfunction, accompanied by depression. Four subjects had diagnoses of paraphrenia or paranoia, and 2 of personality disorder. The physical health of the subjects, as assessed by a physician, was as follows: 5 were in poor health, 14 in fair health, and 9 in good health. Over half the subjects—15 of 28—were widows. Eight subjects were married, 4 were single and 1 was divorced.

Investigation Methods

Several psychological measurement techniques were used throughout the ten-year period of our investigations of the aged. The Community Aged I (1964) sample were given the Minnesota Multiphasic Personality Inventory (Hathaway and McKinlay, 1951), the Hospital Aged III sample provided information on the Maudsley Personality Inventory (Eysenck, 1959), the Community Aged V group were given the 16 Personality Factor Questionnaire (Cattell *et al.*, 1955), the Tennessee Self-Concept Scale (Fitts, 1965), the Life Satisfaction Inventory A and the Activity Inventory (Cavan *et al.*, 1949). The Institutions Aged VI provided valuable information on the new experimental scale by Delhees and Cattell, 1971, called the Clinical Analysis Questionnaire. Our investigations can, therefore, allow us to present normative data on both normal and mentally ill elderly, including both the dimensions of normal personality and a quantitative approach to certain psychopathological characteristics.

The measurement of normal dimensions of personality, in contrast to the psychopathological approach of the two previous scales, was undertaken by using the Maudsley Personality Inventory (Eysenck, 1959) with the Hospital Aged III and the Cattell 16 Personality Factor Questionnaire (Cattell *et al.*, 1970) with the Community Aged V sample. It might be of interest to note at this point that an attempt to use the Cattell 16PF scale with the Community Aged I organic group completely failed. We were only able to give this inventory to one generalised organic case, even though these community cases of senile or arteriosclerotic dementia were fairly mild. They had not been hospitalised.

The measurement of abnormal characteristics in the elderly was carried out in the early and final stages of our investigations. The Community Aged I sample were given the MMPI, the Institutions Aged VI sample the Clinical Analysis Questionnaire, which measures psychopathological dimensions as well as the normal Cattell dimensions of personality.

The measurement of self concept and adjustment was also undertaken with well-tried psychometric tools. The Tennessee Self Concept Scale of Fitts (1965) and The Life Satisfaction Index Scales of Havighurst (1963) and his colleagues.

The major reasons for using these dimensional inventories of various aspects of behaviour is that a great deal of exhaustive research has been devoted to their construction. The scales are not set up in terms of subjective or *a priori* concepts, but are directed to previously located natural personality structures and related to the way personality develops. It is also noted that because the measures deal with basic personality concepts, investigations on the aged with them become increasingly relevant to organised and integrated bodies of practical and theoretical knowledge in a number of important psychological fields.

The Community Aged I Study

PSYCHOPATHOLOGICAL DIMENSIONS OF PERSONALITY

The Minnesota Multiphasic Personality Inventory (Hathaway and McKinlay, 1951) was used with the Community I study in 1964–5 and is, of course, very well known. It is probably the most used and researched upon early attempt at quantification of psychopathology in the U.S.A. Several reviews of the extensive literature on this measure exist and readers are referred once again to O. S. Buros Mental Measurements Year Books for details. Britton and Savage (1966) presented an overview and used the inventory in its basic form.

The MMPI is not so much concerned with discovering normal personality dimensions, but with classification according to some of the accepted psychiatric categories, to give a profile in quantitative as well as qualitative terms of abnormal behaviour. The Inventory, introduced in 1940, was presented to prospective users as an attempt to produce a comprehensive inventory, based on sound psychometric theory and related to psychiatric classifications of mental illness. The individual card form of the MMPI contains some 550 questions, but in order to facilitate scoring in the booklet (group) form some questions are repeated giving a total of 566. These questions have to be answered by the patient on a "Yes", "No", "Cannot Say" basis. The questions were chosen from a larger item pool, consisting of selections from previous questionnaires and inventories, questions based on the psychiatric interview, and other similar sources.

Originally nine clinical scales were developed to distinguish between various distinct psychiatric groups and a normal sample. The psychiatric groups were composed of patients at the University of Minnesota Hospitals, and consisted only of those for whom a clearly defined diagnosis was available. The normal group were visitors to the hospitals who were thought to provide a representative cross-section of the normal population. The original clinical scales measured (1) Hypochondriasis (Hs); (2) Depression (D); (3) Hysteria (Hy); (4) Psychopathic personality (Pd); (5) Masculinity-feminity (Mf); (6) Paranoia (Pa); (7) Psychasthenia (Pt); (8) Schizophrenia (Sc); (9) Hypomania (Ma). The Social Introversion-Extraversion Scale (Si) or Drake (1946) has since become part of the standard inventory. In addition there are four validity scales Cannot-say (?), Lie (L), Faking (F) and the K scale (K); of these the Cannot-say, Lie and Faking scales are overall validity scales and the K scale is used as a suppressor variable. Since its introduction, many "derived scales" have also been produced from the MMPI. These, too, however, usually lack normative data for the aged (Aaronson, 1960; Welsh, 1952, etc.). Our investigation will cast some light on and bring some limited progress in these areas.

Readers will readily appreciate, however, that the application of any psychometric techniques to an elderly group presents a variety of problems; we experienced many, if not all, of them. One of the major difficulties is the choice of the optimal situation for assessment. Three basic solutions were considered: (1) to transport the elderly to our unit; (2) to use a mobile caravan; (3) to visit the home of each person to carry out our investigations. Each of these possibilities has advantages and dsadvantages. To name a few: many of the elderly, particularly the "normal, healthy" group, will not attend a hospital or anything remotely resembling one. A caravan is extremely conspicuous in a suburban street. The home is subject to a wide variety of distractions from the telephone to over-attentive relatives.

Our eventual solution was to visit the homes of our subjects and adapt to the situation as we found it. Initially, the role and intention of the psychologist was explained and our relation to any of the medical or social members of the team who had previously contacted the subject was explained. Every effort was made to reduce distraction and the assessment was interrupted if it was obvious that excessive interference with the subject was taking place. In many instances this resulted in two, three or more sessions before completion of the investigations.

The Hospital Aged III Study

NORMAL PERSONALITY CHARACTERISTICS

The Maudsley Personality Inventoty published by Eysenck in 1959. The questionnaire was developed to allow the quantitative assessment of two major dimensional types of personality characteristics, Neuroticism and Extraversion, and was given to the Hospital Aged III sample. When our personality research began in 1964, the improved Eysenck Personality Inventory (1964) was not available, nor was there any published data on the Eysenckian dimensions of Extraversion and Neuroticism in the elderly. The development of the MPI has been described in detail by Eysenck (1956). Briefly, by means of item and factor analysis of questions, principally from the Guilford Inventory and the Maudsley Medical Questionnaire, he extracted the two dimensions of Extraversion and Neuroticism. Forty-eight questions were finally selected to form the MPI, 24 to measure neuroticism (the N scale) and 24 to measure extraversion (the E scale).

Answers are grouped "Yes", "No", and "?", and in scoring two points are given per item to the designated scale for the keyed neuroticism or extraversion responses and one point to either designated scale for the "?". All the N-scale questions are keyed for "Yes" answers, but only sixteen E-scale questions are so keyed, the others being keyed "No". The possible range of scores on both scales is thus from 0 to 48. Several reviews of the test have been published, readers might wish to refer to the 7th edition of Buros, O.S. (1972) "Mental Measurements Year Book", and Bolton and Savage (1966) for further details.

Jenson (1958), in reviewing a number of earlier studies, reports that no correlation has been found between age and the MPI scales, and that correlations with sex have been negligible in all studies, though there is a tendency for women to score on the average about one point higher than men on both the E and N scales. Apart from its well-established basic factorial construct and content validity, the validity on the MPI in relation to other scales is high. For example, the MPI N scale correlated 0·64 with the Heron Neuroticism Scale and 0·77 with the Taylor Manifest Anxiety Scale, whilst the E Scale correlates −0·80 with Heron's Introversion scale, 0·65 and 0·67 with Cattell's CPF A and B scales and 0·81 with the Minnesota Social Extraversion measure. A further study by Savage and McCawley (1966) (reported later in this book) showed that the MPI loaded 0·78 on a factor of emotionality derived from a factor analysis of 16 scales purporting to measure aspects of emotional behaviour. Data on the aged is needed to allow its potential to be applied by clinicians and other helpers to this area.

The Community Aged V Study

NORMAL PERSONALITY CHARACTERISTICS

The investigation carried out between 1971–74 looked once again at normal personality characteristics in the aged. All the assessment measures were read to the participants, Form C of the 16PF (Cattell *et al.*, 1970) was used, consisting of 105 items. Each of the 16 factors is measured by 6 items, except for the general intelligence factor where 8 items are used. To these 98 items are added 7 experimental motivational distortion items. Three alternative answers are provided for each item.

It measures the primary factors or dimensions of personality derived from multivariate analyses of data which included oblique rotation procedures. There is, therefore, some inter-relationship between some of the factors. The second order factors present a more orthogonal picture of personality. The factors measured by the test are:

Factor

A	Aloof (Schizothymia)	*v*	Warm, Outgoing (Cyclothymia)
B	Dull (Low General Ability)	*v*	Bright (Intelligent)
C	Emotional (General Instability)	*v*	Mature (Ego Strength)
E	Submissive (Submission)	*v*	Dominant (Dominance)
F	Glum, Silent (Desurgency)	*v*	Enthusiastic (Surgency)
G	Casual (Weakness of Character)	*v*	Conscientious (Super Ego Strength)
H	Timid (Withdrawn Schizothymia)	*v*	Adventurous (Adventurous Cyclothymia)
I	Tough (Toughness)	*v*	Sensitive (Sensitivity)
L	Trustful (Lack of Paranoid Tendency)	*v*	Suspecting (Paranoid Tendency)
M	Conventional (Practical Concernedness)	*v*	Eccentric (Bohemian Unconcern)

N Simple (Naive Simplicity) v Sophisticated (Sophistication)
O Confident (Freedom
    from anxiety) v Insecure (Anxious Insecurity)
Q_1 Conservative
    (Conservatism) v Experimenting (Radicalism)
Q_2 Dependent (Group v Self-Sufficient (Self-sufficiency)
    Dependence)
Q_3 Uncontrolled (Poor v Self-Control (High Self-Sentiment)
    Self-Sentiment)
Q_4 Stable (Relaxation) v Tense (Somatic Anxiety)

Added to these source-factors, it has been demonstrated that major clear-cut, second-order factors of Anxiety and Extraversion exist (Cattell and Scheier, 1961) among the primary factors. The Anxiety factor is derived from factors C, H, L, O, Q_3, and Q_4, and the Extraversion factor from A, E, F, H, and Q_2. The next two most important second-order factors have been found to be those of Tough Poise (Alert Poise) and Independence. Cattell and Scheier (1958) derived weight for estimating the degrees of Neuroticism from the scores on factors B, C, E, F, G, H, I, O, Q_1, and Q_4.

It should be noted that Factor B was omitted in the present study as full cognitive investigations had previously been carried out with these samples (Savage *et al.*, 1973).

The 16PFQ probably has the best content and construct validity of any multi-dimensional psychometric measure, as the "Handbook" of 16PF shows (Cattell *et al.*, 1970). The mean correlation of each group of six items with its factor is about $+0 \cdot 71$ which is high for such a brief measure, and the factors themselves are soundly established. Numerous illustrations of relations of factors to external criteria for concurrent and predicting validity for a wide variety of real life situations are also given.

As Cattell (1962) points out, reliability is acceptable even though some of the individual test-retest correlations are not high, they are statistically significant and their departure from unity covers "function-fluctuation".

Raw scores for the primary personality factors and M.D. data are converted to Standard Sten scores, allowing one to place the S in relation to other people in a defined population. In this study, the general population norms were used. These were based on the responses of 1,217 American men and women aged 15–80 years, averaging 35 years of age. At the time of the study British norms were not available.

Sten scores are distributed over ten equal-interval standard score points from 1 through 10, with the population mean fixed at 5·5. Stens 5 and 6 extend respectively a half standard deviation below and above the mean, while the outer limits for Stens 1 and 10 are 2½ S.D.'s above and below the mean. Thus the range of what one would essentially call average score, namely one S.D. range centred on the mean is represented by Sten 5 and 6.

The standardisation sample was carefully chosen to represent occupations, educational levels, geographical areas, etc. Cattell mentions, incidentally, that age correction tables have not been systematically introduced since the age trends are not generally of practical significance over the "typical" adult age.

MEASUREMENT OF SELF CONCEPT

It was decided to use the Tennessee Self-Concept Scale to measure these aspects of personality. This scale fulfils the need for an instrument which is simple for the subject, widely applicable, well standardised, and multi-dimensional in its description of the self-concept. The last is particularly important when one considers the complexity of the self-concept.

Originally developed by Fitts (1955) as a tool used in assessing mental health, it has since found wider use with a manual and norms published by Counselor Recordings and Tests in 1965. The initial scale consisted of a large pool of items compiled by Fitts from previous research in the area of self-concept. Additional items were derived from written self-description of patients and non-patients, and a system was developed for classifying items on the basis of content. The present Tennessee Self Concept Scale consists of 90 items for which there was perfect agreement among seven clinical psychologists employed as judges in sorting the preliminary pool of items into the specified classification scheme. The "face" or content validity is consequently regarded to be satisfactory (Fitts, 1965).

The scale is three-dimensional with each statement classified along (1) a positive-negative continuum; (2) internal categoric continuum and (3) external categoric continuum. The items which constitute the main body of this scale are divided into 45 positive and 45 negative statements about the self.

The internal categories dimension contains three categories:

1. Abstract description. At this level the individual is describing what he *is*—the traits and characteristics he observes as he looks at himself, (e.g. Item 1—I have a healthy body).

2. Self-satisfaction. This category deals with the individual's reaction to what he perceives within himself—how well satisfied he is with the self he perceives (e.g. Item 19—I am a decent sort of person).

3. Function or Behaviour. This category samples the individual's perception of his behaviour—the way he actually functions, acts, operates or behaves (e.g. Item 46—I am not the person I would like to be).

The external categories are divided into five areas:

1. The physical self. Physical characteristics, appearance, state of health, sexuality, physical skill, etc. (e.g. Item 4—I am full of aches and pains).

2. The moral self. The self viewed from the framework of morals, ethics, religion, and general value system, (e.g. Item 21—I am an honest person).

3. The psychological or personal self. The self in terms of intellectual, personality, and mental health factors—one's general adequacy as a person, (e.g. Item 43—I am satisfied to be just what I am).

4. The family self. The kind of person one is in relation to his primary group membership (family and close friends), (e.g. Item 64—I am too sensitive to things my family says).

5. The social self. The self in terms of secondary group membership, or the self as perceived in relation to, and interaction with people in general, (e.g. Item 85—I try to understand the other fellow's point of view).

The remaining ten items on the scale are summed to yield a self-criticism score as an index of validity or truthfulness of the subjects' responses to the other 90 items. The 10 items from this scale were taken from the Lie Scale. The items included on this subscale are mildly derogatory, but are also generally considered applicable to everyone. The self-criticism scale is intended to indicate the degree of defensiveness or deceptiveness of the individual so that the lower the score, the more defensive the individual responding to the scale (Grant, 1969).

With this conceptual scheme a variety of scores were generated which reflect significant information concerning the individual self-concept. In addition to the Self-Criticism Score, the TSCS yield the following six types of scores.

1. Positive (P). A self-esteem or Positive Score may be obtained for each of the eight areas of reported self-concept. Scores on all 90 items are summed to provide the Total P Score, which reflects the general level of self-esteem. Ordering of the scores is as would be expected; high scores represent high levels of self-esteem.

2. (Variability (V). There are three of these scores: Total V, Column Total V, and Raw Total V. These scores are indicative of the amount of variability, or inconsistency, from one area of self-perception to another.

3. Distribution of Responses (D). The D Score weighs and summarises the individual's distribution of scores across five response categories. High D scores indicate a relatively higher use of the "5" and "1" response categories (the extremes) than of the "2", "3" and "4" categories of response and are indicative of an overly-definite or certain self-concept. Low scores represent an uncertain, poorly-differentiated image. Scores in the middle range depict the clearest differentiation.

4. Conflict (C). The Net Conflict Score and the Total Conflict Score are indicative of differences in responses to the positively stated items and the negatively stated items. A tendency to "over-respond" to either the positive or the negative item indicates an over-affirmation of positive attributes, and possible acquiescence conflict. Similarly, an emphasis on the negative items may represent denial conflict. While Net Conflict is indicative of a directional emphasis on the test items, the Total Conflict Score reflects conflict or confusion in general, without regard to its direction.

Net Conflict Score bears a strong resemblance to descriptions often given of response set, or response bias. The Net Conflict Score is, indeed, highly correlated with the T/F Ration Score of the TSCS, which is an indicator of the subject's tendency to agree to, or disagree with, an item regardless of its content. T/F Ratio Scores in the middle range of the distribution are considered optimal, indicating that the subject is able to differentiate between those statements which apply to him and those which do not.

5. Empirical Scales. The Clinical and Research Form of the TSCS provides six scales, empirically derived from the 100 test items, which differentiate among various groups often encountered in a clinical setting. In the development of these six scales, various "deviant" groups of subjects were identified by other criteria and were given the TSCS. The six groups identified were:

Norm	N = 626
Psychotic	N = 100
Neurotic	N = 100
Personality Disorder	N = 100
Defensive Positive	N = 100
Personality Integration	N = 75

The TSCS responses of these groups were subjected to item analysis. Those items which differentiated any one group from all other groups and the norm group. The six scales so developed were as follows:

a. Defensive Positive Scale (DP). This scale consists of 29 items which differentiated psychiatric patients having Total P scores above the norm group mean from the other patient groups and the norm group. It is thought to represent a more subtle measure of defensiveness than the Self Criticism Score.

b. General Maladjustment Scale (GM). This scale comprises 24 items which distinguish psychiatric patients from non-patients, but do not distinguish between psychiatric classifications. As used here the term "psychiatric patients" refers to the psychotic, neurotic and personality disorder groups.

c. Psychosis Scale (Psy). Twenty-three items make up this scale—items which best differentiate psychotic patients from other groups.

d. Personality Disorder Scale (PD). This scale is composed of 27 items which distinguish this psychiatric classification from the norm, psychotic, neurotic, personality integration and defensive positive groups.

e. Neurosis Scale (NS). This scale is also composed of 27 items which distinguish neurotic from other groups. Like the GM and PD Scales, it is an inverse one. Low raw scores on these scales result in high T Score.

f. Personality Integration Scale (PI). Twenty-five items are included in this scale, representing a group of subjects judged, by outside criteria, to have better than average level of adjustment.

6. Number of Deviant Signs (NDS). The final score on the profile sheet is the Number of Deviant Signs Score. The NDS, too, is an empirically-devised measure, being simply a count of the number of deviant features of other scores. It is the Scales' best index of psychological disturbance (Thompson, 1972 pp. 2–4).

The standardisation group from which the norms were developed was a broad sample of 626 people. The sample included people from various parts of the United States, the age ranges of whom were from 12 to 68. There were approximately equal numbers of both sexes, both Negro and white subjects, representative of all social, economic and intellectual levels from 6th grade (1st form in any 11+ entry school) through to Ph.D degree. Subjects were obtained from high school and University classes, employees at state institutions and various other sources (Fitts, 1965). Fitts (1965) points out that it would be possible to expand the norm group considerably and this has not been done for two reasons. First, it is apparent that samples from other populations do not differ appreciably from the norms provided the samples are large enough (N = 75 or more). Second, the effects of such demographic variables such as age, race, education and intelligence on the scores of this scale are quite negligible.

ASSESSING PERSONAL AND SOCIAL ADJUSTMENT

In order to gain insight into the level of personal adjustment or life satisfaction the Life Satisfaction Index A and B were used in their original complete form (Havighurst 1963), the development of which was discussed at length in an earlier section. In short, the Life Satisfaction Index A consists of 20 items covering the five items suggested by Neugarten *et al.* (1961), (namely: zest *vs* apathy; resolution *vs* fortitude; goodness of fit between desired and achieved goals; positive self-concept; and mood tone) including items from the Kutner Morale

Scale and the happiness scale of the Chicago Aptitude Inventory (see Cavan *et al.* 1949). Life Satisfaction B consists of 6 open-ended questions and 6 check-list items scored on a three-point scale. Four of the items come from Kutner's Scale (*see* Kutner *et al.*, 1956).

The scoring of the Life Satisfaction Index was carried out, however, according to the method suggested by Wood *et al.* (1969). This is to say that a score of 2 was given for a "right" answer, 1 for a "don't know" and 0 for a "wrong" answer. Wood (1969) found that when using this scoring system the correlation between LSI A and LSR (*see* Neugarten *et al.*, 1961) was slightly higher than when using the original method of scoring.

The rather ambiguous item: "I feel my age, but it doesn't bother me" was scored "right" if the response to the whole item was "agree" and "wrong" if the response was "agree" to the first half of the question or "disagree" to the whole question. It was felt that this overcame the confusion caused by this question noted by Adams (1969).

The Activity Inventory which measures "role-activity" was chosen for use in the light of the importance of this variable in the development of personality and adjustment theories of old age. As Neugarten (1965) pointed out, "role-activity measures are made of ratings of the extent and intensity of activity in eleven different social roles—parent, spouse, grandparent, kin-group member, worker, homemaker, citizen, friend, neighbor, club and association member and church member."

The Institutions Aged VI Study

NORMAL PERSONALITY CHARACTERISTICS AND ADJUSTMENT

Finally, a number of psychological measurement techniques were used in a series of three small investigations of the aged in various institutional care settings. The first and second studies, undertaken with Institutions Aged VI sample groups (a) and (b) described earlier were on patients and non-patients in Local Authority homes for the elderly, who were given the Eysenck Personality Inventory and the Cattell and Eber 16PFQ. This work in many ways develops that undertaken with the Hospital Aged III sample. The Eysenck Personality Inventory (Eysenck and Eysenck, 1964) is a development of the Maudsley Personality Inventory used in our Hospital Aged III sample. The EPI gives two measures of personality, neuroticism and introversion-extra-version. (Plus a 12-item lie scale to weed out people suspected of faking good). The normative sample consisted of 2,000 people drawn from a wide range of occupations, and several clinical groups (neurotics, prisoners, psychotics, alcoholics). However, in the studies prior to the test itself, 30,000 people are reported to have been involved. Eysenck claims a test retest reliability between $0 \cdot 84$–$0 \cdot 94$. There are two forms of the scale—A and B. Eysenck has in several different studies used the method of nominated groups to establish the validity of the test. Highly consistent results are claimed. Details on the test construction of the EPI are given in full in the test manual

The 16PF Questionnaire (Cattell *et al.*, 1970) as was used on the Aged V sample, was given to these Institution Aged VI (a) and (b). The primary and second order factor dimensions of personality, fully described in Chapter 2 and in relation to the Community Aged IV study, were analysed.

In addition to these, samples (a) and (b) used the Life Satisfaction Index A and B (Cavan *et al.*, 1949), also used for the Community Aged V sample and fully described on pages

NORMAL AND PSYCHOPATHOLOGICAL PERSONALITY FACTORS

The third and final of this small series of experiments, carried out on day centre psychogeriatric patients, used the newly developed Clinical Analysis Questionnaire (Delhees and Cattell, 1971). This test measures the normal 16 primary source traits of Cattell in Part I, but has, in addition, a Part 2, which allows the investigation of 12 abnormal dimensions of personality. It will be helpful at this point to describe this test as only the interim version of the test is available and, at the time that the study began, no information on the aged had been collected with it.

Questionnaire instruments which tap pathological behaviour have been in use for some time: The Minnesota Multiphasic Personality Inventory constitutes an important example. As Cattell *et al.* (1970) point out, however, such instruments give estimates of the severity of clinical syndromes. They do not generally measure personality dimensions.

In Cattell's terminology, the MMPI yields information about "surface traits". It differentiates between people exhibiting various clinically defined syndromes. A syndrome consists of a correlation cluster—of behaviours which tend to be found together.

It may, however, be deemed more useful to gather information about the personality dimensions which underlie, and contribute to, the observed syndromes. These personality dimensions are termed "source traits" since they are believed to have a causal nature. Source traits are unitary structural dimensions defined in terms of factor anlysis. They are repeatable, and they are less susceptible to fluctuation than the surface traits.

The Clinical Analysis Questionnaire (CAQ) consists of two parts. Part 1 comprises the 16 dimensions of the normal personality sphere which have formerly been measured by the Sixteen Personality Factor Questionnaire. There are 8 items for each factor; the CAQ Part 1 is thus a little longer than the 16PF Forms C and D, but rather shorter than Forms A and B.

This study, as indicated above, constitutes but one of a series of investigations, which also included intensive examinations of the phenomenon of depression (e.g. Cattell and Bjerstedt, 1967). The end result—the CAQ Pathological Supplement—contains twelve scales. Seven scales tap aspects of depression: hypochondriasis; zest versus suicidal disgust; brooding discontent; anxious depression; high energy euphoria versus low energy depression; guilt and resentment; and bored depression. The remaining scales cover paranoia, psychopathic deviation, schizophrenia, psychasthenia and general psychosis. There are twelve items for each scale. Reliability coefficients range from $0 \cdot 67$ to $0 \cdot 90$, and concept validity coefficients from $0 \cdot 42$ to $0 \cdot 82$. Three depression factors—anxious depression, guilt and resentment, and bored depression—are not as yet so well measured as the others.

Nine principal second-order factors may be derived from the 28 first order factors. The secondaries consist of Exvia, Anxiety, Cortertia, Independence, Superego, General frustrated depression, Restless depression, Suicidal depression, and General maladjustment depression. It will be noted that these factors do not cover a number of important primary factors: they should not, therefore, be used alone. In any event, procedures for calculating these second order factors have not yet been published.

The Clinical Analysis Questionnaire may be administered in a number of alternative ways which include oral administration, the method used in the present study. The significant words and symbols of the Scale B (Intelligence) items were presented visually as the question was orally administered. Table 24 presents the normal and pathological scales measured by this technique.

The CAQ is, as yet, not fully developed, and reliability and validity data are available for limited groups only. Reliability was assessed in terms of consistency over a one-day retest interval for a sample of 100 largely normal young adults. For the CAQ Part 1 scales, the coefficients range from 0·51 to 0·74. The mean coefficient is almost exactly that expected when the 16PF Form A and B scales are reduced to 8 items each.

Concept validity coefficients were computed for a sample of 300 men and women taken from a mixed population of normal and clinical subjects. The coefficients refer to the correlations of the scales with the pure factors which they are designed to measure. The coefficients for CAQ Part 1 range from 0·52 to 0·70, and are comparable to those derived for other 16PF scales.

Cattell *et al.* (1970) indicate that although much pathological behaviour may be explained in terms of "tangles" in normal processes, clinical use of the 16PF has provided more adequate prediction of neurotic than of psychotic behaviour. It was the possibility that the 16PF omitted to cover some specifically pathological factors which led to the construction of the CAQ Part 2: The Pathological Supplement. Of the series of studies contributing to this end, perhaps the most important one was reported by Cattell and Bolton in 1969. The investigation consisted of a comparison of the factor domains of the 16PF and the MMPI.

The first procedure which was carried out involved a comparison of the MMPI surface traits and the 16PF source traits. A sample of 259 Air Force men was used, which included, for "pathological" variance, 40 cases listed by psychiatrists as being in some need of clinical help. Multiple correlational analysis indicated that the MMPI scales denoting schizophrenia, anxiety, psychasthenia and social introversion could be predicted from the 16PF with some efficiency. An appreciable amount of the material in the MMPI was, however, unaccounted for by the 16PF.

The items of the two instruments were then factor analysed. The somewhat imprecise scaling of the MMPI was thus set aside, and the inherent common dimensionality of the two measures was evaluated. Twenty-one factors, rotated to the best possible simple structure, emerged. Fifteen of these factors were identifiable in terms of dimensions of the 16PF. One factor—the last—was an error factor, containint what Cattell and Bolton designate "garbage". The remaining five factors were named as Hypochondriasis, Psychopathic deviation, Psychasthenia, Religious resignation and General functional psychosis. These factors contained very little of the 16PF variance, but were clearly defined by MMPI variables. "General functional psychosis" was marked by the 16PF Q_3 (self-sentiment strength) variables, but also loaded on MMPI variables denoting loss of contact with reality and inappropriateness of emotional expression. Factor Q_3 had, on previous occasions, been observed to show some relationship to psychoticism; it has been hypothesised that this may derive from a compensatory device being provided when the ego is disturbed.

The analysis thus demonstrated that pathological behaviour, recorded in terms of a broad range of clinical items, could partly be accounted for by normal personality source traits which are common to all. A more adequate explanation of observed behaviour may be obtained, however, when dimensions are included which appear with any appreciable variance only among psychiatric patients.

In the Institutions Aged VI studies, adjustment was investigated on this sample with the Havighurst techniques for measuring life satisfaction, described earlier on pages 86–87.

3

Personality in the Community Aged

A number of studies were carried out between 1964 and 1973 on samples of the Newcastle upon Tyne aged population living in the community. Initially the Minnesota Multiphasic Personality Inventory was used to investigate psychopathological dimensions and levels in the Community Aged I Sample of 86. More extensive investigations of Personality, with Cattell's Sixteen Personality Factor Questionnaire, were undertaken with the Community Aged V group of 82. The measurement of basic personality source traits and second order factors were related to information on self concept and adjustment in these "normal" aged living in the community. The final data have much to offer to an understanding of personality functioning in the aged.

This chapter, however, will concentrate on descriptions of the aged personality characteristics—normal and abnormal—found in our studies and some of their interrelationships. The final chapter of the book will deal with possible analyses of the structure of personality or type of personality in the aged, and their implications.

Psychopathological Characteristics in the Community Aged

At the time of our initial investigation of the Aged in 1964, there was little evidence on whether or not personality characteristics changed dramatically with advancing age. In contrast to the situation in the area of cognitive functioning, there had been very few attempts to obtain age related normative data on existing psychometrically developed psychopathological scales, let alone develop measures specifically for "the aged".

It seemed, at that early stage of our research, very important that a firm basis in adequate normative data on personality characteristics of the aged was available before any major progress could be made. We initially chose the MMPI because of its wide use in clinical psychology, particularly in America, and its relation to problems and methods in clinical psychiatry. The results of our survey are presented here in an examination of the scores of the elderly on basic validity and clinical scales of the MMPI. Age, sex and psychiatric diagnostic group data are examined. In addition, comparison with information from related studies is given, even though such comparisons are limited or complicated by inter-study and other methodological problems.

The scores for the whole of the Newcastle upon Tyne Community I Group were compared with those for the standardised MMPI, which have a mean of 50 and standard deviation of 10. (As can be seen in Table 3, large and significant score differences are evident on all

Table 3. Newcastle upon Tyne Community Aged I
MMPI Basic Clinical and Validity Scales
Means and Standard Deviations of MMPI K corrected T scores

	(N = 83) K corrected T Scores		
	M	*S.D.*	
L	41·3	5·2	**
F	54·8	7·0	**
K	61·5	4·7	**
Hs	73·2	14·2	**
D	67·4	14·5	**
Hy	72·5	10·7	**
Pd	49·6	9·8	
Mf	56·8	11·7	**
Pa	54·5	9·1	**
Pt	58·1	9·5	**
Sc	62·3	10·2	**
Ma	42·3	6·2	**
Si	47·5	6·9	
Standardisation sample	Mean 50	Standard Deviation 10 on all scales	

**Difference from standardisation significant at p < 0·01

except the Psychopathic Deviate and Social Introversion scales. These results highlight the changes which occur with advancing age and suggest that interpretation of MMPI data for research or clinical purposes without adequate age norms may be extremely misleading, indeed inadvisable. Examination of subgroup differences, Tables 4 and 5, suggests that age and sex differences within our sample were not generally of much consequence. Age differences were apparent, however, in the Psychopathic Deviate and Social Introversion scales, perhaps reflecting in their higher scores ($p < 0.05$) a more satisfactory adjustment in those who had survived longest. The only sex difference of note was, not unexpectedly, on the Masculinity-feminity scale. This suggests that, for the greater part, the corrections for sexual bias in response incorporated in the MMPI are adequate. It is not surprising that the Masculinity-feminity scale, which reflects sexual interests, is subject to bias when our sample are compared with young Minnesota subjects.

Table 4. Newcastle upon Tyne Community Aged I
MMPI Basic Clinical and Validity Scales
Means and Standard Deviations of MMPI K corrected T scores. Age Groups

	Age Groups				
	70 — 74 (N = 48)		75 + (N = 35)		
	M	S.D.	M	S.D.	
L	40·9	4·9	41·6	5·7	
F	54·0	6·2	56·1	8·2	
K	61·8	4·9	60·0	4·0	
Hs	71·7	15·2	72·0	13·2	
D	64·9	14·7	68·1	13·9	
Hy	71·4	10·3	73·4	11·2	
Pd	47·8	5·9	53·0	13·0	*
Mf	58·0	11·7	62·5	11·1	
Pa	53·7	6·4	57·1	11·6	
Pt	56·4	9·8	59·3	9·1	
Sc	60·8	9·9	64·0	10·7	
Ma	41·6	5·5	43·6	7·0	
Si	46·3	6·2	49·8	7·7	*

*Difference significant at $p < 0.05$

Table 5. Newcastle upon Tyne Community Aged I
MMPI Basic Clinical and Validity Scales
Means and Standard Deviations of MMPI K corrected T Scores. Sex Groups

	Sex Groups				
	Male (N = 27)		Female (N = 56)		
	M	S.D.	M	S.D.	
L	41·4	5·6	41·2	5·0	
F	54·6	6·6	55·0	7·5	
K	61·9	4·5	61·0	4·7	
Hs	76·8	16·8	69·5	12·5	*
D	70·6	16·2	64·2	13·0	
Hy	73·4	10·6	71·7	10·8	
Pd	48·6	6·2	50·6	11·2	
Mf	48·4	5·1	65·3	9·7	**
Pa	52·5	5·3	56·4	10·2	
Pt	59·2	11·5	56·9	8·6	
Sc	62·9	11·2	61·7	10·0	
Ma	42·0	6·0	42·6	6·4	
Si	46·5	6·9	48·4	7·0	

**Difference significant at $p < 0.01$
*Difference significant at $p < 0.05$

Comparison of the scores of our two major psychiatric classification groups, normal and functionally ill, are shown in Table 6. The score levels obtained reflect the expected bias in the "functional" mental illness group towards a higher score on most scales, reflecting an increased level of psychopathology. This increase in score is particularly evident in the "psychoneurotic triad" of scales, Hysteria, Depression and Hypochondriasis. It should also be remembered that though classified by a psychiatrist as having symptoms of functional mental illness such as anxiety or depression, these elderly people were *not* under psychiatric treatment, or in many cases any medical treatment at all for these conditions. They were relatively mild disorder levels requiring neither hospitalization nor out-patient hospital treatment. This is very important in view of the fact that the MMPI would normally be used where there was evidence or suspicion of mental illness and where one might now expect even greater deviation from the adult normative data of the MMPI as available at this point.

Table 6. Newcastle upon Tyne Community Aged I
MMPI Basic Clinical and Validity Scales
Means and Standard Deviations of MMPI K corrected T Scores. Diagnostic Groups

			Diagnosis		
	Normal (N = 40)		Functional (N = 41)		
	M	S.D.	M	S.D.	
L			41·8	6·4	
F			56·9	7·6	**
K	61·7	4·3	61·0	4·9	
Hs	64·5	11·1	81·3	13·1	**
D	58·7	8·7	75·8	14·7	**
Hy	66·7	8·6	78·5	9·3	**
Pd	46·5	4·7	54·0	12·4	**
Mf	60·7	11·9	52·4	11·4	**
Pa	51·3	5·6	57·5	10·3	**
Pt	53·3	7·8	62·6	9·1	**
Sc	57·0	7·2	67·5	10·4	**
Ma	41·0	4·9	43·1	7·2	
Si	45·0	4·2	49·9	6·9	**

** Difference significant at $p < 0.01$

Previous studies using the MMPI with aged persons have employed a variety of systems of subject selection which made direct comparisons with our own data difficult. However, we have attempted to extract comparable subsets from earlier studies and here present two of the most interesting. The first of these is a comparison between our "normal" subjects and the "nonhospitalised aged" of Swenson (1961). Six of the MMPI clinical scales differ to a significant degree ($p < 0.01$) and the pattern of difference is interesting. The present sample had higher scores on the Sc scale and the Hs and Hy components of the "psychoneurotic triad", the D scale scores being similar. The Swenson sample had higher scores on the Pd, Ma and Si scales (Table 7).

Interesting differences were also obtained between the present male sample and that of Kornetsky (1963). For the K, Hs, D, Hy, Pt and Sc scales our sample had higher scores and for the L, F, Pd, Mf, Ma and Si scales lower scores ($p < 0.01$). These groups of scales represent the "psychopathological" and "abnormal socialisation" aspects

Table 7. The Newcastle upon Tyne Community Aged I *Normal* and the
Swenson (1961) *Nonhospitalised* samples
MMPI Basic Clinical and Validity Scales
Means and Standard Deviations of MMPI K corrected T scores

	Newcastle upon Tyne normal *sample* (N = 40)		*Swenson* nonhospitalised *sample* (N = 95)		
	M	S.D.	M	S.D.	
L	1·1	0·9	6·1	3·6	**
F	4·8	3·3	7·9	3·1	**
K	18·3	2·3	14·4	4·7	**
Hs	64·5	11·1	58·0	12·8	**
D	58·7	8·7	59·2	11·7	
Hy	66·7	8·6	55·9	11·7	**
Pd	46·5	4·7	51·0	9·1	**
Mf	60·7	11·9	55·6	10·5	
Pa	51·3	5·6	52·4	8·7	
Pt	53·3	7·8	53·2	10·4	
Sc	57·0	7·2	52·5	9·7	**
Ma	41·0	4·9	47·2	10·0	**
Si	45·0	4·2	56·5	7·7	**

**Difference significant at p < 0·01

of the MMPI. Thus, whilst the present male subjects differ from the standardisation group in terms of increased psychopathology, the Kornetsky subjects showed primary differences in their lack of adequate adjustment to the social changes necessary in ageing (Table 8).

This difference is, perhaps, best explained in terms of the sampling of the groups which are compared. Kornetsky obtained his aged males as volunteers from community organisations (clubs, etc.). Each subject was screened and those with present or previous psychopathology or overt physical illness were excluded. Thus, an exceptionally healthy group with a mean I.Q. of over 110 was obtained. Hence, it was unlikely that the group would show obvious "psychopathology" on the MMPI. In addition, it is relevant that a previous study by Goodstein (1954) using college students had shown an elevation in "abnormal socialisation" to be associated with higher I.Q.

Table 8. The Newcastle upon Tyne Community Aged I and
the Kornetsky (1963) samples
MMPI Basic Clinical and Validity Scales
Means and Standard Deviations of MMPI K corrected T Scores. Male Subjects

	Newcastle upon Tyne sample (N = 27)		Kornetsky sample (N = 43)		
	M	S.D.	M	S.D.	
L	41·4	5·6	54·2	8·8	**
F	54·6	6·6	57·1	9·1	
K	61·9	4·5	54·8	9·8	**
Hs	76·8	16·8	58·8	8·6	**
D	70·6	16·2	63·6	14·3	**
Hy	73·4	10·6	55·8	9·8	**
Pd	48·6	6·2	54·1	7·9	**
Mf	48·4	5·1	60·0	9·1	**
Pa	52·5	5·3	52·9	8·1	
Pt	59·2	11·5	53·5	10·4	**
Sc	62·9	11·2	54·8	11·8	**
Ma	42·0	6·0	54·1	7·6	**
Si	46·5	6·9	54·0	10·5	**

**Difference significant at p < 0·01

Indices of Ageing

There are a considerable number of scales and indices, which, over the years, have been derived for use with the MMPI. Of these, a number were thought to be of more primary interest, in particular, the Welsh (1956) factor scales A and R, measures of "overt-anxiety" and "repression-denial". These Anxiety Index and Internalisation ratio, Welsh (1952) and the Ageing Index of Aaronson (1964) were calculated as for our own Newcastle upon Tyne Community Aged. They had all been used extensively with younger subjects and it was thought that it would aid MMPI interpretation if some indication of their validity with aged persons was obtained.

The results of our sample are compared with previous studies in Table 9. The Aaronson Ageing Index produces the expected low mean score of 30·3 when compared with the mean of 80·7 quoted by Aaronson for a group of subjects aged about 30. The Welsh Anxiety

Table 9. Newcastle upon Tyne Community Aged I
MMPI Derived Scales and Indices. All Subjects

	Newcastle upon Tyne Community Aged I sample (N = 83)		Previous findings		
	M	S.D	M	S.D.	
Aaronson Ageing Index	30·3	17·2	80·7	29·8	(1)
Welsh Anxiety Index	50·8	17·6	50·0		(2)
Welsh Internalisation Ratio	1·11	0·39	1·0		(2)
Welsh Factor Scale A	40·7	6·2	50·0	10·0	(3)
Welsh Factor Scale R	53·0	14·4	50·0	10·0	(3)

(1) Aaronson (1964); (2) Welsh (1952); (3) Welsh (1956)

Index and Internalisation Ratio do not differ from their respective standardisation data. However, the Welsh A scale mean is significantly (p < 0·01) lower than the standardisation but the R scale does not differ significantly.

Furthermore, the age, sex and diagnostic group differences in these data, presented in Tables 10, 11 and 12, cast some important doubts on the validity of these derived scales and indices. Indeed, the Aaronson ageing index shows an increase with age. Anxiety level slightly increases with age, whilst the tendency to Internalisation is reduced. Sex and diagnostic group comparisons reveal surprisingly few differences and none which are statistically significant (Tables 10, 11 and 12).

Table 10. Newcastle upon Tyne Community Aged I
MMPI Derived Scales and Indices
Means and Standard Deviations. Age Groups

	70 — 74 (N = 48)		75 + (N = 35)	
	M	S.D.	M	S.D.
Aaronson Ageing Index	26·8	13·3	33·4	22·0
Welsh Anxiety Index	47·8	16·7	51·8	22·3
Welsh Internalisation Ratio	1·17	0·22	1·14	0·39
Welsh Factor Scale A	38·8	7·8	41·1	10·3
Welsh Factor Scale R	53·1	11·0	49·9	22·2

No significant differences

Table 11. Newcastle upon Tyne Community Aged I
MMPI Derived Scales and Indices
Means and Standard Deviations. Sex Groups

	Male (N = 27)		Female (N = 56)	
	M	*S.D.*	*M*	*S.D.*
Aaronson Ageing Index	24·0	10·5	23·2	19·7
Welsh Anxiety Index	52·4	20·2	48·1	18·8
Welsh Internalisation Ratio	1·20	0·30	1·13	0·18
Welsh Factor Scale A	38·5	8·9	40·3	8·9
Welsh Factor Scale R	53·6	13·4	50·9	17·9

No significant differences

Table 12. Newcastle upon Tyne Community Aged I
MMPI Derived Scales and Indices
Means and Standard Deviations. Diagnostic Groups

	Normal (N = 40)		Functional (N = 41)	
	M	*S.D.*	*M*	*S.D.*
Aaronson Ageing Index	35·1	39·8	24·2	26·3
Welsh Anxiety Index	46·5	7·7	52·5	25·0
Welsh Internalisation Ratio	1·20	0·20	1·11	0·39
Welsh Factor Scale A	39·1	14·3	40·3	15·6
Welsh Factor Scale R	51·9	17·3	53·0	14·4

No significant differences. Organic subjects (N = 2) not included

One feels somewhat obliged to speculate on the possible causes of the differences, or lack of them, found in this analysis of the MMPI derived scales and indices. In the case of the Aaronson Ageing Index the present data probably appear to deviate from Aaronson's (1958) hypothesised model of age changes on the MMPI. He quotes (Aaronson, 1964):

". . . elevations on Scales Pd, Pt and Sc characterised young entrants into an abnormal population whilst elevations on the Hs and D characterised older entrants".

It will be recalled that the present sample has elevations on *both* Hs, D and Pd, Pt and Sc groupings. This could well have caused the apparent anomaly of a higher score on the Ageing Index in the oldest age group. It seems that the Index may not be applicable in old age, although its relevance to an ageing population appears well proven. Our results suggest also that extreme caution is necessary in the application of the Welsh Scales and Indices to the aged. The derivation of the Indices was based on typical trends in the MMPI profiles of younger adults, and the Factor Scales were based on factor analyses of data from similar populations. If an underlying change in the structure of personality occurs in the aged, it may well be that Scales and Indices based on "neurotic shifts" in the scale-scores of younger persons are not applicable to the aged. This produces a situation analogous to the use of WAIS deterioration indices, based on patterns of decline in the ageing, with the aged. It would appear that in the case of both cognitive and personality indices, clinical application should be confined to the population and age range on which the indices were derived, or on which they had been subsequently validated.

These basic results for the clinical and validity scales are of considerable value to the clinician. It has been shown that the standard normative data, with a mean of 50 and a standard deviation of 10 are of doubtful applicability to the aged. Age and sex differences within the sample were not generally significant. The diagnostic group differences were highly significant, a general elevation in all scale scores, particularly evident on the Hs, D, Hy, M and Sc Scales, was observed. This result would appear to confirm the validity of the Inventory as a measure of general mental illness in the aged. However, the differentiation of the present sample into specific diagnostic groups using the MMPI could not be adequately assessed as the psychiatric diagnoses available were not sufficiently specific.

As the pressure of clinical anxiety was a predominant feature in the diagnosis of many of the subjects in the present "functional" sample, the rather negative results on the Welsh Anxiety Scale and Index are interesting. It would appear that the manifestation of anxiety in the aged may well be different from the typical patterns observed in younger groups. Extreme caution is urged in the clinical application of these scales and indices to the aged.

These results provide a basis for the interpretation of MMPI data from the aged not previously available. There is evidence that the

Inventory is rather cumbersome in its entirety for routine use with the aged and that the information on individual diagnosis which can be obtained may not fully justify such use. This does not detract from the value of the MMPI as a research instrument or as a basis for the extraction of more readily applicable derivatives for use with specific populations, such as the aged, should copyright regulations permit.

Normal Personality Characteristics in the Community Aged

We felt that it was important to provide data on the aged and to shed light on the applicability of using the major psychometric assessment procedure and theoretical approach to personality of R. B. Cattell and his colleagues (Cattell, 1965; Cattell *et al.*, 1970). Although several studies using the 16PF to assess personality changes throughout the life span have been reported (Seally and Cattell, 1965; Goodwin and Schaie, 1969), separate data for an aged sample cannot be readily found. A full description of the Community Aged V Sample and of the investigations administered to these 82 elderly Newcastle upon Tyne residents is given on pages 80–87.

Table 13 presents the data on Cattell's personality characteristics in this aged population alongside Cattell and Porter's normative data on the younger general population sample from the 16PF "Manual" (1962). The initial general population standardisation sample consisted of 1217 men and women ranging from 15–80 years of age (mean 35 years) who were selected to represent occupations, educational levels, geographical areas, etc., in the U.S.A. The British norms of Saville (1972) were not available when this work was done.

The Newcastle upon Tyne Community Aged sample results differed considerably from those of Cattell's general population. The Aged scored significantly lower ($p < 0.01$) than the general population on Factors F (Surgency), A (Sizothymia *vs* Affectothymia) and H (Threctia *vs* Farmia) while scoring significantly higher ($p < 0.05$) on Factor M (Austia *vs* Praxermia). This seems to indicate that the aged as a group are more silent, reticent and introspective than their younger counterparts, having an intense subjectivity and inner life. Likewise, the old-age group tends to be more egocentric. They are inclined to be reserved and detached, exhibiting a temperamental leaning to be cautious in emotional expression; uncompromising and critical in

Table 13. Newcastle upon Tyne Community Aged V
Normative Data on Cattell's Sixteen Personality Factor Questionnaire

	Newcastle upon Tyne Community Aged V (N = 82)		Cattell's General Population (N = 1217)			
	M	S.D.	M	S.D.	t	
A	4·68	2·00	5·50	2·00	3·58	**
C	4·48	1·93	5·50	2·00	4·50	**
E	5·62	1·35	5·50	2·00	0·54	
F	4·13	2·03	5·50	2·00	5·98	**
G	6·61	1·57	5·50	2·00	4·92	**
H	4·72	1·60	5·50	2·00	3·46	**
I	5·88	1·78	5·50	2·00	1·71	
L	7·01	1·90	5·50	2·00	6·65	**
M	5·05	1·89	5·50	2·00	1·98	*
N	6·61	1·79	5·50	2·00	4·90	**
O	6·98	1·79	5·50	2·00	6·57	**
Q_1	4·66	1·57	5·50	2·00	3·73	**
Q_2	6·27	1·98	5·50	2·00	3·37	**
Q_3	5·07	2·05	5·50	2·00	1·87	
Q_4	6·35	1·98	5·50	2·00	3·74	**

*Difference significant at $p < 0.05$
**Difference significant at $p < 0.01$

outlook, and awkwardly aloof in manner. Along with this, the aged report themselves as being shy, experiencing a sense of inferiority, preferring a limited number of associations and not being able to keep in contact with all that is going on around them.

Significantly elevated ($p < 0.01$) scores were obtained on Factors L (Protension vs Relaxed Security), O (Guilt proneness), and Q_4 (Ergic Tension). Added to this, there is a marked decrease in mean scores in the aged sample on Factors C (Ego Strength, $p < 0.01$). The aged personality shows a greater general emotional instability manifesting itself in a lack of frustration tolerance, a proclivity for easily getting upset, and having greater difficulties in coping with affective forces.

Linked with this, the aged personality is characteristically more emotionally sensitive and dependent. In conjunction with this emotional sensitivity, dependence and insecurity, the personality of the aged tends to be more mistrusting and suspecting than the personality generally found in middle life. The older person would seem more contemptuous than the average, thoroughly correct in his behaviour, resentful and indignant of people putting on airs, sceptical of alleged idealistic motives in others and hence exhibiting a greater general paranoid tendency. It is not surprising to find that the older personality shows a higher inner tension which may take the form of feeling frustrated, overwrought and impatient. He is more likely to experience worry, moodiness, social insecurity and general anxiety.

Significant differences were observed on factors G, N and Q_2. Factors G (Super Ego Strength), N (Alertness vs Shrewdness) and Q_2 (Group Adherence vs Self-Sufficiency) are significantly higher (p < 0·01) than the mean scores of the general population. The aged sample have greater super ego strength implying that they are quite conscientious, persistent, moralistic and staid. This greater super ego strength can be readily understood in psychodynamic terms.

Our aged population appears to be appreciably more shrewd and calculating than Cattell's population. This points to the older person's greater alertness to manners, to social obligations and to the social reactions of others. Cattell et $al.$ (1970) posit that this is also related to an objective test factor showing hypomanic and insecure behaviour, suggesting the pattern is motivated by "social climbing". This indeed is compatible with their heightened super ego functioning (G), their tendency to be suspecting (L), and their conventionality—their anxiety to do the "right thing" (M). Moreover, the older individual tends to be more independent, resolute and accustomed to going his own way and making his own decisions than the general population. This, however, does not necessarily imply dominance in his relationships with others, but rather has implications for the personality structure of the older individual and his life style.

The means (sten scores) and standard deviations of the 15 source traits are presented grouped by sex and age in Tables 14 and 15 respectively. Likewise, a two-way analysis of variance (Rao, 1952) was performed for each of the 15 factors and can be seen in Table 16.

It is somewhat surprising to note that on all 15 source traits there were no significant differences (increases or decreases) in mean scores over the later part of the life span (70+) in our sample (i.e. no significant age differences among the age groups used).

In previous comprehensive studies of age differences in personality structure using the 16PF over wider age ranges, this had not been so. Goodwin and Schaie (1969), studying a sample ranging in age from 21 to 75 years, and Seally and Cattell (1965) investigating a sample aged 16–70 years, found marked age differences on several source traits. The former found significant increases in mean scores for factors Q_1 (Guilt Proneness), Q_2 (Group dependent vs self-sufficiency) and Q_3 (Low Integration vs High Self-Concept Control) over the life span while factor E (Dominance) and Q_4 (Ergic Tension) showed significant decreases in mean scores over age. They found that factors A, H and L also showed significant age differences. Factor A (warm, sociable vs aloof, stiff) showed a decline over the middle years (approximately 36–55) followed by an increase and then a further decline after the age of 65. Factor H (adventurous vs shy, timid) showed age trends similar to factor A. Factor L (suspecting, jealous vs acceptable, adaptable) showed a fairly curvilinear U-shaped trend for aged 21–75. Seally and Cattell (1965), however, found increases with age for ego

Table 14. Newcastle upon Tyne Community Aged V
Normative Data on Cattell's Sixteen Personality Factor Questionnaire
Overall and Grouped by Sex

	Overall (N = 82)		Male (N = 26)		Female (N = 56)	
	M	S.D.	M	S.D.	M	S.D.
A	4·68	2·00	4·42	2·08	4·80	1·97
C	4·48	1·93	5·27	1·99	4·14	1·88
E	5·62	1·35	5·85	1·19	5·52	1·19
F	4·13	2·03	4·50	2·37	3·96	1·85
G	6·61	1·57	6·39	1·67	6·71	1·51
H	4·72	1·60	4·85	1·64	4·63	1·56
I	5·88	1·78	4·50	1·77	6·52	1·34
L	7·01	1·90	7·00	2·25	7·02	1·74
M	5·05	1·89	4·50	1·90	5·25	1·88
N	6·61	1·79	6·85	1·41	6·50	1·95
O	6·98	1·79	6·42	1·96	7·27	1·61
Q_1	4·66	1·57	4·96	1·84	4·52	1·43
Q_2	6·27	1·98	6·96	2·24	6·00	1·79
Q_3	5·07	2·05	5·70	1·90	4·75	2·06
Q_4	6·35	1·98	5·35	1·65	6·82	1·96

Table 15. Newcastle upon Tyne Community Aged V
Cattell's Sixteen Personality Factor Questionnaire
Sten Scores Means and Standard Deviations by Age and Sex

| | | 70 — 74 | | 75 — 79 | | 80 — 84 | | 85 + | |
		M = 4	F = 7	M = 13	F = 23	M = 6	F = 14	M = 3	F = 12
	Sex	M	S.D.	M	S.D.	M	S.D.	M	S.D.
A	M	3·50	2·08	4·08	1·75	5·67	2·58	4·67	2·31
	F	5·00	1·73	4·74	2·22	4·86	1·92	4·75	1·87
C	M	5·25	2·87	4·54	1·71	6·00	1·55	7·00	2·00
	F	4·43	2·30	3·65	1·77	4·36	1·65	4·67	1·88
E	M	6·25	1·71	5·77	1·01	5·33	1·03	6·67	1·53
	F	6·00	2·16	5·35	1·11	5·71	1·33	5·33	1·61
F	M	2·50	1·73	4·08	1·89	6·33	2·66	5·33	2·52
	F	4·29	2·29	3·87	1·94	4·21	1·89	3·67	1·50
G	M	4·75	0·96	6·54	1·51	6·67	1·75	7·33	2·52
	F	6·71	1·11	6·39	1·59	6·64	1·50	7·42	1·51
H	M	5·75	1·71	4·31	1·32	6·00	1·67	3·67	1·53
	F	4·00	1·00	5·13	1·60	4·57	1·74	4·08	1·31
I	M	5·75	1·71	3·92	2·06	5·17	0·98	4·00	0·00
	F	6·71	1·38	6·35	1·43	6·71	1·21	6·50	1·62
L	M	5·00	3·16	7·54	1·94	6·67	2·25	8·00	1·00
	F	7·86	1·07	6·87	2·05	7·29	1·68	6·50	1·38
M	M	4·50	2·38	4·46	2·15	4·50	1·76	4·67	1·16
	F	5·71	2·99	5·35	1·87	5·29	1·77	4·75	1·29
N	M	7·00	0·82	6·61	1·45	6·83	1·94	7·67	0·58
	F	6·71	1·38	6·74	1·79	6·71	2·05	5·67	2·35
O	M	7·00	1·41	6·62	1·94	5·67	2·16	6·33	2·89
	F	7·57	1·13	7·39	1·53	7·64	1·74	6·42	1·73
Q₁	M	5·50	3·11	4·69	1·84	5·17	1·47	5·00	1·00
	F	4·29	0·95	4·39	1·78	4·86	1·10	4·50	1·31
Q₂	M	8·00	0·82	6·77	2·59	6·83	2·40	6·67	2·08
	F	5·00	1·63	5·61	2·08	6·43	1·16	6·83	1·53
Q₃	M	5·25	1·71	6·15	1·86	5·00	2·24	6·00	1·73
	F	4·86	2·41	5·39	2·04	4·07	1·82	4·25	2·01
Q₄	M	5·50	1·00	5·15	1·95	5·50	1·87	5·67	0·58
	F	6·43	1·62	6·87	1·84	7·64	2·02	6·00	2·13

strength (C), super ego (G), and autia (M), and a decrease with age in surgency (F).

This Newcastle upon Tyne Community IV result seems to support Swenson's (1966) observation that compared to younger age groups

Table 16. Newcastle upon Tyne Community Aged V
Sixteen Personality Factor Questionnaire (Form C)
Summary Analyses of Variance by Age and Sex

	Age	df	Sex	df	Age × Sex	df
A	0·43	3, 74	0·65	1, 74	0·81	3, 74
C	2·39	3, 74	8·14**	1, 74	0·49	3, 74
E	0·29	3, 74	1·01	1, 74	0·82	3, 74
F	0·78	3, 3	1·03	1, 3	2·06	3, 74
G	1·49	3, 3	0·63	1, 3	1·29	3, 74
H	0·17	3, 3	0·04	1, 3	3·23*	2, 74
I	1·30	3, 74	31·02**	1, 74	0·83	3, 74
L	0·03	3, 3	0·02	1, 74	3·00*	3, 74
M	0·23	3, 74	2·89	1, 74	0·18	3, 74
N	0·42	3, 74	0·62	1, 74	0·87	3, 74
O	1·07	3, 74	5·30*	1, 74	0·76	3, 74
Q_1	0·33	3, 74	1·37	1, 74	0·02	3, 74
Q_2	0·36	3, 3	2·23	1, 3	1·79	3, 74
Q_3	2·17	3, 3	3·89	1, 3	0·02	3, 74
Q_4	1·30	3, 3	11·58**	1, 3	0·59	3, 74

**Difference significant at p < 0·01
*Difference significant at p < 0·05

those 60 through 69 years and 70 years and older display comparatively more stability in personality functioning.

Turning our attention to sex differences, we note that ego strength (C) showed a significant (p < 0·01) sex difference with men scoring higher than women on this trait. This would seem to indicate that women tend to be more affected by feelings and less stable emotionally than their male counterparts. Coupled with this, the women are more lacking in frustration tolerance, more apt to be easily upset and more worried than the men.

Consistent with this result the females scored significantly higher on factors I (Tough vs Tenderminded, p < 0·01), O (Guilt Proneness, p < 0·05) as well as Q_4 (Tension, p < 0·01). It would appear then, that a rather well-defined pattern regarding sex differences in the ageing personality emerges within our sample. The women are prone to be more tender-minded, sensitive dependent and over-protected than men, even in the aged. There is a clinging, insecure quality to their personality which most likely manifests itself in seeking help and sympathy. They would also appear more timid, gentle and indulgent to self and others than the men. This sex difference (factor I) seems to be most prominent in the 74–79 age group (t = 4·16, df = 34, p < 0·01) and exists in the 80–84 and 85+ groups to a less marked degree (t = 2·76, df = 18, p < 0·05; t = 2·59, df = 13, p < 0·05). One might also note that Cattell *et al.* (1970) suggested that there is increasing evidence which points to Tendermindedness (I+) being clinically the matrix of attitudes out of which neurotic maladjustments can arise.

At the same time the men's significantly lower scores on this factor (I) attests to their greater tough-mindedness, unsentimentality, self-reliance and a greater willingness to accept responsibility.

The women's higher scores on factor O (Guilt Proneness, p < 0·05) point to a proclivity towards being apprehensive, self-reproaching and insecure. They seem to feel a greater sense of general unworthiness, occasioning a more sensitive reaction to super ego infringements and perhaps other types of personal inadequacy too. This difference between males and females is most acute in the 80–84 age group (t = 2·17, df = 18, p < 0·05). Cattell's work suggests that an O+ person feels he is unstable, reports over-fatigue from exciting situations, is unable to sleep through worrying, is easily downhearted and remorseful, feels that people are not as moral as they should be and is inclined to piety. Furthermore, on the basis of their O scores, we would expect the aged women to exhibit a mixture of hypochondriacal and neurasthenic symptoms, with phobias and anxieties prominent when their normal state of functioning is diminished.

Goodwin and Schaie (1969) and Seally and Cattell (1965) have also found consistent sex differences in Ego Strength (factor C), Tough and Tendermindedness (factor I), and Guilt Proneness (factor O). These differences were of the same magnitude and direction as found in the present aged sample.

The fourth source trait on which there were significant sex differences was that of Ergic Tension (Factor Q_4 p < 0·01). By virtue of their significantly elevated scores the women demonstrate a marked propensity towards being more tense, frustrated, driven, overwrought and fretful than the males. This is especially true within the 74–79 and 80–84 age groups (t = 2·6387, df 34, p < 0·05; t = 2·2156, df = 18, p < 0·05). In psychodynamic terms, high ergic tension is best interpreted as an "id" energy excited in excess of the ego strength capacity to discharge it and which is therefore misdirected, converted int psychosomatic disturbances, anxiety etc., and is generally disruptive of steady application and emotional balance. It must be remembered that this undischarged drive can be a function of (a) level of situational, environmental frustration and difficulty as well as (b) some temperamental incapacity of the ego to handle discharge well even in an environment of ordinary difficulty. Clinically, Q_4 shares with C, O, and I much of the differentiation of neurotics from normals. Interestingly enough, Goodwin and Schaie (1969) found no sex differences on this factor throughout the life span. Although statistically insignificant, it is interesting to note that within our aged sample the males had tended to score higher than the females on factor Q_3. This implies that the male has a tendency to be somewhat more controlled and socially precise having a higher self-concept control than the female.

This tight constellation of sex differences in the present aged population is quite meaningful and substantiates trends in personality structure throughout the life span. This is borne out by Shepherd et al. (1966). The personality structure of Aged women (as opposed to their male counterparts) is characterised by a lowered ego strength being more affected by feelings and emotionally less stable than men, more tender-minded and dependent, more apprehensive and frustrated. Thus the women have an overall tendency to exhibit neurotic traits.

Statistically significant (Table 16) Age Sex interactions occur in this British Newcastle upon Tyne Community Aged data on factors H (Timid vs Adventurous) and L (Trustful vs Suspecting) indicating that within each age group the sexes behaved differently. The men seem to have scored more than the women on factor H within the 70–74 and 80–84 age groups, while the women tend to achieve higher mean scores within the 75–79 and 85+ age groups. This would seem to imply that the males are more socially bold than the women between the ages of 70–74 and 80–84 and less so between the ages of 75–79 and 85+. Likewise, the men seem to be less suspecting and dogmatic than the women between the ages of 70–74 and 80–84 and more so between the ages of 75–79 and 85+.

Self Concept in the Community Aged

One can well argue on a number of grounds that no attempt to understand personality in the aged would be complete without reference to the "self concept", a central theme in many major works on personality measurement and theory. Self theorists have claimed that utilization of the internal frame of reference adds materially to the understanding and prediction of human behaviour and that the knowledge of a person's self concept increases an understanding of him beyond what can be known from externally observable clues like age, sex, etc. (Thompson, 1972). Fitts *et al.* (1971), for example, propose that knowledge of a person's self concept is a short cut to other information about the person, such as his feelings, attitudes, interpersonal relationships and mental health. The nature of the self concept and its change with age, however, need to be more fully understood. Considering self concept as a unidimensional concept, various investigators reported that the elderly exhibit a more negative self concept than younger samples (Sward, 1945; Norman, 1949; Lehner and Gunderson, 1953; Mason, 1954; Dodge, 1961). On the other hand, some authors have observed a trend towards increasing self confidence with increasing age (Brozek, 1955; Kelly, 1955). It seems, therefore, that evidence regarding self concept in old age is quite inconsistent. The solution to this problem might well involve clarification concerning the multidimensional nature of the self-concept in the elderly and the development of more sensitive measures. For, it is possible that old age is typically a time in which "old labels" of self concept are no longer applicable. One's earlier way of defining oneself in relation to one's body, role in life, family and social life and personal worth may become inappropriate. Knowledge of self concept in old age—by the aged themselves and those who plan on their behalf—may provide "significant inputs" in helping to design programmes for the aged or predict the success of various schemes to help them.

The Community Aged V population were used in this study. A comparison between our data on the aged and the original normative data information on a general population is of considerable interest. Fitt's (1965) standardization group was a broad sample of 626 people from various parts of the U.S.A. His subjects ranged in age from 12 to 68 years and comprised approximately equal numbers of both sexes, both negro and white subjects, representatives of all social, economic and intellectual levels. The means and standard deviations from the general population and the elderly population on the TSCS are produced in Table 17.

Table 17. Newcastle upon Tyne Community Aged V
Self Concept

	Newcastle Old Age Community Norms (N = 82)		Fitts' TSCS Norms Age 12—68 (N = 626)		t
	M	S.D.	M	S.D.	
Self Criticism	30·44	6·57	35·54	6·70	6·51**
True/False Ratio	1·47	0·41	1·03	·29	12·31**
Net Conflict	19·23	16·40	−4·91	13·01	15·32**
Total Conflict	33·49	10·99	30·10	8·21	3·37**
Total Self Esteem	384·31	24·77	345·57	30·70	10·99**
S_1	128·46	8·30	127·10	9·96	1·19
R_2	131·83	10·20	103·67	13·79	17·90**
Behaviour	123·99	9·46	115·01	11·22	6·94**
Col. A	73·95	7·95	71·78	7·67	2·40 *
Col. B	82·10	5·63	70·83	8·70	11·95**
Col. C	75·27	7·06	64·55	7·41	12·41**
Col. D	81·10	4·86	70·83	8·43	10·82**
Col. E	72·04	8·27	68·15	7·86	4·20**
Total Variability	41·24	10·84	48·53	12·42	5·08**
Col. Total Variability	21·04	5·49	29·03	9·12	7·78**
Row Total Variability	20·33	6·52	19·60	5·76	1·07
Defensive Personality Scale	76·22	9·24	54·40	12·38	15·44**
General Maladjustment Scale	98·12	9·31	98·80	9·15	0·63
Psychotic Scale	53·28	6·61	46·10	6·49	9·42**
Personality Disorder Scale	91·54	8·38	76·39	11·72	11·49**
Neurosis Scale	90·45	11·01	84·31	11·10	4·72**
Personality Integration Scale	5·67	2·66	10·42	3·88	10·78**
Distribution	153·98	15·71	120·44	24·19	12·24**
5	32·79	8·17	18·11	9·24	13·83**
4	21·06	8·76	24·36	7·55	3·66**
3	7·50	3·83	18·03	8·89	10·62**
2	9·90	5·08	18·83	7·99	9·90**
1	28·73	7·46	20·63	9·01	6·94**

**Difference significant at $p < 0·01$

*Difference significant at $p < 0·05$

df = 706

It is quite evident that there are extensive significant differences in the scores on several aspects of self concept between our present elderly sample and that studied by Fitts (1965). The Newcastle Aged showed significant elevated mean scores on the Defensive Personality (DP) Scale while significantly lowered mean scores on the Self Criticism (SC) Scale. This indicates a heightened level of defensiveness on the part of the older persons which seems to operate on two levels of functioning—an obvious, manifest level (SC) and a subtle level (DP). The greater defensiveness of the elderly cause them to make more of a conscious, deliberate effort to present a more favourable picture of themselves than do the general population. This, of course, may stem from a weakened capacity to cope with self-criticism. Likewise, they also exhibit what may be called subtle defensiveness to a significantly greater extent than do the general population. Hence, regardless of how they describe themselves on a self-report instrument, they have at some level of awareness negative elements of their self concepts about which they are defensive. It is possible that this increased defensiveness during the latter part of the life span may partially account for the significantly higher self esteem (P scores) attained by these individuals, as our data are consistent with that of Grant (1969). By exhibiting a greater overall level of self esteem, it would seem that these old people tend to like themselves, feel that they are persons of value and worth, have confidence in themselves and act accordingly, all to a larger extent than the general population.

This higher level of self esteem cannot be accounted for by different levels of perception of Identity (Row 1 P Score) of "This is what I am" on the part of the old folks for there were no significant differences in mean scores on this variable. Although we note that the positive way in which the older individual views his behaviour (Row 3 P Score) contributes to his elevated level of self esteem, the major contribution to this elevated level lies in the older person's self satisfaction (Row 2 P Score). It would appear then that the older person is able to derive greater self-satisfaction and able to accept himself and his functioning more than his younger counterpart while viewing his own identity or "what he is", as very much like his counterpart in the general population. It must be remembered, however, that this high level of self esteem may well be due to defensive distortion.

While in younger years defensive attitudes and behaviour are negatively associated with a positive self concept and adjustment (Hogan,

1948; Haigh, 1949), it seems that the ability to defend oneself adequately and efficiently is an asset in later life. Hinton (1967) arrived at this same general observation.

The self concept of the aged can also be viewed in terms of a more external frame of reference, namely the way in which they view their physical self (Column A), moral-ethical self (Column B), personal self (Column C), family Self (Column D) and social self (Column E).

This aged sample population generally views itself as being more adequate in relation to these Column Scores than do the general population. They scored significantly higher than the general population on Column C, Column B and Column D. It would appear that the older folk are generally more satisfied with their personal and moral worth in their evaluation of their personality than the general population.

Likewise, these elderly express a heightened sense of worth within the family context.

This aged sample also achieved significantly elevated mean scores when describing their Social Self—Column E and their Physical Self —Column A compared to the general population.

In scoring significantly higher than the general population on the True-False Ratio (T/F), it is evident that the old age group—unlike the general population—achieves self definition by focusing on what they are and are relatively unable to accomplish the same thing by eliminating or rejecting what they are *not*. This observation is reaffirmed by the fact that the old-age group's mean Net Conflict scores are significantly greater than those of the standardization sample.

This aged group's Total Conflict Scores are also significantly lower, reflecting less extensive confusion, contradiction and general conflict in self conflict than Fitt's sample population.

It is rather noteworthy that the aged sample demonstrated significantly lower mean Total Variability scores as well as the Column Total Variability while there were no significant differences in mean Row Total Variability scores between the two groups. The old folk have significantly less of a tendency to compartmentalize certain areas of the self. This is to say that the aged demonstrate greater unity or integration of the self than the general population. They have a greater consistency between the various aspects of the self (physical self, moral-ethical self, personal self, family self, social self) as compared to the younger group. Along with this, however, there are no significant differences between the two groups so far as the consistency among the internal frame of reference, i.e. identity, self satisfaction and behaviour.

It would seem, then, that the aged have a heightened, integrated awareness of the functioning of their "self", and do not have the need to compartmentalize certain aspects of their "self" as much as the general population does. However, increased self-consistency on the part of the aged is accompanied by an increased tendency toward conflict (as defined by the TSCS). This might indicate that although the aged person may possess an appreciable amount of consistency and integration of the self—which allows for greater awareness and insight into functioning—he may not have the means whereby to resolve some of the conflicts brought about by this greater awareness and insight into the self.

These older individuals define themselves in more definite terms than do the general population. They attain a greater decisiveness in their attempts at self-description and are more certain as to the way in which they perceive their self functioning. This can be seen by their significantly higher mean Distribution Score (D), as well as by their constellation of sub-scores. They score significantly greater mean D5 and D1 scores while scoring significantly lower than the general population on D4, D3 and D2. Their sub-scores indicate that they are much less likely to hedge about and avoid committing themselves in their self description than the general population sample who tend to be more extremely uncertain and non-committal in their self evaluations.

The present results confirm Thompson's (1972) observation that the Empirical Scales for elderly people are general deviant. Significant elevations occur on the Psychosis Scale (Pay) while the Neurosis Scale (N), Personality Disorder Scale (PD) and Personality Integration Scale Scores are significantly (PI) lower than average. There were no significant differences on the General Maladjustment Scale (GM). This is to say that the elderly score significantly higher on the items which best differentiate psychotic patients from other groups. It is interesting that the aged are less like Neurotic and Personality Disorder groups than are the general population. The old folks share less an affinity to the Personality Integration group than do the general population. There are no significant differences between the aged group and the general population on the GM scale—a general index of adjustment-maladjustment.

This elderly sample of community residents show high self esteem in all areas of self concept but less so regarding the Physical and Social aspects of the self. The high self regard, however, seems to be partially a product of unrealistic self enhancement due to defensiveness. This defensiveness may very well be an asset in old age. The self image of the elderly is quite pronounced, sharply differentiated and perhaps— at times—rigid. Attaining self definition may be a problem resulting in contradiction. Although these elderly people appear to have more self awareness than the general population, they have less capacity for self criticism and a much stronger set of defences. It is felt that these defences may well, in part, be used to cope with the conflict that their increased self awareness causes.

The means and standard deviations of the 29 TSCS scores are presented grouped by sex and age in Table 18.

A two-way analysis of variance (Rao, 1952) for the 29 scores was carried out and can be seen in Table 19.

As individuals progress through the later part of the life span (70+), they have a greater tendency to be very definite and certain in what they say about themselves and how they see themselves. This is indicated by the distribution sub-scores—the way in which answers are distributed across the five available choices in responding to the items of the Scale. Thus, with increasing age, there was a significant ($p < 0.01$) increase in D5 scores as well as a significant ($p < 0.05$) increase in D1 scores. Accompanying these increases in mean distribution sub-scores, there was a marked decrease ($p < 0.01$) in D4 scores, again attesting to the greater certainty and definiteness with increases in age in what the old folk say about themselves.

Another significant increase ($p < 0.01$) in mean scores over the later part of the life span was found for Column B of the TSCS. It would seem that with increasing age there is a marked tendency toward a heightened level of satisfaction with one's moral worth, relationship to God, feelings of being a "good" or "bad" person, and satisfaction with one's religion or lack of it. Likewise, there is a significant increase ($p < 0.05$) in Row 2 scores with advancing age within our sample population. In general, these scores reflect the individual's self-satisfaction or self-acceptance. Hence, with increasing age there is a proclivity for a heightened level of self satisfaction and a greater ability to accept oneself. While with age there is a greater self acceptance, there also seems to be a significant increase ($p < 0.05$) in mean scores of the Defensive Position (DP) Scale. This is a subtle measure of

Table 18. Newcastle upon Tyne Community Aged V
Age self concept mean TSCS and standard deviations

	Sex	70–74 Mean	S.D.	75–79 Mean	S.D.	80–84 Mean	S.D.	85+ Mean	S.D.	Overall Mean	S.D.
Self	M	28·00	4·23	31·01	7·58	31·67	6·62	28·33	8·16	30·42	6·77
Criticism	F	34·71	5·34	30·78	5·61	29·00	7·44	28·17	6·55	30·27	6·43
	T	32·27	5·83	30·89	6·29	29·80	7·14	28·20	6·57		
True False	M	1·34	0·21	1·40	0·46	1·33	0·24	1·54	0·46	1·39	0·38
Ratio	F	1·54	0·64	1·61	0·47	1·38	0·32	1·46	0·29	1·51	0·43
	T	1·47	0·52	1·54	0·47	1·36	0·29	1·47	0·31		
Net	M	9·50	6·95	16·39	16·64	18·67	9·27	21·67	23·71	16·46	14·59
Conflict	F	24·57	23·22	21·87	17·53	16·64	17·53	20·08	12·86	20·52	17·15
	T	19·09	19·90	19·89	17·18	17·25	15·29	20·40	14·52		
Total	M	27·50	8·43	30·39	11·77	28·33	8·71	34·33	11·85	29·92	10·26
Conflict	F	37·43	12·03	36·74	11·94	32·29	10·16	34·08	9·98	35·14	11·01
	T	33·82	11·54	34·44	12·11	31·10	9·70	34·13	9·91		
Total	M	380·25	28·62	381·39	33·78	401·50	22·01	393·00	21·00	397·19	29·27
Positive	F	373·43	38·05	379·39	19·61	390·93	12·22	386·17	25·07	382·98	22·54
Score	T	375·91	33·56	380·11	25·18	394·10	15·95	387·53	23·77		
Row 1	M	130·75	7·50	127·64	9·07	130·50	6·72	135·33	3·51	129·58	7·94
	F	124·14	12·59	127·83	7·54	130·71	6·80	127·17	9·23	127·95	8·48
	T	126·55	11·09	127·69	8·00	130·65	6·60	128·80	8·95		
Row 2	M	125·75	13·82	128·92	13·38	139·50	8·50	134·33	9·24	131·50	12·45
	F	128·00	15·35	130·35	8·14	135·07	4·76	133·83	9·67	131·98	9·09
	T	127·18	14·14	129·83	10·17	136·40	6·23	133·93	9·25		
Row 3	M	123·75	9·22	124·92	13·45	131·50	1·31	123·33	9·50	126·08	11·30
	F	121·29	11·77	121·43	7·92	124·43	6·62	125·33	9·08	123·00	8·38
	T	122·18	10·50	122·69	10·21	126·55	7·70	124·93	8·86		
Column A	M	71·75	7·93	75·61	7·92	38·67	10·63	77·00	7·94	75·89	8·37
	F	71·00	11·42	71·87	7·01	75·29	6·71	73·92	7·61	73·05	7·66
	T	71·27	9·86	73·22	7·47	76·30	7·94	74·53	7·49		
Column B	M	80·00	5·60	78·00	8·28	83·67	5·32	83·33	1·53	80·23	7·01
	F	79·86	6·36	81·74	4·06	85·79	3·36	83·83	4·59	82·96	4·68
	T	79·91	5·81	80·39	6·10	85·15	4·02	83·73	4·11		
Column C	M	74·00	5·35	77·15	7·15	78·83	6·34	78·67	3·79	77·23	6·30
	F	70·57	11·70	73·57	6·63	75·50	4·92	77·17	6·79	74·45	7·15
	T	71·82	9·68	74·86	6·94	76·50	5·32	77·47	6·22		
Column D	M	82·00	2·94	78·54	7·20	84·67	2·42	80·67	1·53	80·96	5·98
	F	81·57	5·03	80·70	4·58	82·86	2·45	79·83	4·84	81·16	4·30
	T	81·73	4·22	79·92	5·66	83·70	2·72	80·00	4·34		
Column E	M	72·50	9·11	72·08	9·71	75·50	5·96	73·33	8·02	73·08	8·33
	T	70·43	6·66	71·78	8·33	71·86	7·97	71·42	10·14	71·55	8·27
	T	71·18	7·25	71·89	8·72	72·95	7·47	71·80	9·52		
Total	M	31·25	6·24	38·92	11·37	41·33	13·65	35·00	15·72	37·85	11·63
Variability	F	44·86	11·98	41·17	8·41	45·71	9·29	41·42	13·26	42·82	10·18
	T	39·91	12·04	40·36	9·48	44·00	10·60	41·13	13·43		
Column	M	15·50	3·69	20·85	5·83	20·83	6·62	19·33	8·74	19·85	6·06
Total	F	23·14	5·15	20·70	4·90	24·29	6·32	24·00	6·45	21·96	5·72
Variability	T	20·36	5·92	20·75	5·17	23·25	6·44	20·67	6·64		
Row Total	M	15·75	2·99	18·08	6·02	20·50	8·55	15·67	7·23	18·00	6·34
Variability	T	21·71	8·26	20·96	5·24	22·93	5·97	20·42	7·99	21·43	6·36
	T	19·55	7·26	19·92	5·62	22·20	6·70	19·47	7·85		

(Continued on page 117)

	Sex	70–74 Mean	S.D.	75–79 Mean	S.D.	80–84 Mean	S.D.	85+ Mean	S.D.	Overall Mean	S.D.
Defensive	M	73·75	6·24	77·08	12·41	79·17	6·52	85·00	3·00	77·96	9·87
Personality	F	69·29	9·00	73·78	7·57	78·21	8·12	78·83	10·38	75·41	8·91
Scale	T	70·91	8·08	74·97	9·56	78·50	7·52	80·07	9·62		
General	M	102·25	4·99	98·46	10·03	102·17	9·97	101·67	4·93	100·27	8·75
Maladjust-	F	95·14	14·28	96·04	8·99	101·07	5·72	95·75	10·49	97·13	9·47
ment Scale	T	97·73	11·94	96·92	9·31	101·40	6·98	96·93	9·79		
Psychotic	M	52·00	5·35	54·39	9·28	53·50	3·78	56·67	8·51	54·08	7·42
Scale	F	49·86	6·89	52·96	6·55	52·86	6·18	54·67	5·30	52·91	6·23
	T	50·64	6·18	53·47	7·55	53·05	5·47	55·07	5·75		
Personality	M	93·00	6·06	83·92	10·58	93·00	7·24	94·67	7·64	88·65	9·94
Disorder	F	87·71	7·34	91·65	7·80	95·71	4·84	94·92	7·40	92·88	7·33
Scale	T	89·64	7·10	88·86	9·53	94·90	5·61	94·87	7·17		
Neurosis	M	91·25	11·30	95·08	11·57	93·83	13·81	96·33	8·39	94·34	11·21
Scale	F	84·14	13·21	87·61	9·05	90·71	8·37	90·75	13·70	88·63	10·54
	T	86·73	12·48	90·31	10·52	91·65	10·01	91·87	12·76		
Personality	M	7·00	4·08	6·46	3·36	4·47	1·03	5·67	2·52	6·04	2·97
Integration	F	6·10	2·08	6·39	2·64	5·14	2·21	3·92	2·15	5·50	2·51
Scale	T	6·36	2·80	6·42	2·87	5·00	1·60	4·27	2·25		
Distribution	M	138·00	23·48	147·69	24·56	165·17	10·27	143·00	9·54	149·69	21·70
Score	F	149·86	9·70	152·35	9·66	161·93	5·36	159·50	17·34	155·96	11·68
	T	145·55	16·05	150·67	16·45	162·90	7·05	156·20	17·21		
5	M	23·75	9·00	30·15	11·62	39·33	1·75	35·00	14·42	31·85	10·88
	F	28·86	3·89	31·65	6·16	35·57	5·60	34·33	9·02	32·97	6·77
	T	27·00	6·33	31·11	8·41	36·70	5·04	34·87	9·68		
4	M	26·25	8·66	22·08	11·66	13·00	4·69	18·33	10·02	20·19	10·35
	F	24·86	5·82	24·52	7·63	17·36	4·31	19·33	10·74	21·66	8·06
	T	25·36	6·56	23·64	9·20	16·05	4·76	19·13	10·25		
3	M	9·75	8·73	8·69	5·56	7·50	4·32	8·67	3·06	8·58	5·38
	F	7·57	3·55	7·57	2·84	6·36	2·21	6·17	2·95	6·96	2·82
	T	8·36	5·63	7·97	4·00	6·70	2·92	6·67	3·04		
2	M	13·75	6·65	13·00	9·03	8·50	1·64	8·00	4·00	11·50	7·20
	F	10·14	5·76	9·35	3·17	8·00	2·66	9·58	3·78	9·16	3·56
	T	11·46	6·04	19·67	6·12	8·15	2·37	9·27	3·73		
1	M	26·50	8·89	26·23	10·50	31·67	5·01	30·00	6·56	27·96	8·75
	F	26·43	8·46	27·17	5·82	32·71	5·17	30·09	8·07	29·09	6·83
	T	26·46	8·17	26·83	7·70	32·40	5·01	30·07	7·57		
Number of	M	17·00	6·48	27·08	13·51	31·17	10·87	30·67	15·57	26·89	12·55
Deviant	F	26·00	23·66	30·09	17·61	29·07	13·98	37·00	11·55	30·80	16·44
Signs	T	22·73	19·21	29·00	16·12	29·70	12·88	35·73	12·10		

defensiveness, and would imply that over the later part of the life span, individuals' positive self description may—to a certain extent—stem from defensive distortion. In light of the lack of personality differences with advancing age groups within the sample, it is interesting to note that there is a significant decrease ($p < 0.05$) in the Personality Integration Scale (PI) mean scores between advancing age groups within the sample.

Table 19. Newcastle upon Tyne Community Aged V
Age Self Concept mean TSCS Scores and Standard Deviations
Two-way Analyses of Variance on the TSCS

	Age	df	Sex	df	Age × Sex	df
Self Criticism	0·88	3, 3	0·02	1, 3	4·77**	3, 74
True/False Ratio	0·89	3, 3	1·69	1, 3	0·40	3, 74
Net Conflict	0·14	3, 74	0·75	1, 74	0·56	3, 74
Total Conflict	0·56	3, 74	4·45**	1, 74	0·31	3, 74
Total Positive Score	2·00	3, 74	0·84	1, 74	0·12	3, 74
R_1	0·83	3, 3	0·90	1, 3	1·02	3, 74
R_2	2·85*	3, 74	0·00	1, 74	0·37	3, 74
R_3	1·26	3, 74	2·34	1, 74	0·48	3, 74
Col. A	1·26	3, 74	2·71	1, 74	0·09	3, 74
Col. B	4·51**	3, 74	3·05	1, 74	0·62	3, 74
Col. C	1·99	3, 74	3·80	1, 74	0·06	3, 74
Col. D	2·79	3, 74	0·02	1, 74	1·14	3, 74
Col. E	0·05	3, 74	0·37	1, 74	0·23	3, 74
Total Variance	0·78	3, 74	3·76	1, 74	0·74	3, 74
Column Total Variability	0·79	3, 3	1·80	1, 3	1·27	3, 74
Row Total Variability	0·76	3, 74	5·27*	1, 74	0·22	3, 74
Defensive Personality Scale	3·15*	3, 74	2·35	1, 74	0·19	3, 74
General Maladjustment Scale	1·15	3, 74	2·12	1, 74	0·31	3, 74
Psychotic Scale	1·01	3, 3	0·81	1, 3	0·03	3, 74
Personality Disorder Scale	1·58	3, 74	1·77	1, 74	2·11	3, 74
Neurosis Scale	0·78	3, 74	4·57*	1, 74	0·16	3, 74
Personality Integration Scale	3·16*	3, 74	3·36	1, 74	0·48	3, 74
Distribution Score	3·70	3, 3	2·15	1, 3	1·12	3, 74
5	4·47**	3, 74	0·07	1, 74	0·76	3, 74
4	15·23**	3, 74	1·40	1, 74	0·27	3, 74
3	0·57	3, 74	0·25	1, 74	0·03	3, 74
2	1·35	3, 74	3·32	1, 74	0·93	3, 74
1	2·88*	3, 74	0·16	1, 74	0·02	3, 74
Number of Deviant Signs	1·20	3, 74	0·13	1, 74	0·51	3, 74

**Difference significant at $p < 0.01$
*Difference significant at $p < 0.05$

Turning to sex differences on the TSCS within our aged sample, a rather well-defined pattern of differences emerges. The women demonstrate significantly elevated mean Total Conflict ($p < 0.01$) and

Total Variance ($p < 0.05$) scores, while scoring significantly lower ($p < 0.05$) on the Neurosis Scale (which is an inverse scale) than their male counterparts.

The women in our sample tend to have a significantly higher degree of confusion, contradiction and general conflict in self-perception than do the males. The conflict scores are reflections of conflicting responses to positive and negative items within the same area of self perception (Total Conflict). The women exhibit a definite propensity for scoring higher on the Row Total Variability than their male counterparts. This implies that the women measure a greater amount of inconsistency from one area of self-perception to another, and have a greater tendency to compartmentalize certain areas of the self apart from the remainder of the self. To be more specific, they show greater inconsistency in self-perception between their basic identity, their self acceptance and the way in which they perceive their own behavioural functioning. Their significantly lower mean scores on the Neuroses (N) Scale point to the fact that women show greater similarity to the standardization group for the empirical scales of neurotic patients than do the men.

A significant age x sex interaction ($p < 0.01$) was found for the Self Criticism Score (SC). This is to say, there is some complex interaction between age and sex on this variable. It is noticeable that male and female scores on this variable converge with age.

Adjustment in the Community Aged

It has been said that the practical purpose of gerontology is to help people live better in their later years (Havighurst, 1963). There has been no agreement, however, as to what constitutes good living in later life. As has been seen in an earlier section, there is agreement on some of the determining contributors of good living such as health, economic security, presence of friends and family, but there is disagreement on the actual signs of good living in the feelings and behaviour of a person as he grows older. Havighurst (1963) mentions two general approaches to the definition and measurement of successful ageing, or adjustment—an inner, subjective entity and an outer, behavioural entity. The definition of personal adjustment used in the present study and advocated by Cavan et al. (1949), Havighurst (1957) and others, is the overall happiness or life satisfaction of the individual with his past life and present situation. A person, therefore, can be said to be ageing successfully or personally adjusted if he is happy and satisfied with his life. Personal adjustment in the aged was assessed by means of the (previously described) Life Satisfaction Indexes A and B. The other definition of social adjustment or successful ageing was that of competent behaviour in the common social roles of worker, parent, spouse, homemaker, citizen, friend, association member and church member, and was measured by an Activity Inventory (Havighurst and Albrecht, 1953).

The means and standard deviations for the aged sample on the LSI A, LSI B and Activity Inventory were calculated and are presented grouped according to age and sex in Table 20. In order to assess the

Table 20. Newcastle upon Tyne Community Aged V
Adjustment LSI A, LSI B and Activity Inventory

| | Overall and Grouped According to Sex | | | | | |
	Total		Male		Female	
	M	*S.D.*	*M*	*S.D.*	*M*	*S.D.*
LSI A	28·32	5·84	28·77	6·84	28·11	5·17
LSI B	17·54	4·30	18·58	4·21	17·05	4·30
Active Inventory	22·31	6·97	22·73	6·95	22·11	7·03

| | | Grouped According to Age | | | | | | | |
| | | 70 — 74 | | 75 — 79 | | 80 — 84 | | 85 + | |
		M	*S.D.*	*M*	*S.D.*	*M*	*S.D.*	*M*	*S.D.*
LSI A	M	25·25	10·63	29·46	6·64	28·67	6·74	30·67	2·08
	F	27·14	7·93	27·65	3·94	28·14	6·37	29·50	4·15
	Total	26·46	8·51	28·31	5·06	28·30	6·31	29·73	3·79
LSI B	M	16·25	4·99	18·92	4·52	18·83	3·55	19·67	4·04
	F	17·43	5·22	15·70	4·40	18·57	3·18	17·67	4·42
	Total	17·00	4·92	16·86	4·65	18·65	3·29	18·07	4·28
Activity	M	24·00	3·56	21·00	7·04	27·17	7·41	19·67	7·37
Inventory	F	21·71	8·86	22·61	5·77	22·71	7·13	20·67	8·61
	Total	22·55	7·23	22·03	6·20	24·05	7·32	20·47	8·13

| | | Two-way Analysis of Variance | | | | |
	Age	*df*	*Sex*	*df*	*Age × Sex*	*df*
LSI A	0·75	3, 74	0·38	1, 74	0·28	3, 74
LSI B	1·05	3, 74	2·77	1, 74	0·90	3, 74
Activity						
Inventory	0·62	3, 74	0·05	1, 74	0·66	3, 74

contribution of age, sex and age x sex variables to differences within the aged sample, two-way analyses of variance were computed for the three measures of life satisfaction. The results of these analyses can be seen in Table 20. Upon inspection of the results, it is of interest that age groups (70–74; 75–79; 80–84; 85+) within our aged sample population did not differ significantly on any of the measures of life satisfaction—be it the inner, subjective measures or the outer, behavioural measure. In a like manner, men did not differ from women—or vice versa—with regard to life satisfaction. No age x sex interaction was observed. This seems to imply that with advancing age within the later part of the life span, there is no significant increase or decrease in personal or social adjustment as measured in terms of overall life satisfaction. The lack of sex differences in life satisfaction within our aged sample population is quite interesting, especially when considering consistent sex trends in the personality (16PF) and self concept (TSCS) results.

We hope that future research workers and clinicians will find the information presented in this chapter on the normal and abnormal personality dimensions and their quantification in the Aged both practically and theoretically useful. It could and should lead to improved investigation and understanding of individual elderly in both the patient and social situation, so that better, or at least more, appropriate treatment and provision can be made for them. The final chapter in this book will try to illustrate how research into the theory of personality and eventually help for the aged can be improved by this basic knowledge.

4

Personality and Mental Illness

We would now like to present one fairly comprehensive and a series of small pilot studies on personality and mental illness. We appreciate that there are many difficulties and limitations in this section but we feel, on balance, that readers and research workers would welcome the basic data and forgive the presentation, which results from the nature of these small interrelated, but separate, investigations. These were begun on Newcastle upon Tyne Hospital III and continued on the Institutions VI aged populations, a total of 243 in all. The first larger study, initiated in 1964, looked into the application of Eysenckian theory and methods of measuring personality (Eysenck, 1966) in the aged. A further study in 1968 followed similar lines on new clinical populations. A second series, completed in 1973, looked at Cattell's approach to personality, combining the measurement and analysis of normal and psychopathological dimensions with some normal, but primarily the mentally ill aged living in various settings.

The Newcastle upon Tyne Hospital Aged III Study

NORMAL PERSONALITY CHARACTERISTICS

In this investigation the Maudsley Personality Inventory was administered to 144 of the elderly representing organic, functional and normal states. The sample divided into four groups: Normal (i.e. subjects

122

judged by a psychiatrist to be mentally stable), 29; Affective Disorders, consisting of cases of endogenous depression, reactive depression and anxiety states, 42; late recurring schizophrenia and paraphrenia, 31; and Organic Psychosis, consisting of cases of senile and arteriosclerotic dementia, 42. The normal subjects were drawn from the Newcastle Community Aged Survey (Kay, Beamish and Roth, 1964a,b), while the other subjects were in-patients at a large mental hospital, fully described in Chapter 2, page 69.

The development of the Maudsley Personality Inventory (MPI) has been described in detail by Eysenck (1956). By means of item and factor analysis of questions drawn principally from the Guilford Inventory and the Maudsley Medical Questionnaire, he extracted the two dimensions of Extraversion and Neuroticism. Forty-eight questions were finally selected for the MPI, 24 to measure neuroticism (N) and 24 to measure Extraversion (E). Answers are grouped "Yes", "No" and "?" (i.e. "not sure"), and in scoring 2 points are given to the designated scale for the keyed responses and 1 point to the designated scale for the "not sure" responses. All the N scale items are keyed for "Yes" answers, but only 16 E scale answers are so keyed, the others being keyed "No". The possible range of scores on both scales is thus from 0 to 48.

Table 21 presents the means, standard deviations, reliability coefficients and correlations between E and N for various groups. Jensen (1958), in reviewing a number of early studies, reported that no correlation had been found between age and the MPI scales, and that correlations with sex had been negligible in all studies, although there is a tendency for women to score on the average about 1 point higher than men on both E and N Scales. A later study, however, by Guttmann (1966) analysed the MPI scores of 1,419 Canadian Ss between the ages of 17 and 94 and found a low but significant correlation ($r = -0.069$, $p < 0.05$) between extraversion and age, thus confirming Lynn's (1964) suggestion that behaviour patterns become more introverted with increasing age. As can be seen from Table 21, split-half reliability is high, and test-retest reliability has been quoted as $+0.73$ for the E scale and $+0.62$ for the N scale (Bartholomew and Marley, 1959).

In view of these considerations, the MPI was selected as a useful instrument for the assessment of personality in a group of old persons suffering from various kinds of mental disorder.

The relationship between MPI scores and psychiatric diagnosis in an elderly sample of Ss had not, hitherto, been investigated. It is intended, therefore, to present data bearing upon this relationship. Previous work indicates that neurotics have higher N scores than other Ss (Sainsbury, 1960; McGuire *et al.*, 1963) and that schizophrenics score low on E (McGuire *et al.*, 1963). Further, theories advanced by Eysenck (1957) and Shapiro (1956) predict that organics should have higher E scores than other groups, since brain damage is assumed to generate reactive inhibition in the CNS which, in turn, leads to extraverted behaviour patterns. There is also the finding of Choppy and Eysenck (in Eysenck, 1963) that Ss with generalised brain damage

Table 21. Extraversion and Neuroticism Studies
Means, Standard Deviations, Reliability and Intercorrelation of
E and N Scales on the MPI

Study	Sample	N	Extraversion M	S.D.	Neuroticism M	S.D.	rEN	Reliability E	N
Eysenck (1956a)	Normal adult males	200	24·26	10·04	17·81	11·32	−0·15	0·85*	0·90*
	Normal adult females	200	24·17	9·33	19·45	11·02	−0·04	0·82*	0·87*
	Males and females	400	24·89	9·67	18·63	11·19	−0·09	0·83*	0·88*
Eysenck (1956b)	English University students, male	50	28·86	8·36	19·04	11·24	0·12		
Star (1957)	English University students, male	213	25·26	8·85	23·23	11·27	−0·07		
Das (1957)	Polytechnic and Art school students, mixed	68	24·57	19·04	27·06	11·56	−0·08		
Bendig (1957)	American University students, male	714	28·40	8·06	20·19	10·71			
Referred to by Jensen (1958)	American University students, female	350	29·41	8·37	21·63	10·45			
Sigal, Star and Franks (1958)	Dysthymics Hysterics and psychopaths	25	21·00	11·96	36·80	10·48			
		27	25·22	9·96	28·82	12·76			
Eysenck (1959)	English "normals"	1800	24·91	9·71	19·89	11·02			
Sainsbury (1960)	O.P. controls, mixed	546	25·70	8·50	18·40	10·80			
	O.P. neurotics,	116	21·40	10·10	32·00	9·20			

Table 21—*Continued*

Study	Sample	Extraversion			Neuroticism			Reliability	
		N	M	S.D.	M	S.D.	rEN	E	N
McGuire et al. (1963)	Depressed patients, mixed	42	21·90	8·50	28·30	12·40	−0·42		
	Character neurosis, mixed	35	21·40	8·90	32·10	13·4	−0·36		
	Dysthymia, males and females	30	19·70	9·90	34·20	8·90	−0·11		
	Hysteria, males and females	12	19·30	8·40	28·20	13·60	−0·33		
	Organic psychosis, males and females	15	25·90	11·20	29·90	10·80	−0·38		
	Schizophrenia, males and females	12	16·70	5·70	28·70	10·10	−0·31		
	Mania, males and females	5	22·00	4·80	30·00	8·10	−0·10		
	Whole sample, males and females	151	21·20	9·10	30·60	12–00	−0·32		
Savage (1962)	University students	168	27·30		27·70				

*Corrected split-half reliability

have high neuroticism scores. The present chapter ascertains whether these findings occur with older Ss. The influences of age and sex on the E and N scales is also a matter of concern. Lynn (1964) and Guttmann (1966) have demonstrated that behaviour patterns become more introverted with increasing age. Other studies of personality and ageing (*see*, for example, Birren, 1964), stress that older people have less opportunity and appear to have less desire for social interaction, and this factor may represent itself in the present data by lowered E scores in older groups. The normative data on the MPI suggest that sex differences are minimal.

A final issue is that of the orthogonality of E and N scales. This is discussed in Chapter 4. Other studies have examined the correlation of E and N for younger samples than the present one. The independence or interdependence of E and N scales for older normal and abnormal Ss is, as yet, unknown. No significant differences from normal younger age groups on E and N scales were found for the normal elderly; an interesting result in view of the Community I neurologically related scales. This normal group were, of course, "hyper" normal in psychiatric terms.

Extraversion, Neuroticism and Psychiatric Diagnosis

Table 22 presents means and S.D.'s of E and N scores overall and for the diagnostic groups of the Newcastle upon Tyne Hospital Aged III. There are no significant differences among the E scale comparisons between groups: the predictions that organics would score highly on E and that the schizophrenics would be more introverted than other groups are not, therefore, supported. With respect to the Neuroticism dimension, the prediction that the affectives would score significantly differently from the other groups is not borne out. On the other hand, the difference between organics and normals on the N scale reaches significance (p < 0·01). This is due to the high N score of the organic Ss, which exceeds, although not significantly, that of the affectives.

In general, the MPI does not produce the differences in scores on E and N dimensions that one would expect on the basis of previous work and on theoretical grounds. This may, of course, be due, in part, to the inadequacies inherent in psychiatric diagnosis; it is common practice, for example, to discriminate between different types of schizophrenia, but, unfortunately, the present sample is not large enough for us to do this. Again, that the N score of the affectives is as

Table 22. Newcastle upon Tyne Hospital Aged III
Neuroticism, Extraversion Normative Data for Elderly Psychiatric Groups

		Normals (N = 29)	Affectives (N = 42)	Schizo-phrenics (N = 31)	Organics (N = 42)	All subjects (N = 144)
Age:	Mean	73·7	68·5	69·7	74·3	71·5
	S.D.	8·2	6·7	7·5	9·7	8·1
N:	Mean	20·0	24·2	18·7	26·8	22·9
	S.D.	11·2	13·1	10·8	9·8	11·7
E:	Mean	25·8	24·0	22·3	25·8	24·5
	S.D.	8·2	8·9	8·0	8·0	8·3
E.N. correlations		−0·11	0·22	−0·01	−0·18	−0·12

low as 24·2 is perhaps not so surprising since the N scale is primarily a measure of anxiety (it correlates highly with Taylor's Manifest Anxiety Scale) whereas the majority of elderly affectives are depressed.

The chief positive finding in this section is the high mean N score of the organics in comparison with the other groups. This confirms the finding of Choppy and Eysenck (in Eysenck, 1963). There seem to be three possibilities which might account for this finding:

(a) the higher neuroticism may be the direct consequence of the cortical changes themselves.

(b) organic Ss are anxious over their reduced capacities and the social situation (hospitalisation) into which dementia has led them. This view is supported by clinical experience with such patients who frequently voice grievances about their stay in hospital or express concern about their abilities. This concern and anxiety is encountered less among hospitalised schizophrenics and endogenous depressives.

(c) it may be an artefact due to all of the N scale items being keyed for "Yes" answers. Organic Ss are, according to this view, simply agreeing with the questioner more than other Ss.

Further studies are needed to substantiate these speculations.

It is interesting to note that neither Extraversion nor Neuroticism are statistically significantly related to age in the present sample, although there is a slight tendency for older organics to score higher on the E scale. Indeed, there are no sex differences on E and N, either for the whole sample or for each of the diagnostic groups.

Unpublished data from sample (a) Institutions VI on psychiatric patients aged 60–79 (means 67) in 1968 provides some useful supplementary data to the Hospital Aged III study, using the Eysenck Personality Inventory, an improved revision of the MPI (Eysenck, 1964), with three groups of hospitalised aged psychiatric patients. The 57 patients included 19 affectives, all depressives, 20 thought disordered schizophrenics and 18 schizophrenics with no signs of thought disorder, as described in the Institutions Aged VI sample in Chapter 2 page 73. Table 23 shows that there were no statistically significant differences between the mentally ill groups in extraversion but that the affective group, despite being all depressives, were more neurotic than the schizophrenics.

Table 23. Newcastle upon Tyne Institutions Aged VI(a)
E.P.I. Extraversion and Neuroticism Scores Means and Standard Deviation

	Affectives (N = 19)		Thought Disordered Schizophrenics (N = 20)		Schizophrenics (N = 18)	
	M	*S.D.*	*M*	*S.D.*	*M*	*S.D.*
Extraversion	13·89	3·70	11·90	2·86	12·39	4·00
Neuroticism	13·26	5·58	10·05	5·96	9·11	4·60

Analysis of Variance—Extraversion and Neuroticism

Source of Variance	Sum of squares	d.f.	m.s.v.	F	
Extraversion					
Total variance	715·53	56			
Variance between					
groups	41·64	2	20·82	1·67	n.s.
Variance within groups	673·89	54	12·48		
Neuroticism					
Total variance	1172·25	56			
Variance between					
groups	177·84	2	88·92	4·82	0·05
Variance within groups	994·41	54	18·42		

The Institutions Aged VI Study

NORMAL AND PATHOLOGICAL PERSONALITY CHARACTERISTICS

This section consisted of three studies, VI(a), (b) and (c). Readers will recall that details of these small aged samples are given in Chapter 2 under Institutions Aged VI information. In sample (c) personality was investigated with the Clinical Analysis Questionnaire (Delhees and Cattell, 1971) on the small sample of out-patient, short-stay psychogeriatric group fully described on page 74 as the Newcastle upon Tyne Institutions Aged VI(c) sample. Though essentially a pilot study, some interesting findings emerged. This instrument measures the normal dimensions of the 16PFQ, but, in addition, allows the investigation of 12 clinical or psychopathological scales. The normative data

Table 24. Newcastle upon Tyne Institutions Aged VI(c)
Clinical Analysis Questionnaire
Cattell's 16PF

		Old Age Sample (N = 20)		College Students (N = 273)	
	Factor	M	S.D.	M	S.D.
Part I					
A	Warmhearted, outgoing	5·90	1·89	7·8	2·6
B	Intelligence	2·15	1·27	6·5	1·4
C	Emotionally stable, mature	4·65	2·62	11·7	2·7
E	Assertive, aggressive	5·50	1·96	9·1	3·2
F	Happy-go-lucky, lively	1·65	0·93	9·9	2·8
G	Conscientious, persistent	7·95	1·64	10·4	3·3
H	Venturesome, uninhibited	4·45	1·99	8·8	4·0
I	Tender-minded, sensitive	4·40	2·21	7·7	3·3
L	Suspicious, hard to fool	5·95	1·67	9·1	2·7
M	Imaginative, bohemian	3·80	1·88	8·8	2·8
N	Astute, polished	6·70	1·53	7·0	2·4
O	Apprehensive, self-reproaching	5·45	2·44	7·2	3·0
Q_1	Experimenting, liberal	1·85	1·27	9·2	2·9
Q_2	Self-sufficient, resourceful	4·30	1·66	8·8	3·2
Q_3	Controlled, exacting will power	7·70	1·53	9·2	3·1
Q_4	Tense, frustrated	4·90	2·49	7·3	3·0
Part II					
D_1	Overconcerned with health, etc.	7·90	1·59	4·0	4·6
D_2	Disgusted with life	7·05	2·26	4·4	4·5
D_3	Seeks excitement, is restless	4·25	1·62	13·1	3·6
D_4	Has disturbing dreams, tense	6·65	2·89	6·8	4·1
D_5	Has feelings of weariness, worries	5·95	2·11	8·2	5·5
D_6	Has feelings of guilt, critical of self	5·75	2·20	7·1	4·6
D_7	Avoids contact with people	7·50	2·19	5·8	3·9
Pa	Believes he is being persecuted	6·15	1·42	6·4	4·0
Pp	Complacent towards antisocial behaviour	4·20	1·44	15·4	3·9
Sc	Retreats from reality	5·75	2·38	6·4	4·2
As	Suffers compulsive habits	5·25	2·24	8·7	4·2
Ps	Feels inferior and unworthy, timid	6·20	1·74	5·6	4·6

are illustrated in Table 24. Sten scores are used in terms of the 16PFQ and CAQ in this study. The general population norms of Cattell's 16PFQ (Cattell *et al.*, 1970) and the college norms for Part I presented in the CAQ interim experimental edition used a mean sten of 5·5 and an S.D. of ±2. The Institutions Aged VI(c) group were significantly less intelligent, much more serious-minded and prudent, much more conscientious, more practical, very conservative and traditional and well-controlled, with few personal or interpersonal problems than Cattell's general population norms (Table 24).

A more complicated comparison of personality characteristics of the resident elderly in various settings can be made between the sub-samples (a), (b), (c) of the Institutions Aged VI, as well as relating the data to other published studies.

Here, analysis of variance indicated that there were significant differences between these samples on each of the 16 dimensions. F was significant at the 0·01 level in every analysis of normal personality dimension, but that for Factor E, where F was significant at the 0·05 level. The means for the present and the standardisation samples were then compared, in terms of the Scheffe criterion. The results indicate that the psychogeriatric day-patients sample is less intelligent (Factor B), more sober, conventional and conservative (Factors F, M and Q_1) and shows a higher degree of conscientiousness (Factor G) and control (Factor Q_3) than the standardisation sample (Table 24).

If we regard the mean scores of the standardisation sample as representing mean scores for the adult population, we may then regard the differences observed above, as age differences. As such, they may be compared with results obtained by Cattell *et al.* (1970), Fozard and Nuttall (1971) and Goodwin and Schaie (1969).

As with the Newcastle upon Tyne Institution Aged VI(c) Aged, a decline with age on Factor B (Intelligence) was observed by Fozard and Nuttall (1971) and by Cattell *et al.* (1970) for women. It will be remembered that the present sample also consisted predominantly of female subjects.

The fall in Surgency (Factor F) with age, for both sexes, was similarly observed both by Cattell *et al.* (1970) and by Fozard and Nuttall (1971).

Neither Fozard and Nuttall (1971), nor Goodwin and Schaie (1969) report any age change in Factor M, while Cattell *et al.* (1970) observed a marked increase in unconventionality with age for men. The significantly higher degree of conventionality observed in the present sample may, it seems, be due to something other than age, or perhaps age plus cultural and social differences between U.K. and U.S.A.

The same conclusion appears to apply to the significantly higher degree of conservatism (Factor Q_1) found in the present sample. No age trend for this Factor is reported by either Fozard and Nuttall (1971), nor by Goodwin and Schaie (1969). Cattell *et al.* (1970) observed an increase in radicalism for men, and for women until the age of 35. We, of course, were dealing with the very elderly compared to this.

Super-ego strength (Factor G) was found to be significantly higher in the present sample than in the standardisation sample, as did Fozard and Nuttall (1971). The significantly higher degree of self-concept control in our Aged (Factor Q_3) is also consistent with the previous findings that scores on this factor tend to increase with age.

The trends observed in the present sample which are thus inconsistent with age-related studies are the high level of conventionality (M) and conservatism (Q_1). Furthermore, the present sample showed an "average" mean score of 5·5 on Factor E (Dominance). In all three age-trend studies, a fall in score on this factor had been observed. Goodwin and Schaie (1969) and Fozard and Nuttall (1971) had additionally found an increase in age with self-sufficiency (Factor Q_2); a higher score on this factor than in the standardisation sample was not presently observed.

Thus, some of the significant differences between the psychogeriatric day-patient sample and the standardisation sample appear to be accountable for in terms of the age of the geriatric sample. Others, however, do not.

Comparison of the present sample with other aged samples drawn from the Newcastle area was thus carried out, in order to attempt to identify the characteristics which were peculiar to the present sample. The psychogeriatric day-patient sample (VIc) was first compared to Gaber's (1974) Community Aged V. The means, standard deviations and values of F are shown in Table 25. Significant differences between the two samples emerged in relation to seven dimensions. The psychogeriatric sample appears to be more conscientious (G), controlled (Q_3), and conservative (Q_1) than the community sample; it was also more sober (Factor F). While being more group-dependent (Q_2), the psychogeriatric sample seemed to be more tough-minded (I) and less

Table 25. Comparison of Normal Personality in Institutions Aged VI(c)
and Community Aged V

Factor	Institutions Aged VI(c) (N = 20)		Community Aged V (N = 82)		
	M	S.D.	M	S.D.	F
A	5·90	1·89	4·68	2·00	5·95
B	2·15	1·27	—	—	—
C	4·65	2·62	4·48	1·93	0·11
E	5·50	1·96	5·62	1·35	0·16
F	1·65	0·93	4·13	2·03	27·96**
G	7·95	1·64	6·61	1·57	11·22*
H	4·45	1·99	4·72	1·60	0·43
I	4·40	2·21	5·88	1·78	10·43
L	5·95	1·67	7·01	1·90	5·35
M	3·80	1·88	5·05	1·89	7·10
N	6·70	1·53	6·61	1·79	0·04
O	5·45	2·44	6·98	1·79	9·75
Q_1	1·85	1·27	4·66	1·57	56·40**
Q_2	4·30	1·66	6·27	1·98	16·87**
Q_3	7·70	1·53	5·07	2·05	28·82**
Q_4	4·90	2·49	6·35	1·98	8·09

*Difference significant at $p < 0.05$
**Difference significant at $p < 0.01$

guilt-prone (O) than the community residents. Thus, in some respects the psychogeriatric sample appear to be more vulnerable than the community residents, but in others they appear to be less troubled.

When the day-patient sample is examined in relation to the hospitalised psychiatric group, Institutions Aged VI(b) studies by Pidwell (1971), significant differences are found for six dimensions. The relevant data are shown in Table 26. The day-patient sample subjects are less intelligent (B), more conservative (Q_1), sober (F), conventional (M), and controlled (Q_3) than the hospitalised subjects. They are, however, more tough-minded (Factor I).

Comparative data for the present sample and the nursing-home sample (Pidwell, 1971) are shown in Table 27. Day-patient subjects are again less intelligent (B), more sober (F), conventional (M) and conservative (Q_1) than the nursing-home subjects. They show, however, higher super-ego strength (conscientiousness, Factor G).

Thus the day-patient subjects are consistently more conservative (Q_1) and sober (F) than all other groups. They appear also to be less intelligent—Factor B scores were, unfortunately, not available for the community sample. The day-patients are more controlled (Q_3) and tough-minded (I) than the community and the hospitalised subjects.

Table 26. Newcastle upon Tyne Community Aged VI(b)
Means and Standard Deviations of 16PF factor scores and LSI-A and B
for the three residence groups

	Residence					
	Community (N = 14)		Old Age Home (N = 14)		Psychiatric Hospital (N = 14)	
Factors	M	S.D.	M	S.D.	M	S.D.
MD	4·64	1·82	5·36	2·10	6·00	1·62
A	5·07	2·47	5·00	1·80	4·86	2·11
B	5·21	1·67	4·00	1·52	4·14	1·83
C	3·79	2·67	4·07	2·76	6·36	1·87**
E	6·00	1·84	6·29	2·09	7·00	2·11
F	6·00	2·15	5·93	2·62	5·50	2·35
G	6·36	2·92	5·71	2·13	6·79	2·01
H	5·50	1·61	4·79	1·80	5·57	1·91
I	6·00	1·62	6·50	1·70	7·21	1·89
L	6·86	1·66	7·79	1·85	6·14	2·03
M	5·21	1·97	7·43	1·40	6·79	1·85*
N	6·86	1·51	6·93	1·86	4·79	2·23**
O	6·43	2·35	5·29	2·34	5·79	2·15
Q_1	4·93	1·73	4·14	2·25	5·07	1·44
Q_2	5·79	2·52	6·00	2·42	5·07	2·02
						almost
Q_3	5·00	1·30	6·86	2·28	5·57	2·28*
Q_4	6·57	1·56	4·29	1·82	4·43	2·31**
Anxiety	6·86	1·16	5·50	2·17	4·93	2·09*
1 − E	5·50	1·60	5·21	1·81	5·64	1·82
Neuroticism	6·93	1·64	5·86	2·45	5·29	2·09
Alert-Poise	5·43	1·56	4·86	1·51	4·64	1·69
Independence	5·57	2·24	6·36	2·06	6·07	1·59
LS1 − A	27·64	9·49	25·29	8·61	27·14	6·82
LS1 − B	16·29	5·73	16·53	4·24	15·43	4·76

**Difference significant at $p < 0.01$
*Difference significant at $p < 0.05$

Table 27. Newcastle upon Tyne Aged—Aged VI(b) and VI(c)
Cattell's 16PFQ

| | Ahed VI(b) | | | | | | Aged VI(c) | |
| | Community (N = 14) | | Old Age Home (N = 14) | | Psychiatric Hospital (N = 14) | | Day-Patients (N = 20) | |
Factor	M	S.D.	M	S.D.	M	S.D.	M	S.D.
MD	4·64	1·82	5·36	2·10	6·00	1·62		
A	5·07	2·47	5·00	1·80	4·86	2·11	5·90	1·89
B	5·21	1·67	4·00	1·52	4·14	1·83	2·15	1·27
C	3·79	2·67	4·07	2·76	6·36	1·87	4·65	2·62
E	6·00	1·84	6·29	2·09	7·00	2·11	5·50	1·96
F	6·00	2·15	5·93	2·62	5·50	2·35	1·65	0·93
G	6·36	2·92	5·71	2·13	6·79	2·01	7·95	1·64
H	5·50	1·61	4·79	1·80	5·57	1·91	4·45	1·99
I	6·00	1·62	6·50	1·70	7·21	1·89	4·40	2·21
L	6·86	1·66	7·79	1·85	6·14	2·03	5·95	1·67
M	5·21	1·97	7·43	1·40	6·79	1·85	3·80	1·88
N	6·86	1·51	6·93	1·86	4·79	2·23	6·70	1·53
O	6·43	2·35	5·29	2·34	5·79	2·15	5·45	2·44
Q_1	4·93	1·73	4·14	2·25	5·07	1·44	1·85	1·27
Q_2	5·79	2·52	6·00	2·42	5·07	2·02	4·30	1·66
Q_3	5·00	1·30	6·86	2·28	5·57	2·28	7·70	1·53
Q_4	6·57	1·56	4·29	1·82	4·43	2·31	4·90	2·49

They show greater super-ego strength (G) than the community and the nursing-home subjects, while they are more conventional (M) than both hospital and nursing-home subjects. Although they are more group-dependent (Q_2) than the community residents, they are, however, less guilt-prone (O).

A picture thus emerges whereby the day-patients are characterised by a quality of restrainedness, which might be consistent both with their patient and their community resident status. The very qualities which enable them to behave in a socially acceptable manner would also seem to imply an inflexibility which may militate against successful adjustment to the changes in circumstances which accompany increasing age.

In terms of a multi-dimensional description of personality then, the psychiatric day-patient sample appears to differ significantly from community and institutionalised aged samples, and also from the younger standardisation sample of Cattell and his colleagues.

It might also be helpful at this point to have a look at the subsample (a) of Institutions VI data on the 16PFQ with psychiatric elderly patients in terms of normal personality characteristics. Table 28 presents the means and standard deviations for the 16 primary source traits and profile coefficients of similarity for the affective-depressive, schizophrenic and schizophrenic thought-disordered aged patient groups. In general they illustrate significant differences on normal personality

Table 28. Newcastle upon Tyne Institutions Aged VI(a)
Cattell's Sixteen Personality Factor Questionnaire

Factor	Affectives (N = 19)		Thought-Disordered Schizophrenics (N = 20)		Schizophrenics (N = 18)		F
	M	S.D.	M	S.D.	M	S.D.	
A	4·00	1·60	4·35	1·42	3·94	1·86	
B	3·58	1·57	4·00	2·10	3·00	1·33	
C	4·05	2·22	3·85	1·95	5·67	1·91	4·44
E	5·47	1·93	6·55	1·85	7·00	1·61	3·50
F	4·63	1·95	3·00	1·38	3·78	2·37	3·50
G	6·68	1·46	6·85	1·35	7·00	1·72	
H	5·58	2·14	3·90	1·41	4·56	1·50	4·73
I	6·21	2·25	6·10	2·55	5·83	2·07	
L	6·11	1·66	6·50	1·79	6·33	2·05	
M	4·84	2·12	5·20	1·69	6·11	1·81	
N	6·21	1·72	6·25	2·71	5·67	1·85	
O	6·95	1·99	6·70	2·27	5·28	2·32	3·68
Q_1	4·84	2·24	4·40	2·04	4·89	1·23	
Q_2	6·11	1·59	5·10	2·07	5·94	2·67	
Q_3	4·58	2·09	4·75	1·77	6·39	2·52	4·40
Q_4	6·00	2·60	5·10	1·71	5·06	2·04	

r_p between the profiles

	Affectives (N = 19)	TDS (N = 20)	Schizophrenics (N = 18)
Affectives			
Thought-Disordered Schizophrenics	0·87		
Schizophrenics	0·75	0·79	

characteristics between differentially diagnosed psychiatric state aged patients.

The thought-disordered schizophrenics were found on Cattell's factor C to be more emotionally unstable than either of the other two groups who did not differ between themselves to any significant degree. Rather suprisingly, the affectives were found to be more neurotic than either of the schizophrenic groups on Eysenck's neuroticism factor which correlated highly with factor C.

The affective group was also found, on Cattell's factor E to be more submissive than the non-thought disordered schizophrenics. All three groups, however, remained within the normal range on this dominance-submission factor. This difference between the three groups would be expected on the basis of Cattell's manic-depressive and schizophrenic profiles, Cattell *et al.* (1970) where a similar difference was found for younger age groups.

All three groups scored low on factor F (surgency). The thought-disordered schizophrenics were significantly less surgent than the affective group ($P = < 0.05$). The difference between affectives and the non-thought disordered schizophrenics was not statistically significant in this study. Cattell found no difference between the groups on this factor with adults, both being equally abnormally desurgent. Such a difference, however, might well be expected—since factor F is one of the major components of introversion, one of noted features of schizophrenia but less commonly observed in depressives.

The mentally ill group means on the factor measuring venturesome, thick-skinned *vs* inhibited, withdrawn characteristics were also found to be significantly different. Both schizophrenic patient groups appeared to be more withdrawn and retiring than the affectives, but only between the thought-disordered schizophrenics and the affectives did this difference reach statistical significance ($p < 0.01$).

On factor O, self-assurance *vs* apprehension, non-thought-disordered schizophrenics were found significantly less guilt prone and apprehensive than affectives and thought-disordered schizophrenics (at the 0.05 and 0.02 significance respectively). One might expect and, indeed, found greater guilt proneness in affectives than schizophrenics.

The last significant distinction between the patient groups was found on factor Q_3, where schizophrenics were seen to be more highly controlled than affectives ($p < 0.01$) and thought-disordered schizophrenics ($p < 0.02$). These factors O and Q_3 results with the aged agree with Cattell's profiles for the two psychoses, where schizophrenic adults were found more highly controlled and less apprehensive than affectives.

The investigation of psychopathological dimensions in the aged was also carried out on the Institutions Aged VI(c) sample and is of considerable interest. In detail, the CAQ Part II data on psychopathology in old age can only be related to the Delhees and Cattell (1971) normative data on students in terms of stens. The means and SD's are presented in Table 24.

It can be seen than on 4 of the 12 clinical scales the norms for the aged differ significantly from those for the college students. Even allowing for the strong limitation of both samples, the results are indicative of important differences. These hospitalised aged were generally more hypochondriacal, suicidal and paranoid. They were, however, less discontent and less psychopathic. More detailed work on Aged samples relating analysis from the CAQ dimensional approach to psychopathological investigation and the more traditional psychiatric categorization of patients, would be most illuminating. We hope to do these in the near future.

Adjustment

The small hospitalised, institution and psychogeriatric day hospital samples also provided data of Life Satisfaction as a measure of adjustment in the mentally ill aged. Mean scores for the LSIA and B using Wood's system of scoring are given in comparison to the similar scores

Table 29. Newcastle upon Tyne Aged
Life Satisfaction

	Sample	N	Score		F
			M	S.D.	
LSIA	Institutions Aged VI(c)	28	18·9	6·8	
	Institutions Aged VI(b)	42	26·6	7·7	20·0
	Community Aged V	82	28·3	5·8	50·5
LSIB	Institutions Aged VI(c)	28	11·6	5·2	
	Institutions Aged VI(b)	42	15·9	4·9	12·3
	Community Aged V	82	17·5	4·3	35·2

from the Community Aged V population and the Pidwell/Savage unpublished study (Table 29). Analysis of variance and appropriate Scheffe tests indicated that the Institutions Aged sample of psychogeriatric patients were less well adjusted than the Community Aged V and those in nursing home and hospital care. Interestingly, the latter two groups' adjustment was not significantly different. It might lead one to think that the concept of adjustment or life satisfaction needs to be more fully described; or perhaps both groups adequately adjusted to their different and perhaps appropriate surroundings or life situation! Only further research will clarify this problem.

The relationships between personality and adjustment were also investigated in this study. Stepwise multiple regression was unable to locate any normal personality variable which accounted for a significant amount of the variance in LSIB score. When the two indices were combined, Intelligence again emerged as a predictor of life satisfaction which was as efficient as was the use of all sixteen variables. Here it accounted for twenty-one per cent of the variance in total LSI score.

The predictive power of the Intelligence scale is consistent with the findings of Lowenthal (1964, 1968) and Gilberstadt (1968); that the presence or absence of intellectual deficit is highly significant to adjustment. It is also in line with Cattell's (1970) observation that there tends to be an association between intelligence, as measured by the B scale, and morale. The only variable which showed a significant simple correlation with intelligence was the activities variable; intelligence may be related to morale by means of its permitting the individual to maintain a degree of self-help and interest in life. The early work on intellectual functioning in the Aged (Savage *et al.* 1973, remarked on this.

However, as Cattell *et al.* (1970) point out, intelligence is an important dimension in individual differences, but cannot truly be regarded as forming part of the personality sphere. The emergence of Scale B as the only predictor variable also leads to reflection upon the mode of operation of the "self-appraisal of mental health" variable, which was discussed above. Such self-assessment may include an appraisal of cognitive deficits; such deficits may be perceived by the individual before they become sufficiently overt to warrant a diagnosis of dementia.

Psychopathological variables were, however, important in relation to adjustment in these small Sample VI investigations. Multiple regression of the twelve pathological personality variables of the Clinical Analysis Questionnaire upon the three measures of life satisfaction indicated that, in each case, Factor D5 (low energy depression) provided as good a prediction of LSI score as did the use of all twelve variables. In the case of the LSIA, Factor D5 accounted for 40 per cent of the variance. It controlled 55 per cent of the variance in both the LSIB and the total LSI score.

Low energy depression showed significant simple correlations with self-assessed mental health ($+0\cdot49$) and with activities ($-0\cdot61$). This would seem to confirm that it derives its predictive power from its connotations of negative self-concept and apathy. It may be recalled that the activities variable also correlated significantly with Intelligence —the most powerful normal personality predictor of satisfaction. The evidence appears to be accumulating for the significance of the solitary activity variable in the context of the present sample. Again, only one personality variable provides as good a prediction of satisfaction as might the use of the complete set. The "Low energy depression" predictor does, however, account for a more substantial amount of the total variance than did the "Intelligence" factor in the previous analysis.

The examination of the relationship between personality and adjustment has been limited by the small size and composition of the VI(c) sample under investigation. The results which have been presented do, however, appear to lend some support to the view that the study of personality among the aged is necessary for a proper understanding of adjustment in old age in normal and mentally ill aged.

5

The Structure of Personality
in the Aged

An attempt to improve the measurement of personality characteristics in the aged must depend on and relate to a better understanding of the structure of personality at this age and, indeed, a sound basis for analysing possible changes or differences. In order to clarify some of these issues, we will now present some of the multivariate analyses of the Newcastle upon Tyne aged populations. Are there some major dimensions on which we ought to concentrate? Does personality change in normal as well as pathological ageing? Can personality types be identified? Is there any validity in so doing? We will first present analyses of the pathological dimensional approach to personality in the Community Aged I group.

Earlier discussion has concentrated on an examination of the individual aspects of the MMPI; scales, and derived indices. The practical and theoretical implications of how these aspects interact and change with age, and their relation to other features of the people seen are, however, also of considerable importance. One of the ways in which a clarification of these complex inter-relationships between variables can be obtained, is with the use of techniques of factor analysis. Several such analyses of our MMPI data, alone, and in combination with certain other significant variables, seemed to point to some useful integration of theoretical views and empirical fact. Previous multivariate analysis of the MMPI data on adult populations wholly below 65 have yielded a variety of interpretations, confused by differences in methodology and terminology. However, there has been a broad general agreement on the existence of two or three basic factors. One of these would seem to be a measure of susceptability to general maladjustment or pathology, the other a factor related to degree and intensity of interaction with others. As Slater and Scarr (1964) have pointed out, these interpretations are not dissimilar to Eysenck's Extraversion and Neuroticism.

The present analyses of the MMPI data with Aged Community subjects were carried out using the K corrected T scores of the MMPI and the A and R scales of Welsh (1956). These data were first subjected to Principal Component analysis, then, in order to break down the

Table 30. Structure of Psychopathology
Newcastle upon Tyne Community Aged I

MMPI Factor Loadings for Aged Sample
(N = 83)

Scale	Principal components			Varimax rotation		
	I	II	III	I	II	III
	Factor Loadings					
L	−0·29	0·05	0·66	0·05	−0·06	0·72
F	−0·73	−0·19	0·14	−0·42	−0·51	0·40
K	0·18	0·84	0·25	−0·12	0·84	0·28
Hs	−0·82	0·32	−0·31	−0·92	−0·13	0·12
D	−0·86	0·12	−0·19	−0·81	−0·31	0·22
Hy	−0·73	0·30	−0·44	−0·90	−0·11	−0·04
Pd	−0·74	−0·05	0·47	−0·34	−0·36	0·72
Mf	0·41	0·12	0·00	0·26	0·31	−0·15
Pa	−0·75	−0·36	0·19	−0·34	−0·36	0·43
Pt	−0·87	0·22	−0·12	−0·83	−0·22	0·30
Sc	−0·91	0·16	−0·05	−0·75	−0·29	0·45
Ma	−0·43	0·27	0·45	−0·25	0·07	0·63
Si	−0·72	−0·28	0·13	−0·37	−0·58	0·37
A	−0·76	−0·45	−0·17	−0·47	−0·76	0·09
R	−0·65	−0·13	−0·13	−0·62	−0·20	0·17
	Latent Root					
	7·18	1·56	1·39	4·86	2·85	2·41
	Percentage of Variance					
	48·0%	10·4%	9·3%	32·4%	19·0%	16·1%

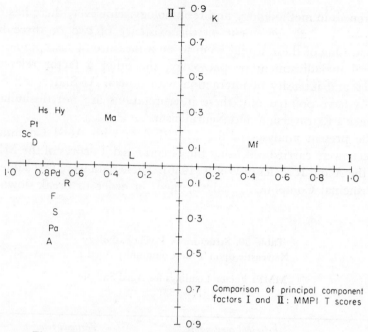

Fig. 1. Structural psychopathology in the Community Aged

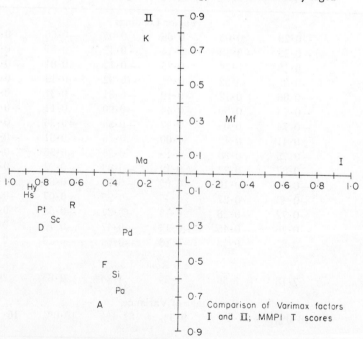

Fig. 2. Structural psychopathology in the Community Aged

structure obtained, rotated to a statistically and psychologically meaningful Varimax solution. The results of these analyses are presented in Table 30 and Figs. 1 and 2 illustrate a plot of the first two Varimax factors.

Inspection of the Principal Component solution revealed the expected statistically highly significant factor, which appears to express psychologically a factor of adjustment leading fairly uniformly throughout all the clinical scales of the MMPI. Factor II seems to have a relationship to neuroticism, whilst the third factor is probably associated with an "aggressive-defensive" reaction to the ageing process.

Varimax rotation does indeed break down the general factor into a useful, more multidimensional picture. The first Varimax factor (Table 30, Fig. 2) loads most highly the Depression, Hysteria, Hypochondriasis, Psychosthenia, Schizophrenia and Welsh (1956) R scales. This combination of scales seems related to *maladjustment*, concentrating on neurotic problems, with, perhaps, a somatic component.

The second factor appears to relate to a dimension of Introversion-Extraversion. The Social Introversion-Extraversion, Paranoia, F and Welsh A scales have high positive loadings and the K scale a high negative loading. These scales seem to measure withdrawal from social influences and contact.

When the MMPI variables used above are combined with I.Q., Age, Sex and other data, it is possible to obtain even further clarification of the factor structure underlying these measures.

The first Principal Component factor (Table 31, Fig. 3) is again a general factor reflecting cognitive personality and diagnostic change in the Aged Community population. The second factor contrasts personality characteristics. Varimax rotation extracts a first factor of cognitive change (Table 32, Fig. 4). The second factor similarly relates personality change and psychiatric diagnosis. The third factor again links age and sex related changes, with loadings on such variables as the Ageing Index of the MMPI and WAIS Picture Completion.

It is interesting to examine these findings in the light of other studies and of theoretical approaches to the ageing process. It would appear that, increasingly, age *per se* is not seen as the most important underlying variable in relation to personality change. In our earlier book (Savage et al., 1973), we discussed the findings of extensive studies of the cognitive abilities of older people and concluded that a theoretical model including level and learning aspects of intellectual functioning in both

Table 31. Structure of Psychopathology
Newcastle upon Tyne Community Aged I
Principal Component Factor Loadings: WAIS, MMFI and Project Variables

Variable		Factor I	II	III	IV
1	Diagnosis 1964	−0·60	−0·22	−0·13	−0·06
2	Diagnosis 1961	−0·62	−0·21	−0·17	+0·04
3	Age	−0·19	+0·04	−0·25	+0·38
4	Sex	−0·02	+0·27	−0·53	+0·43
5	WAIS I	+0·78	−0·46	+0·07	+0·14
6	C	+0·81	−0·28	+0·17	+0·12
7	A	+0·76	−0·30	−0·09	−0·11
8	S	+0·73	−0·40	−0·03	+0·01
9	D	+0·74	−0·21	−0·31	−0·06
10	V	+0·76	−0·45	+0·08	+0·09
11	DS	+0·59	−0·35	−0·24	−0·41
12	PO	+0·69	−0·30	+0·32	−0·29
13	BD	+0·76	−0·39	−0·19	−0·23
14	PA	+0·76	−0·34	−0·03	−0·11
15	OA	+0·66	−0·39	+0·01	−0·13
16	V IQ	+0·85	−0·41	−0·08	+0·13
17	F IQ	+0·80	−0·37	−0·13	−0·16
18	FS IQ	+0·87	−0·42	−0·11	+0·01
19	WAIS DQ	−0·11	−0·24	+0·73	+0·26
20	WB DQ	+0·06	−0·22	+0·72	+0·35
21	Reynell	+0·09	−0·15	+0·61	+0·36
22	Hewzon	−0·00	+0·09	+0·21	+0·21
23	V-P disc.	+0·27	−0·15	+0·08	+0·43
24	Allen	+0·25	−0·22	+0·60	+0·52
25	MMFI L	+0·05	−0·35	+0·06	+0·16
26	F	−0·54	−0·43	−0·35	−0·09
27	E	+0·26	+0·01	+0·26	+0·15
28	Hs	−0·67	−0·48	+0·18	−0·23
29	D	−0·70	−0·57	+0·17	−0·15
30	Hy	−0·63	−0·51	+0·06	−0·08
31	Fd	−0·33	−0·61	−0·46	+0·27
32	Mf	+0·09	+0·57	−0·26	+0·26
33	Pa	−0;41	−0·59	−0·37	+0·14
34	Pt	−0·64	−0·60	+0·05	+0·04
35	Sc	−0·62	−0·61	−0·12	+0·07
36	Ma	−0·18	−0·30	−0·27	+0·46
37	Si	−0·49	−0·54	−0·15	+0·19
38	AgI	+0·27	−0·19	−0·60	+0·45
39	AI	−0·55	−0·49	+0·11	−0·04
40	IR	−0·57	−0·25	+0·47	−0·43
41	A	−0·59	−0·49	−0·14	+0·03
42	R	−0·38	−0·54	−0·07	−0·11
Percentage of Variance		31·4%	15·2%	9·6%	6·2%

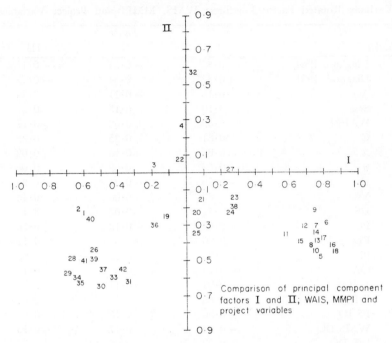

Comparison of principal component factors I and II; WAIS, MMPI and project variables

Fig. 3. Structural psychopathology in the Community Aged

verbal and motor perceptual areas, was appropriate to devising adequate methods of measuring "stable" and "sensitive" areas of functioning and their change in the elderly. Satisfactory adjustment to advancing years in personality may well reflect a similar combination between "sensitive" and "stable" aspects of personality.

Examination of our data in clinical or pathological dimensions of personality in the community aged gives support to this hypothesis. The first general factor of mental health or illness may represent the "sensitive" aspects of personality, that is those characteristics variables most vulnerable to change, whilst the second factor reflects the more stable and enduring characteristics (Table 31). The Varimax rotation simply strengthens the first and second factor variable loadings in these terms. On the first factor the WAIS subtests Information and Vocabulary have the highest loadings; Digit Span, Object Assembly and Digit Symbol the lowest, reflecting stable and sensitive areas of cognitive functioning. The second factor suggests an equivalent structure in personality with a sensitive group of scales, probably reflecting internal, somatic, change, contrasted with a more stable

Table 32. Structure of Psychopathology
Newcastle upon Tyne Community Aged I
Varimax Rotated Factor Loadings: WAIS, MMPI and Project Variables

Variable		Factor I	II	III
1	Diagnosis 1964	+0·35	−0·53	−0·11
2	Diagnosis 1961	+0·37	−0·54	−0·15
3	Age	+0·15	−0·11	−0·26
4	Sex	+0·10	+0·15	−0·57
5	WAIS I	−0·89	+0·08	+0·17
6	C	−0·81	+0·25	+0·23
7	A	−0·80	+0·18	+0·02
8	S	−0·83	+0·09	+0·06
9	D	−0·76	+0·21	−0·25
10	V	−0·86	+0·08	+0·18
11	DS	−0·71	+0·02	−0·17
12	PC	−0·69	+0·18	+0·38
13	BD	−0·86	+0·09	−0·11
14	Pi	−0·81	+0·15	+0·05
15	OA	−0·75	+0·06	+0·10
16	V IQ	−0·94	+0·14	+0·02
17	P IQ	−0·88	+0·14	−0·04
18	FS IQ	−0·96	+0·15	−0·01
19	WAIS DQ	+0·04	−0·17	+0·75
20	WB DQ	−0·08	−0·06	+0·75
21	Reynell	−0·08	+0·00	+0·63
22	Hewson	+0·03	+0·10	+0·19
23	V-P disc.	−0·29	+0·04	+0·11
24	Allen	−0·26	+0·03	+0·63
25	MMPI L	−0·23	−0·25	+0·11
26	F	+0·17	−0·70	−0·30
27	K	−0·18	+0·18	+0·27
28	Ha	+0·31	−0·75	+0·23
29	D	+0·28	−0·83	+0·24
30	Hy	+0·24	−0·77	+0·12
31	Pd	−0·12	−0·74	−0·37
32	Mf	+0·21	+0·48	−0·35
33	Pa	−0·04	−0·75	−0·28
34	Pt	+0·20	−0·85	+0·12
35	Sc	+0·16	−0·87	−0·04
36	Ma	−0·05	−0·38	−0·22
37	Si	+0·08	−0·73	−0·08
38	AgI	−0·40	−0·07	−0·55
39	AI	+0·19	−0·69	+0·17
40	IR	+0·39	−0·48	−0·49
41	A	+0·19	−0·57	−0·07
42	R	+0·02	−0·65	+0·14

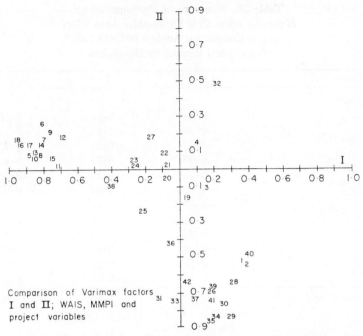

Fig. 4. Structural psychopathology in the Community Aged

group of scales relating to the individual's reaction to the external environment (Table 32).

The very recent small study using Cattell's Clinical Analysis Questionnaire on Newcastle Institutions Aged VI(c) is of interest at this point. An important feature of the Clinical Analysis Questionnaire is, of course, the fact that it yields a comprehensive assessment of personality by including twelve pathological dimensions. Delhees and Cattell (1971), as described earlier, indicate that nine second-order factors may be derived from analysis of Parts 1 and 2 of the CAQ combined. These factors, however, do not cover, to any extent, five important pathological primary factors.

The size of the sample presently under investigation, moreover, precludes the possibility of analysis of the combined normal and pathological personality dimensions.

It was in a purely exploratory fashion, then, that the twelve pathological factor scores were intercorrelated and subjected to principal component analysis.

Table 33. Structure of Psychopathology
Newcastle upon Tyne Community Aged VI(c)
Principal Component Analysis of CAQ Part 2
Pathological Personality Dimensions

Components	1	2	3
Source trait			
D1	−0·69	−0·37	0·16
D2	−0·79	−0·44	−0·27
D3	0·30	−0·52	0·43
D4	−0·69	0·07	0·45
D5	−0·86	−0·29	−0·03
D6	−0·82	0·26	0·09
D7	−0·45	−0·45	−0·63
Pa	−0·31	0·49	−0·41
Pp	0·66	−0·22	−0·48
Sc	−0·76	0·13	−0·05
As	−0·67	0·47	−0·15
Ps	−0·86	−0·09	0·13
Percentage of total variance	46·5	12·4	11·2

Three components with an eigenvalue of 1·0 or greater emerged, which together accounted for 70 per cent of the total variance observed. These three components are presented in Table 33.

Component 1, controlling 46·5 per cent of the variance, appears to comprise a "general psychopathology" factor, with all dimensions loading significantly upon it. Two dimensions, however, contribute loadings in a direction opposite to that of the other ten. These were Factor D3 (Brooding discontent) and Factor Pp (Psychopathic deviation). These two traits appear to represent a less passive and withdrawn aspect of "pathological" personality. It is speculatively suggested that such an aspect of personality might be comparable to the strong assertiveness found by Turner *et al.* (1972) and Kleban *et al.* (1971; Kleban and Brody, 1972) to characterise "survivor" members of institutionalised samples.

Component 2 accounts for a further 12·4 per cent of the variance. Factors D3 (Brooding discontent), D7 (Bored depression), D2 (Suicidal disgust) and D1 (Hypochondriasis) load upon one pole: the other consists of Pa (Paranoia) and As (Psychasthenia). Factors As denotes insistent repetitive ideas and impulses to perform certain acts. In this component, a self-centred, perhaps neurotic, malcontent appears to be contrasted with traits denoting a more fundamental disturbance of thought and behaviour patterns.

The third component controls $11 \cdot 2$ per cent of the variance. At one pole are found Factors D7 (Bored depression), Pp (Psychopathic deviation) and Pa (Paranoia), while the other pole loads significantly upon D3 (Brooding discontent) and D4 (Anxious depression). The component might, therefore, be interpreted as "Antisocial and suspicious versus Restless and agitated".

The major components found are not, however, inconsistent with those from the MMPI (Britton and Savage, 1966) and from the psychiatric data of Garside *et al.* (1965). One is encouraged by the possible long term possibilities for the CAQ with its ability to measure and interrelate normal and pathological aspects of personality.

These analyses have given rise to many interesting features of the personality dimensions in the aged. However, the MMPI is, perhaps, only one of the personality inventories which are available to the research or practising psychologist. It is by nature tending to look at the pathological rather than the normal psychological characteristics of the Aged. This work is, therefore, useful to the extent that it presents a clear picture of the distribution of clinical dimensions in the normal community population, thus allowing a better definition of the abnormal, but limited in that it tells us little or nothing of the personality of the community aged in terms of a non-pathological personality structure. Our investigations, therefore, proceeded with other types of personality measure as an aid to the understanding of the structure of personality in the Aged: namely, the techniques of Eysenck and Cattell.

The factorial techniques employed on the first Community Aged sample are useful as far as they go. They identify symptom interrelationships and possible categories of diagnosis or dimensions of description for personality. The perennial problem in clinical practice, as the literature of depression has shown, however, is not to confuse diagnostic categories and dimensions with people. Types of depression, endogenous or reactive, are one thing—clusters of symptoms or behaviours, types of people are another. A patient may have mixed or both types of depressive symptoms when presenting clinically. In our Community V Aged study we tackled the problem by investigating "people types", not "symptom categories" using Cluster Analysis (Ward, 1963).

The Community Aged V Study

In order to assess personality structure and functioning in the aged, the Cattell 16 Personality Factor Questionnaire (Form C) was given, with the exception of Factor B which measures verbal reasoning intelligence, and a cluster analysis of this data on the Personality of the Aged, using Ward's method of "hierarchical fusion" was carried out. Four clusters or groups of aged were obtained by this procedure (Fig. 5). The first had 44, the second 16, the third 9 and the fourth 13 aged people in it. The means and standard deviations on fifteen of Cattell's personality characteristics for each group can be seen in Table 34. Profile analysis (Greenhouse and Geisser, 1959) was also employed to look at the differences between the personality types of the four groups of aged. The results of the profile analysis can be seen in Table 35. Of particular interest here is that the personality profile of each of the four groups, as defined by the 15 personality variables, is significantly different, suggesting that distinctive "types" or groups of personality may have been identified.

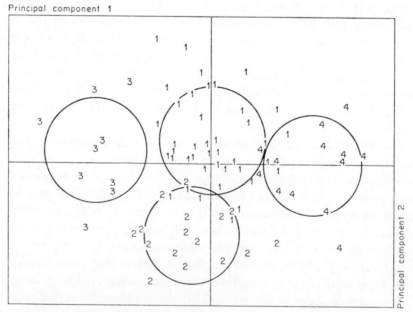

Fig. 5. Types of personality in the aged. Diagrammatic representation of Cluster Analysis by Ward's Method: two principal components

Table 34. Personality Types in the Aged.
Newcastle upon Tyne Community Aged V
Cattell Dimension and Adjustment Scores for the Four Aged Personality Groups

	Normal Group I N = 44		Introverted Group II N = 16		Perturbed Group III N = 9		Mature Group IV N = 13		
	Mean	S.D.	Mean	S.D.	Mean	S.D.	Mean	S.D.	
A Reserved *v* Outgoing	4·72	1·89	3·50	1·90	6·22	1·54	4·92	1·77	
C Affected by Feelings Emotionally Stable	4·00	1·56	5·06	1·47	2·77	1·22	6·53	1·90	
E Humble *v* Assertive	5·79	1·43	5·18	1·18	5·55	1·43	5·61	0·92	
F Sober *v* Happy-go-Lucky	4·84	2·07	2·62	1·45	3·33	1·76	4·15	1·16	
G Expedient Conscientious	6·29	1·19	7·18	1·70	7·33	1·88	6·46	1·82	
H Shy *v* Venturesome	5·15	1·50	3·37	1·05	4·44	1·83	5·07	1·20	
I Tough-minded Tender-minded	6·13	1·15	6·43	1·53	7·44	1·16	3·23	1·42	
L Trusting *v* Suspicious	7·34	1·44	5·75	2·01	9·11	0·73	6·00	1·92	
M Practical *v* Imaginative	5·18	1·91	5·06	1·34	6·66	1·56	3·46	1·27	
N Forthright *v* Shrewd	7·15	1·53	4·75	1·71	6·33	1·15	7·23	1·31	
O Placid *v* Apprehensive	7·13	1·65	6·93	1·14	8·77	0·91	5·23	1·76	
Q_1 Conservation Experimenting	4·88	1·56	4·68	1·40	3·44	1·25	4·69	1·53	
Q_2 Group-dependent Self-Sufficient	6·50	1·50	5·62	1·89	3·83	1·72	7·92	1·68	
Q_3 Undisciplined Self-conflict *v* Controlled	5·52	1·72	3·68	1·57	2·55	0·86	7·00	1·24	
Q_4 Relaxed *v* Tense	6·47	1·65	6·50	1·83	8·55	1·34	5·23	1·36	F

Activity Inventory	* p < 0·05	22·73	6·52	19·69	7·20	17·67	5·32	27·31	6·21 4·79**
LSI A	** p < 0·01	27·27	5·56	29·06	4·12	26·11	8·68	32·46	3·36 3·43*
LSI B	df 3, 78	17·09	3·81	17·38	5·42	15·00	5·24	21·00	2·24 4·08**

Table 35. Newcastle upon Tyne Community Aged V
Profile Analysis of the Four Aged Personality Groups on the 16PF

	df	SOS	F
Factors	14	1108·2	$F_1 = 30·15$
Groups	3	99·1	$F_2 = 17·09$
S's (within groups)	78	150·8	
Groups × Factors	42	930·2	$F_3 = 8·44**$
S's × Factors (within groups)	1092	2866·7	
Total	1147	5154·5	

**Difference significant at p < 0·01

GROUP I. The "Normal". This, the largest group, comprised 44 individuals (54 per cent of the sample population) whose mean age was 78·8 years. As the name implies, this group seems to represent the bulk of the older individuals residing within the community.

This normal group of people tends to be somewhat more intense and apprehensive than younger age groups. They are shown to be suspicious of outward interference in matters concerning themselves and rather wary. These old people are not very happy with changes, are self-sufficient and can be intolerant. Coupled with this, however, they are fairly deliberate in their actions and quite shrewd, analytic and calculating.

GROUP II. The "Introverted". The Aged group consists of 16 individuals whose mean age is 83·8 years. The 16 people were 19·5 per cent of the total sample population. This group is clearly very sober and taciturn. They are reserved, introspective, conscientious people who stick to their inner sense of values. Sometimes, however, they have a tendency to be apprehensive and even melancholic. These elderly people do not enjoy meeting people, are not adventurous, but shy and withdrawn, preferring one or two friends to large groups. Self-restraint and seriousmindedness typify the group, along with sensitivity to others and some tension in themselves.

GROUP III. The "Perturbed". This type, whose mean age is 76·4 years, made up 11 per cent of the sample population under investigation. As a group, they seem rather perturbed, very suspicious and difficult to get along with. They have very weak ego-strength, and are to a marked degree emotionally unstable and uncontrolled. Likewise, they demonstrate considerable indisciplined self-conflict with consequent personal and interpersonal problems. These people tend to be emotionally immature and get emotionally upset. They aspire to be conscientious, but also exhibit inner apprehension and self-reproach. Irrational worry, tenseness, irritability, anxiety and being in an inner state of turmoil also characterise this group. It is of interest that almost all of these individuals in the Perturbed group were independently and blindly assessed by a psychiatrist as being sufficiently disturbed to require psychiatric treatment. Although there are only a small number of these individuals in our sample, these people with functional disorders would tend to loom large in any psychiatric population.

GROUP IV. The "Mature". This type or group is comprised of 13 individuals, 16 per cent of the sample population, whose mean age is 79·1 years. They are highly self-sufficient and resourceful people, enjoying their independence and taking pride in their ability to make their own decisions. This mature-tempered group exhibits considerable ego-strength in terms of emotional stability. They are shrewd, worldly and tough-minded.

As a complementary method of investigating the validity of the four groups derived from the cluster analysis, a discriminant function analysis was carried out by computer. The results of the discriminant function analysis, including the D-square statistic coefficients, constants, evaluation and classification matrix, can be seen in Tables 36 and 37 respectively. There were significant $(0 < 0·01)$ differences in the mean values of the 15 variables in all the four groups. Likewise, the Discriminant Function for each group is provided and may be used to place

Table 36. Personality Types in the Aged
Newcastle upon Tyne Community Aged V
Discriminant Function Analysis

Function Coefficient	Generalised Mahalanobis D-Square 583·53			
	1	2	3	4
1	1·21	0·57	1·11	1·90
2	1·97	2·23	1·24	3·37
3	5·37	4·82	5·22	5·29
4	3·64	2·59	3·35	2·63
5	1·32	2·13	2·02	1·73
6	6·28	4·95	6·42	5·79
7	4·26	4·16	5·04	1·65
8	6·86	5·29	6·90	6·27
9	4·46	3·97	5·21	3·35
10	1·91	0·95	1·08	2·51
11	5·74	5·48	7·04	4·39
12	0·45	0·22	−0·87	0·78
13	4·89	4·18	4·18	5·17
14	6·30	4·55	4·86	6·64
15	4·91	4·65	5·98	3·22
Constant	−178·94	−134·25	−187·27	−156·53

Table 37. Discriminant Function Analysis: Classification Matric

Function Group	1	2	3	4	Total
1	43	0	1	0	44
2	0	16	0	0	16
3	0	0	9	0	9
4	0	0	0	13	13

new individuals into one of the established four groups. We found that each of the experimental groups were widely separated. This is also demonstrated by the largest probability that each case falls into its respective group. The classification matrix (Table 37) is a summary of the evaluation of classification functions for each case.

Both of the statistical analytic procedures employed, profile analysis and discriminant function analysis, gave complementary evidence for the significant differences among our four original clusters. It would seem then, that there is sound evidence as to the validity or statistical uniqueness of the four groups obtained by the cluster analytic methods.

The importance and the validity of these groups were further established in terms of their adjustment and self-concept. The means and standard deviations for the four aged personality groups on the LSIA, Activity Inventory and the Tennessee Self-Concept Scale as well as the "F-score" for each variable can be seen in Tables 38 and 39.

There are significant differences between the four aged personality groups as measured by the Activity Inventory. It is evident that the Mature Tempered group achieve the highest mean score on this measure of social adjustment. Showing greater competence in social spheres, they are significantly better adjusted in this area than the Perturbed group who score the lowest of all four groups. Not unexpectedly, the Mature Tempered also score significantly higher than both the Silent Majority and Introvert groups (t = 2·21, df = 55, p < 0·05 and t = 2·91, df = 27, p < 0·01 respectively). The difference in social adjustment mean scores between the Perturbed group and the Introverted group is minimal (t = 0·71, df = 23); there is, however, a substantial trend for the Silent Majority to achieve higher scores than the Introverted in this realm. The Silent Majority

Table 38. Adjustment in the Aged
Grouped According to Personality Types

	Group I Normal		Group II Introverted		Group III Perturbed		Group IV Mature		F
	M	*S.D.*	*M*	*S.D.*	*M*	*S.D.*	*M*	*S.D.*	
LSI A	27·27	5·56	29·06	4·12	26·11	8·68	32·46	3·36	3·43*
LSI B	17·09	3·81	17·36	5·42	15·00	5·24	21·00	2·24	4·08**
Activity Inventory	22·73	6·52	19·69	7·20	17·67	5·32	27·31	6·21	4·79**

"t" Tests between the Four Aged Personality Groups on the LSI A and
LSI B and Activity Inventory

			df	LSI A "t"	LSI B "t"	Activity Inventory "t"
Group I	*v*	Group II	58	1·55	0·22	1·53
Group I	*v*	Group III	51	0·52	1·37	2·14
Group I	*v*	Group IV	55	3·14**	3·46**	2·21*
Group II	*v*	Group III	23	1·10	1·02	0·71
Group II	*v*	Group IV	27	2·31*	2·18*	2·91**
Group III	*v*	Group IV	20	2·39*	3·67**	3·79**

*Difference significant at p < 0·05
**Difference significant at p < 0·01

seem to be significantly better adjusted in social terms than are the Perturbed (t = 2·14, p < 0·05).

It seems that personal adjustment or life satisfaction as measured by the LSI B, points to a lowered level of personal adjustment in the Perturbed group. Both the Introverted and the Normal group show a trend toward achieving higher levels of life satisfaction than the Perturbed group.

There is no significant difference in mean life satisfaction scores between the Silent Majority and the Introverted groups attesting to the presence of a satisfactory level of personal adjustment in both groups. The Mature group, however, exhibits a highly significant disposition for having a superior level of personal adjustment in relation to the Perturbed, the Introverted and the Normal (t = 6·7, p < 0·05, t = 2·18, p < 0·05 and t = 3·46, p < 0·05).

Table 39. Newcastle upon Tyne Community Aged V
Tennessee Self-Concept Scale—Four Personality Groups

	Group I Silent Majority N = 44		Group II Introverted N = 16		Group III Perturbed N = 9		Group IV Mature Tempered N = 13		F
	M	S.D.	M	S.D.	M	S.D.	M	S.D.	
SC	31·00	5·21	26·44	7·04	38·49	5·20	28·00	6·11	8·85**
TF	1·42	0·35	1·54	0·42	1·94	0·47	1·25	0·31	6·59**
Net Conflict	18·34	15·93	20·88	14·56	33·56	18·95	12·48		3·88*
Total Conflict	33·64	8·82	35·13	10·84	43·33	13·97	23·23	10·30	7·03**
Total P	385·25	18·60	383·38	21·00	362·56	30·68	397·46	34·27	3·71*
Row 1	128·75	6·67	127·75	8·35	122·89	11·84	132·23	9·25	2·28
Row 2	131·64	8·64	132·31	7·96	124·89	12·40	136·85	13·69	2·46
Row 3	124·96	6·77	122·69	8·61	114·89	10·90	128·62	13·33	4·89**
Col. A	72·71	6·64	73·63	8·16	70·67	10·09	80·62	6·98	4·23**
Col. B	82·52	4·72	84·06	4·45	77·89	5·47	81·15	8·33	2·54
Col. C	74·59	6·07	77·56	3·79	68·44	10·88	79·46	6·72	5·58**
Col. D	81·52	4·51	79·67	5·25	78·56	3·91	83·15	5·40	2·08
Col. E	74·86	6·65	68·44	9·63	66·67	6·71	73·77	10·19	4·18**
Total Var.	40·98	9·58	44·94	13·03	48·00	6·96	35·08	12·58	3·13*
Col. Total Var.	20·68	4·82	21·19	6·35	25·22	2·86	19·15	6·87	2·31
Row Total Var.	20·30	6·00	22·63	6·89	24·00	7·44	15·92	6·53	3·49*
DP	75·50	8·39	79·81	7·57	68·33	6·27	79·69	12·16	3·91*
GM	100·86	16·40	94·75	8·79	90·67	12·88	104·08	9·39	2·31
Psy	52·00	6·68	55·75	7·84	54·11	4·91	54·00	5·15	1·36
PD	91·77	8·94	93·00	8·09	83·78	6·36	91·23	11·57	2·18
N	89·98	8·70	90·31	11·72	81·44	10·62	98·46	12·98	4·66**
PI	5·80	2·82	4·88	2·13	5·67	2·65	6·23	2·77	0·68
D	153·14	14·67	158·94	10·71	148·33	9·38	154·62	25·15	0·93
5	32·18	7·61	34·19	5·48	34·11	8·01	32·23	12·54	0·31
4	20·91	8·03	19·69	6·44	27·33	7·25	18·92	12·79	1·90
3	8·14	4·10	7·13	2·53	8·00	2·50	5·39	4·46	1·81
2	10·41	4·21	7·69	2·06	8·33	3·35	12·00	9·16	2·16
1	28·27	6·42	31·13	6·20	22·22	6·61	31·62	10·11	3·70*
NDS	26·84	15·06	34·44	13·20	38·22	17·81	26·77	11·87	3·60*

* Difference significant at p < 0·05
** Difference significant at p < 0·01
   df = 3, 78

A profile analysis (Greenhouse and Geisser, 1959) of the Newcastle upon Tyne Community Aged V personality groups' self-concept profiles was carried out. There is a significant group x variance interaction demonstrating that the group profiles are significantly different from each other. A Diagram of the self concept profile for each group of the personality types in the aged is given in Fig. 6.

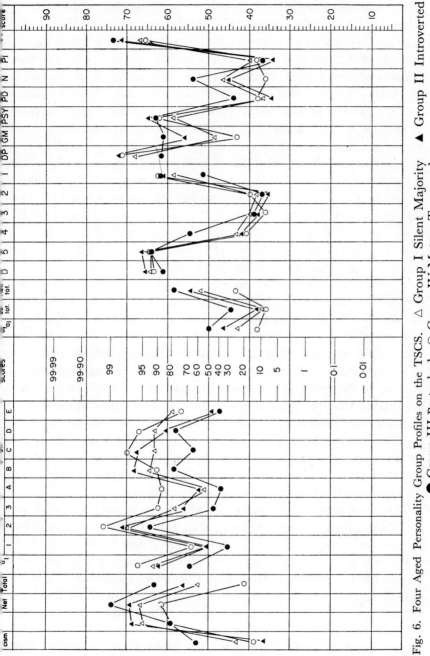

Fig. 6. Four Aged Personality Group Profiles on the TSCS. △ Group I Silent Majority ▲ Group II Introverted ● Group III Perturbed ○ Group IV Mature Tempered

The mature elderly who are clearly more emotionally stable than the other aged personality groups are able to maintain a high level of personal and social adjustment. This is not surprising when the self concept of this group is considered. The Mature aged not only have significantly less conflict (Total Conflict) and confusion in the way in which they perceive themselves, they also have a substantially higher level of self concept integration (Row Total Variability) than the other three groups. As compared to the Normal, the Introverted and the Perturbed, they display a greater unity among the Identity, Self-Satisfaction and Behavioural facets of their self concepts and are less likely to compartmentalise these aspects of self concept. While exhibiting low conflict and variability of self concept this group attained elevated defensiveness scores (DP). It seems as if an ability to maintain viable defences superimposed upon a bulwark of low conflict and good self concept integration heightens phenomenological satisfaction and results in significantly better personal and social adjustment.

While in terms of personality composition the Perturbed Aged are emotionally less stable than the other groups, Life Satisfaction Index B did not record statistically significant differences in personal adjustment between this group and the Normal or the Introverted. It must be stressed, however, that on LSI B, the Perturbed tended to score lower on personal adjustment than the Introverted group. There was a marked tendency for the Perturbed to have a lower level of personal adjustment than the Normal group. In light of the limited numbers of members in the Perturbed group (N = 9) the probability of obtaining significant differences is low; furthermore, it is felt that the trend toward low personal adjustment on the part of the Perturbed displayed on the LSI B is of descriptive and clinical importance. This group demonstrates the lowest social adjustment scores.

Their self concept scores further clarify their poor personal and social adjustment. This Perturbed group display a considerable lack of defences as compared with the other personality groups (SC, DP). While being significantly more lacking in defences, this group has a greater level of conflict in self concept with which to contend. They also have significantly more difficulty in achieving a balanced self definition, for they find it hard to reject those parts of their self concept that they are *not*. The Perturbed display significantly more variability in self description than do the Normal and the Mature aged. Likewise, there is a tendency for this group to have less self esteem than the Introverted.

They have a significantly depreciated sense of personal self worth as compared to the Normal, the Introverted and the Mature. The Perturbed perceive their social selves as being less adequate than the Normal and the Mature groups and derive less satisfaction from social relationships in particular—and their behavioural functioning in general—than the aforementioned groups. Their inner feelings of inadequacy in social relationships correspond closely with their social adjustment scores.

A better understanding of the adjustment scores is afforded when the self concept of the Introvered group is examined. The Introverted group does not score statistically different from the Normal on scores of conflict in self perception. Both groups exhibit, more or less, the same level of confusion and contradiction in self concept (Net Conflict, Total Conflict). In a like manner, there is an absence of significant statistical differences between the Introverted and the Normal so far as variability of self concept is concerned. It should be noted, however, that the Introverted group demonstrates a proclivity toward less conflict and variability in self definition than the Perturbed. Despite the significantly lesser degree of emotional stability by the Introverted in terms of personality type, there are no significant differences in personal adjustment scores between these groups. The positive value of defensiveness—both manifest and subtle—in self description seems crucial here. The Introverted group exhibit a marked tendency toward being substantially more defensive than the Normal, both on the obvious measure of defensiveness (SC) and on an unconscious level (DP). These strong defences may well compensate for the lesser amount of emotional stability on the part of the Introverted. These protective defensive mechanisms in self description may also account for the tendency of the Introverted group to have a heightened level of self worth as compared with the Normal. This is to say that perhaps the defensiveness in self perception makes it possible for the Introverted to experience such subjective feelings as a heightened sense of personal adequacy, hence no difference in personal adjustment scores. There is no difference between these two groups (Normal and Introverted) in overall self esteem.

The Introverted are significantly less satisfied, however, with their "social self" than the Normal, having a reduced sense of adequacy and worth in social interaction with others.

In terms of the dimension of emotional stability and in relation to the other three personality groups, the Normal of the aged population are found in the centre of the continuum. They exhibit a satisfactory level of emotional stability. They are significantly more stable in this area of functioning than the Perturbed and the Introverted. They are, however, significantly less stable than the very stable and self reliant Mature group. While being significantly more extroverted than the Introverted and demonstrating a proclivity toward being more socially bold than the Mature group, these Normals show no difference to the Perturbed group on this dimension (Gaber, 1974).

This Normal group exhibits satisfactory personal adjustment. As might be expected, they score significantly less than the Mature Tempered group on the measure of life satisfaction. The Normals do not differ significantly from the Introverted on the variable of personal adjustment. They do, however, exhibit a trend on the LSIB, to achieve higher personal adjustment scores than the Perturbed group.

The Normal aged have significantly less conflict in their perception of themselves and less total variability of self concept than do the Perturbed group. While not differing substantially in this respect from the Introverted group, they experience significantly more inner conflict than the Mature group. As compared with the Perturbed, the Normal aged seem to handle this conflict and variability through their defensive systems in a significantly more effective way. As mentioned earlier, these Normal aged have a marked tendency to be less able to effectively maintain their defensiveness than the Introverted group. Thus, even while the Introverted are less emotionally stable, there is little difference between the two groups regarding personal adjustment.

Although the Normal aged tend to score lower than the Mature group, they demonstrate—not unlike the Introverted—a high level of self esteem and derive satisfaction from their behavioural functioning (Row 3 score). They tend, however, to feel themselves of less personal worth than the Introverted and the Mature groups. In interpersonal relationships the Normal aged experience a heightened level of adequacy. They are able to reap significantly greater satisfaction from their social functioning than do the Perturbed or Introverted, thus accounting for their greater tendency toward heightened social adjustment in relation to the two aforementioned groups.

DISCUSSION

While there is a need on the part of personality theorists and clincians alike to compare broad sample populations, it must be remembered that much valuable information is lost in this homogenizing process; hence, extrapolations from such material must be made with this limitation in mind. This needed caution can be best understood when viewed against the finding that there are four aged personality groups that comprise the present sample population. In literature dealing with broad comparisons between aged samples and younger populations, there has been no mention of the nucleus of highly integrated and well functioning aged. This Mature group of individuals who compare favourably—in the realm of personality functioning—with younger samples are lost or give way to the stereotyped description of the aged in such comparisons. Likewise, individuals in the small Perturbed group, who may well be considered psychiatrically "at risk" are left unassessed and undifferentiated from the other old age groups. Furthermore, it may be that extremely high and/or low mean scores achieved by these two groups (Mature and Perturbed) on the various personality variables, may cancel each other out.

The results of this study confirm and substantiate the point of view first put forth by Havighurst (1963), that both theories—activity and disengagement—may be applicable to the explanation and understanding of aged personality functioning depending on *individual* and social differences. Neugarten's (1965) assertion that personality is a "pivotal dimension in predicting relationships between levels of social role activity and life satisfaction" has been reaffirmed and has gained further credence on the basis of the present study. Indeed, present results indicate that each of these two theories alone are shown to be an insufficient framework from which to view the ageing personality. The Introverted group and the Normal aged both demonstrate adequate personal adjustment as defined by LSI B. These two groups with different personalities, attitudes toward social interaction and life styles (Activity *vs* Disengagement) are both able to achieve satisfactory life satisfaction in accordance with their particular personalities and self concepts.

Figuring prominently in past research into adjustment in ageing is self concept. It is of utmost importance to note however, that although self concept is regarded today as a multidimensional concept, most work that has been done in this area in connection with adjustment in old age, has used self concept in a unidimensional way. When considering the four aged personality groups—the Normal, the Introverted, the Perturbed, and the Mature—in relation to self concept in old age, it becomes rather evident that such aspects of self concept as defensiveness and variability of self concept, conflict in self definition and various facets of self esteem, are essential in gaining a fuller understanding of the role of self concept in the elderly and figure prominently in the way in which the four groups achieve personal satisfaction. Unfortunately, however, most previous investigations deal only with the measurement of loss of self concept, self confidence, self acceptance etc., and therefore only give but restrictive insights into self concept and ageing.

In this connection, the positive contribution and role of defensiveness in the aged personality merit further research. The Perturbed whose personality functioning is characterised by a lack of emotional stability also demonstrate the lowest adjustment scores. It is quite noticeable that this group scores significantly lower than the remaining three groups on measures of defensiveness. On the other hand, the Introverted are significantly less emotionally stable than the Normal group; nevertheless, there is no significant difference between these groups so far as personal adjustment is concerned. The Introverted group tend to be, however, considerably more defensive than the Normal aged.

The study of human ageing has never been as important as it is today. In light of the ever-increasing proportion of the population that now survives well into old age, it had become necessary to relieve the suffering of the elderly as well as to plan for the future needs of a large elderly population. The results of this study may well have practical implications for those in the helping professions who are involved with the elderly.

The Normals, the Introverted, the Perturbed and the Mature view themselves and their functioning in distinctly different or unique ways. Likewise, the psychological adjustment—both personal and social—of the individuals within these four groups is consistent with their different patterns of personality and self concept. It seems that each group of elderly individuals has its particular life style and *needs* which are highly influenced by its personality and perhaps mediated by its self concept.

A first step in helping to provide for the needs of the elderly population and plan for the future is to understand the needs and requirements of the various segments of the aged population. It is conceivable that the Perturbed group may have needs and requirements that are both quantitatively and qualitatively different from those—let us say —in the Introverted, Normal or Mature groups. Differences in personality and self concept among the groups may influence the acceptance, effectiveness, utility and success of programs designed to aid the elderly. Understanding the personality and self concept of these four groups of aged individuals may well be an essential step in dealing with psychological problems of ageing encountered by the elderly community.

These results are most interesting but considerably more work is needed, particularly longitudinal investigations of personality in the aged. Furthermore, the integration of the personality models with those of cognitive functioning in the aged is essential. The empirical research on this and its implications are essential if we are to help the aged in future generations, or perhaps even our own. To a small extent, research work along these lines is under way in Newcastle upon Tyne. One major weakness in the model is the rather limited procedures for investigating adjustment in the aged. Much more needs to be done to analyse exactly what adjustment means to the aged. A direct observation of what appears to be known and an ethological approach to this problem is needed to strengthen the criteria of adjustment and relate them to intellect and personality.

The cognitive model proposed by Savage and his colleagues in 1973 can be integrated with the present personality model to provide a framework for a more comprehensive theory of the aged person with real possibilities of a useful practical pay-off. In essence, further research is obviously essential to verify the implications of this approach, but the cumulative evidence of our eleven years of investigation with both the community and institutionalised aged gives a basis for positive prediction and hope in our understanding of the problems and suggestions for their alleviation.

Bibliography

Aaronson, B.S. (1958). Age and sex influences on MMPI profile peak in an abnormal population. *J. consult. Psychol.* **22**, 203–206.

Aaronson, B. S. (1960). A dimension of personality change with ageing. *J. clin. Psychol.* **16**, 63–65.

Aaronson, B. S. (1964). Ageing, personality change and psychiatric diagnosis. *J. Gerontol.* **19**, 144–148.

Adams, D. L. (1969). Analysis of a life satisfaction index. *J. Gerontol.* **24**, 270–274.

Albert, E. (1964). Senile demenz und Alzheimersche krankheit als ansdruck des gleichen krankheits geschehens. *Fortsch. neurol. Psychiat.* **32**, 625.

Allport, G. W. (1961). "Pattern and Growth of Personality". Holt, Rhinehart and Winston, New York.

Ames, L. B. (1960*a*). Age changes in the Rorschach responses of individual elderly subjects. *J. genet. Psychol.* **97**, 257–285.

Ames, L. B. (1960*b*). Age changes in the Rorschach responses of a group of elderly individuals. *J. genet. Psychol.* **97**, 287–315.

Baizerman, M. and Ellison, D. L. (1971). A social role analysis of senility. *Gerontologist*, **11**, 163–169.

Bartholomew, A. A. and Marley, E. (1959). The temporal reliability of the Maudsley Personality Inventory. *J. Ment. Sci.* **105**, 238–240.

Beckman, R. O., Williams, C. O. and Fisher, G. C. (1958). Adjustment to life in later maturity. *Geriatrics*, **13**, 662–667.

Bergmann, K. (1966). Observations on the causation of neurotic disorder in old age with special reference to physical illness. *Proc. 7th Int. Congr. Geront.*, pp. 623. Vienna.

Bergmann, K. (1972). Psychogeriatrics. *Medicine*, **9**, 643–653.

Bergmann, K. (1974). Nosology in psychogeriatrics. *In* "Modern Perspectives in Psychogeriatrics" (Howell, J., ed.). In press.

Birren, J. E. (ed.). (1959). "Handbook of Ageing and the Individual". Univ. of Chicago Press, Chicago.

Birren, J. E. (1960). Psychological aspects of ageing. *Ann. Rev. Psychol.* **2**, 161–198.

Birren, J. E. (1964). "The Psychology of Aging". Prentice-Hall, Englewood Cliffs.

Blessed, G., Tomlinson, B. E. and Roth, M. (1968). The association between quantitative measures of dementia and of degenerative changes in the cerebral grey matter of elderly subjects. *Brit. J. Psychiat.* **114**, 797–811.

Bleuler, E. (1943). The clinical features of the late schizophrenics. *Fortschr. neurol. Psychiat.* **15**, 259.

Bolton, N. and Savage, R. D. (1966). The Maudsley Personality Inventory: a review in "Readings in Clinical Psychology" (R. D. Savage, ed.). Pergamon Press, Oxford.

Botwinick, J. (1967). "Cognitive Processes in Maturity and Old Age". Springer, New York.

Botwinick, J. (1970). Geropsychology. *Ann. Rev. Psychol.* **21**, 239–272.

Botwinick, J. and Birren, J. E. (1951*b*). The measurement of intellectual decline in senile psychoses. *J. consult. Psychol.* **15**, 145–150.

Bower, H. M. (1969). The first psychogeriatric day centre in Victoria. *Med. J. Austral.* **11**, 1047–1050.

Bremer, J. (1951). A social-psychiatric investigation of a small community in Northern Norway. *Acta psychiat. Neurol. Kbh.*, Suppl. 62.

Britton, J. H. (1949). A study of the adjustment of retired school teachers. *Amer. Psychologist*, **4**, 308.

Britton, J. H. and Britton, J. O. (1972). "Personality Changes in Ageing: A Longitudinal Study of Community Residents in New York". Springer Publishing Co.

Britton, P. G. and Savage, R. D. (1966). A short form of WAIS for use with the aged. *Brit. J. Psychiat.* **112**, 417–418.

Britton, P. G. and Savage, R. D. (1967). A short scale for the assessment of mental health in the community aged. *Brit. J. Psychiat.* **113**, 521–523.

Brody, E. M. and Gummer, A. C. (1967). Aged applicants and non-applicants to a voluntary home; an exploratory comparison. *Gerontologist*, **7**, 234–243.

Brody, E. M., Kleban, M. H., Lawton, M. P. and Silverman, H. A. (1971). Excess disabilities of mentally impaired aged: impact of individualised treatment. *Gerontologist*, **11**, 124–133.

Brownfair, J. J. (1952). Stability of self concept as a dimension of personality. *J. abnorm. Soc. Psychol.* **47**, 597–606.

Brozek, J. (1955). Personality of young and middle-aged normal men: item analysis of a psychosomatic inventory. *J. Gerontol.* **7**, 410–418.

Brozek, J. (1955). Personality changes with age: an item analysis of the MMPI. *J. Gerontol.* **10**, 194–206.

Buhler, C. (1951). Maturation and Motivation. *Personality*, **1**, 184–211.

Burdach, K. F. (1890–1926). "Von Baue und Leben des Gehirns". Leipzig.

Burstein, S. R. (1949). Aspects of the psychopathology of old age. *Brit. Med. Bull.* **6**, 63.

Byrd, E. (1959). Measured anxiety in old age. *Psychol. Rep.* **5**, 439–440.

Calden, G. and Hokanson, J. E. (1959). The influence of age on MMPI responses. *J. clin. Psychol.* **15**, 194–195.

Caldwell, B. (1954). The use of the Rorschach in personality research with the aged. *J. Gerontol.* **9**, 316–323.

Cameron, P. (1967). Introversion and egocentricity among the aged. *J. Gerontol.* **22**, 465–468.

Canter, A., Day, E. W., Imboden, J. B. and Cluff, J. E. (1962). The influence of age and health status on the MMPI scores of a normal population. *J. clin. Psychol.* **18**, 71–73.

Caplan, G. (1964). "Principles of Preventative Psychiatry". Basic Books, New York.

Capstick, A. (1960). Recognition of emotional disturbance and the prevention of suicide. *Brit. Med. J.* **1**, 1179–1182.

Cattell, R. B. (1957). "Personality and Motivation Structure and Measurement". World Books, New York.

Cattell, R. B. (1962). "Handbook Supplement for Form C of the 16PF Questionnaire". Institute for Personality and Ability Testing, Illinois.

Cattell, R. B. (1965). "The Scientific Analysis of Personality". Penguin Books, Middlesex, England.

Cattell, R. B. and Bjerstedt, A. (1967). The structure of depression by factoring Q-data, in relation to general personality source traits. *Scand. J. Psychol.* **8**, 17–24.

Cattell, R. B. and Bolton, L. S. (1969). What pathological dimensions lie beyond the normal dimensions of the 16PF? *J. consult. Clin. Psychol.* **33**, 18–29.

Cattell, R. B., Eber, H. W. and Tatsuoka, M. M. (1970). "Handbook for the Sixteen Personality Factor Questionnaire". N.F.E.R. Publishing Co., Berks., England.

Cattell, R. B. and Scheier, I. H. (1961). "The Meaning and Measurement of Neuroticism and Anxiety". Ronald, New York.

Cattell, R. B. and Scheier, I. H. (1958). The nature of anxiety: a review of 13 multivariate analyses comprising 814 variables. *Psychol. Rep.* **4**, 351–388.

Cavan, R. S., Burgess, E. W., Havighurst, R. J. and Goldhamer, H. (1949). "Personal Adjustment in Old Age". Science Research Associates, Chicago.

Chesser, E. S. (1965). A study of some aetiological factors in the affective disorders of old age. Unpublished dissertation, Institute of Psychiatry, London.

Chown, Sheila M. and Heron, A. (1965). Psychological aspects of ageing in man. *Ann. Rev. Psychol.* **16**, 417–450.

Clark, F. Legros (1959). "Age and the Working Lives of Men". Nuffield Foundation, London.

Clausen, J. A. (1968). Conceptual and methodologic issues in the assessment of mental health in the aged. *Psychiat. res. Reps.* **23**, 151–160.

Clow, H. E. (1940). A study of one hundred patients suffering from psychosis with cerebral arteriosclerosis. *Amer. J. Psychiat.* **97**, 16–26.

Clow, H. E. and Allen, E. B. (1951). Manifestations of psychoneuroses occurring in later life. *Geriatrics*, **6**, 31–39.

Combs, A. W. (1949). A phenomenological approach to adjustment theory. *J. abnorm. Soc. Psychol.* **44**, 29–35.

Conkey, F. (1933). The adaptation of fifty men and women to old age. *J. home Economics*, **25**, 387–389.

Coppinger, N. W., Bortner, R. W. and Saucer, R. T. (1963). A factor analysis of psychological deficit. *J. genet. Psychol.* **103**, 23–43.

Corsellis, J. A. N. (1962). "Mental Illness and the Ageing Brain". Oxford University Press, London.

Coser, R. L. (1956). A home away from home. *Soc. Probs.* **4**, 3–17.

Craik, F. M. (1964). An observed age difference in response to a personality inventory. *Brit. J. Psychol.* **55**, 453–462.

Cumming, Elaine, Dean, Lois R., Newell, D. S. and McCaffrey, Isobel (1960). Disengagement: a tentative theory of ageing. *Sociometry*, **23**, 23–35.

Cumming, Elaine and Henry, W. E. (1961). "Growing Old". Basic Books, New York.

Cumming, Elaine and McCaffrey, Isobel (1960). Some conditions associated with morale among the ageing. Paper presented at the Annual Meeting of the American Psychopathological Association, New York.

Davidson, H. H. and Kruglov, L. (1952). Personality characteristics in the institutionalised aged. *J. Consult. Psychol.* **16**, 6–12.

Davis, R. W. (1968). Psychological aspects of geriatric nursing. *Amer. J. Nursing*, **68**, 802–804.

Dean, L. R. (1962). Ageing and the decline of affect. *J. Gerontol.* **17**, 440–446.

Delhees, K. H. and Cattell, R. B. (1971). "Manual for the Clinical Analysis Questionnaire". Institute for Personality and Ability Testing, Illinois.

Dobson, W. R. and Patterson, T. W. (1961). A behavioural evaluation of geriatric patients living in nursing homes as compared to a hospitalised group. *Geronto-logist*, **1**, 135–139.

Dodge, J. S. (1961). Changes in self perception with age. *Percept. Mot. Skills*, **13**, 88.

Donahue, Wilma (1949). *In* "Living Through the Older Years" (C. Tibbits, ed.) pp. 63–68. University of Michigan Press, Ann Arbor, Michigan.

Donahue, E. (1962). A brief report on the rehabilitation of long-term aged patients. *In* "Ageing Around the World: Social and Psychological Aspects of Ageing" (C. Tibbits and W. Donahue, eds.). Columbia University Press, New York.

Doppelt, J. E. and Wallace, W. L. (1955). Standardization of the WAIS scale for older persons. *J. Abnorm. Soc. Psychol.* **51**, 312–320.

Drake, L. E. (1946). A social I.E. scale for the MMPI. *J. Appl. Psychol.* **30**, 51–54.

Edwards, A. E. and Wine, D. B. (1963). Personality changes with age; their dependency on concomitant intellectual decline. *J. Gerontol.* **18**, 182–184.

Emerson, A. R. (1959). The first year of retirement. *Occup. Psychiat.* **33**, 197–208.

Erikson, E. (1959). The healthy personality. *Psychological Issues*, volume 1. International University Press, New York.

Essen-Moller, E. (1956). Individual traits and morbidity in a Swedish rural population. *Acta Psychiat. Neurol. Scand.* Supplement 100.

Evans, V. L. (1943). Convulsive shock therapy in elderly patients: risks and results. *Amer. J. Phychiat.* **99**, 531–533.

Eysenck, H. J. (1956a). The questionnaire measurement of neuroticism and extra-version. *Riv. Psicol.* **50**, 113–140.

Eysenck, H. J. (1956b). Reminiscence, drive and personality theory. *J. Abnorm. Soc. Psychol.* **53**, 328–333.

Eysenck, H. J. (1957). "The Dynamics of Anxiety and Hysteria". Routledge and Kegan Paul, London.

Eysenck, H. J. (1959). "The Maudsley Personality Inventory Questionnaire". London University Press, London.

Eysenck, H. J. (1963). "Experiments with Drugs". Pergamon Press, London.

Eysenck, H. J. and Eysenck, S. B. G. (1964). "Eysenck Personality Inventory". London University Press, London.

Feldman, F., Susselman, S., Lipetz, B. and Barrera, S. E. (1946). Electric shock therapy of elderly patients. *Arch. Neurol. Psychiat.* **56**, 133–142.

Feifel, H. (1954). Psychiatric patients look at old age: level of adjustment and attitudes towards ageing. *Amer. J. Phychiat.* **111**, 459–465.

Fiedler, F., Dodge, J., Jones, R. and Hutchins, E. (1958). Inter-relations among measures of personality and adjustment in non-clinical populations. *J. Abnorm. Soc. Psychol.* **56**, 345–351.

Fisher, J. (1957). An empirical study of the relation of physical disease to body-object cathexis. Unpublished manuscript.

Fitts, W. H. (1955). "Preliminary Manual. The Tennessee Department of Mental Health Self Concept Scale". Department of Mental Health, Nashville, Tennessee.

Fitts, W. H. (1965) "Manual: Tennessee Self Concept Scale". Counselor Recordings and Tests, Nashville, Tennessee.

Fitts, W. H., Adams, J. L., Radford, G., Richard, W. C., Thomas, B. K., Thomas,

M. M. and Thompson, W. (1971). "The Self Concept and Self Actualization". Dede Wallace Center Monograph No. 3. Nashville, Tennessee.

Fowler, F. L. and McCalla, M. E. (1969). Correlates of morale among aged in Greater Boston. *Proc. 77th Ann. Conv. Amer. Psychol. Assn.*, **4**, 933–934.

Fozard, J. L. and Nuttall, R. L. (1971). Effects of age and socio-economic status differences on the 16PF questionnaire scores. *Proc. 79th Ann. Conv. Amer. Psychol. Assn.*, **6**, 597–598.

Fried, Edrita G. (1949). Attitudes of the older population groups towards activity and inactivity. *J. Gerontol.* **4**, 141–151.

Friedman, J. H. and Strachan, J. (1972). A self-insured free policy for geriatric mental health. *J. Amer. Geriatrics Soc.* **20**, 490–496.

Gaber, L. B. (1974). Self concept and adjustment in the aged. Ph.D. Thesis, unpublished. University of Newcastle upon Tyne.

Gaitz, C. M. and Baer, P. E. (1970). Diagnostic assessment of the elderly: a multifunctional model. *Gerontologist*, **10**, 47–52.

Gardner, L. Pearl (1948). Attitudes and activities of the middle-aged and aged. *Amer. Psychologist*, **3**, 307.

Garside, R. F., Kay, D. W. K. and Roth, M. (1965). Old age mental disorders in Newcastle upon Tyne. Part III: a factorial study of medical, psychiatric and social characteristics. *Brit. J. Psychiat.* **111**, 939–946.

Gellerstedt, N. (1932–1933). Our knowledge of cerebral changes in normal involution of old age. *Uppsala Lak Fören Förh.* **38**, 193.

Geidt, F. and Lehner, G. (1951). Assignment of ages on the Draw a Person Test by male neuropsychiatric patients. *J. Personality*, **19**, 440–448.

Gilberstadt, H. (1968). Relationships among scores of tests suitable for the assessment of adjustment and intellectual functioning. *J. Gerontol.* **23**, 483–487.

Goldstein, S., Sevriuk, J. and Graver, H. (1968). The establishment of a psychogeriatric day hospital. *Canada Med. Assn. J.* **98**, 955–959.

Goodstein, L. D. (1954). Regional differences in MMPI responses among male college students. *J. Consult. Psychol.* **18**, 437–441.

Goodwin, K. S. and Schaie, K. W. (1969). Age differences in personality structure. *Proc. 77th Ann. Conv. Amer. Psychol. Assn.*, **4**, 713–714.

Gordon, M. S. (1960). Changing patterns of retirement. *J. Gerontol.* **15**, 300–304.

Granick, S. (1950). Studies of psychopathology in later maturity: a review. *J. Gerontol.* **5**, 44–58.

Grant, C. H. (1969). Age differences in self concept from early adulthood through old age. Ph.D Dissertation, unpublished. University of Nebraska, Nebraska.

Gray, H. (1947). Psychological types and changes with age. *J. Clin. Psychol.* **3**, 273–277.

Greenhouse, S. W. and Geisser, S. (1959). On methods in the analysis of profile data. *Psychometrika*, **24**, 95–112.

Grewel, F. (1953). Testing psychology of dementias. *Folia Psychiat. Neur.* **56**, 305–339.

Gruenberg, E. (1961). "A Mental Health Survey of Older People". Utica, New York.

Grunthal, E. (1927). Clinical and anatomical investigations on senile dementia. *Z. ges. Neurol. Psychiat.* **111**, 763.

Gubrium, J. F. (1971). Self conceptions of mental health among the aged. *Mental Hygiene*, **55**, 398–403.

Gurel, L., Linn, M. W. and Linn, B. S. (1972). Physical and mentaɫ impairment-of-function evaluation in the aged: the PAMIE scale. *J. Gerontol.* **27**, 83–90.

Gutman, D. L., Henry, W. E. and Neugarten, B. L. (1959). Personality development in middle-aged men. Paper read at Amer. Psychol. Assn., Cincinatti.

Guttmann, G. M. (1966). A note on the MPI. *Brit. J. Soc. Clin. Psychol.* **5**, 128–129.

Gynther, M. D. and Shimkunas, A. M. (1966). Age and MMPI performance. *J. Consult. Psychol.* **30**, 118–121.

Haigh, C. (1949). Defensive behaviour in client-centred therapy. *J. Consult. Psychol.* **13**, 181–189.

Hall, C. S. and Lindzey, G. (1957). "Theories of Personality". Wiley, New York.

Hanlon, T., Hofstaetter, P. and O'Connor, J. (1954). Congruence of self and ideal self in relation to personality adjustment. *J. Consult. Psychol.* **18**, 215–218.

Hardyck, C. D. (1964). Sex differences in personality changes with age. *J. Gerontol.* **19**, 78–82.

Hathaway, S. R. and McKinley, J. C. (1951). "The Minnesota Multiphasic Personality Inventory Manual" (revised). The Psychological Corporation, New York.

Havighurst, R. J. (1949). Old age: an American problem. *J. Gerontol.* **4**, 298–304.

Havighurst, R. J. (1950). Public attitudes towards various activities of older people. *In* "Planning the Older Years" (Donahue, Wilma and Tibbits, C., eds), pp. 141–148. University of Michigan Press, Ann Arbor.

Havighurst, R. J. (1953). "Human Development and Education". Longmans Green, New York.

Havighurst, R. J. (1957). The social competence of middle-aged people. *Genet. Psychol. Monogr.* **56**, 297–375.

Havighurst, R. J. (1959). Life styles of middle aged people. *Vita Humana*, **2**, 25–34.

Havighurst, R. J. (1963). Successful Ageing. *In* "Processes of Ageing" (R. G. Williams, C. Tibbits and Wilma Donahue, eds.). Vol. 1. Longmans Green, New York.

Havighurst, R. J. and Albrecht, R. (1953). "Older People". Longmans Green, New York.

Havighurst, R. J. and Shanas, E. (1950). Adjustment to retirement. *Sociol. Soc. Res.* **34**, 169–176.

Herbert, M. E. and Jacobson, S. (1967). Late paraphrenia. *Brit. J. Psychiat.* **113**, 461.

Heron, A. (1963). Retirement attitudes among industrial workers in the sixth decade of life. *Vita Humana*, **6**, 152–159.

Heron, A. and Chown, Sheila (1967). "Age and Function". Churchill, London.

Hess, A. L. and Bradshaw, H. L. (1970). Positiveness of self concept and ideal self as a function of age. *J. Genet. Psychol.* **117**, 57–67.

Hinton, J. (1967). "Dying". Penguin Books, Harmondsworth, England.

Hobson, W. and Pemberton, J. (1955). "The Health of the Elderly at Home". Churchill, London.

Hogan, R. (1948). The development of a measure of client defensiveness in a counseling relationship. Ph.D Dissertation, unpublished. University of Chicago.

Hopkins, Barbara and Roth, M. (1953). Psychological test performance in patients over sixty: (II) paraphrenics, arteriosclerotic psychosis and acute confusion. *J. Ment. Sci.* **99**, 451–463.

Jensen, A. R. (1958). The Maudsley Personality Inventory. *Acta Psychol.* **14**, 314–325.

Jones, H. E. (1961). The age-relative study of personality. *Acta Psychol.* **19**, 140–142.

Kahn, R. L., Seaman, F. D. and Goldfarb, A. J. (1958). Attitudes towards illness in the aged. *Geriatrics*, **13**, 246–250.

Kallmann, F. J. (1948). Preliminary data on life histories of senescent twins. *Amer. Psychologist*, **3**, 307–308.

Kallmann, F. J. (1951). Comparative adaptational, social and psychometric data on life histories of senescent twin pairs. *Amer. J. Hum. Genet.* **3**, 65.

Kaplan, O. J. (ed.) (1945). "Mental Disorders in Later Life". Stanford University Press, Stanford, California.

Kaplan, O. J. (1956). The Aged Subnormal. *In* "Mental Disorders in Later Life" (O. J. Kaplan, ed.) 2nd edn., pp. 383–397. Stanford University Press, Stanford, California.

Kassebaum, G. G., Couch, A. S. and Slater, P. E. (1959). The factorial dimensions of the MMPI. *J. Consult. Psychol.* **23**, 226–236.

Katz, L., Neal, M. W. and Simon, A. (1961). Observations on psychic mechanisms in organic psychoses of the aged. *In* "Psychopathology of Aging" (P. H. Hoch and J. Zubin, eds). Grune & Stratton, New York.

Kay, D. W. K. (1959). Observations on the natural history and genetics of old-age psychoses: a Stockholm material, 1931–1937 (abridged). *Proc. Roy. Soc. Med.* **52**, 791–794.

Kay, D. W. K. (1962). Outcome and cause of death in mental disorders of old age: a long-term follow-up of functional and organic psychoses. *Acta Psychiat. Scand.* **38**, 249–276.

Kay, D. W. K., Beamish, Pamela and Roth, M. (1962). Some medical and social characterists of elderly people under state care. *The Sociology Rev. Monogr.* **15**, 173–193.

Kay, D. W. K., Beamish, Pamela and Roth, M. (1964a). Old age mental disorders in Newcastle upon Tyne, Part I: a study of prevalence. *Brit. J. Psychiat.* **110**, 146–158.

Kay, D. W. K., Beamish, Pamela and Roth, M. (1964b). Old age mental disorders in Newcastle upon Tyne, Part II: a study of possible social and medical causes. *Brit. J. Psychiat.* **110**, 668–682.

Kay, D. W. K. and Bergmann, K. (1966). Physical disability and mental health in old age: a follow-up of elderly people seen at home. *J. Psychosomat. Res.* **10**, 3–10.

Kay, D. W. K., Bergmann, K., Foster, Eleanor and Garside, R. F. (1966). A four year follow-up of a random sample of old people originally seen in their own homes: a physical, social and psychiatry enquiry. *Excerpta Medica Internat. Congr. Series No.* 250, 1668–1670. *Proc. IVth World Congr. Psychiat.*

Kay, D. W. K. and Roth, M. (1955). Physical accompaniments of mental disorder in old age. *Lancet*, **ii**, 740–745.

Kelly, E. L. (1955). Consistency of adult personality. *Amer. J. Psychology*, **10**, 659–681.

Kessell, W. I. N. (1960). Psychiatric morbidity in a London general practice. *Brit. J. Prev. Soc. Med.* **14**, 16–22.

Kessell, W. I. N. and Shepherd, M. (1962). Neurosis in hospital and general practice. *J. Ment. Sci.* **108**, 159–166.

Kidd, C. B. and Smith, V. E. M. (1966). A regional survey of old people in North-East Scottish mental hospitals. *Scot. Med. J.* **11**, 132–136.

Kleban, M. M. and Brody, E. M. (1972). Prediction of improvement in mentally impaired aged: personality ratings by social workers. *J. Gerontol.* **27**, 69–76.

Kleban, M. M., Brody, E. M. and Lawton, M. P. (1971). Personality traits in the mentally impaired aged and their relationship to improvements in current functioning. *Gerontologist,* **11**, 134–140.

Kleemeier, R. W. (1961). The use and meaning of time in special settings: retirement communities, homes for the aged, hospitals and other group settings. *In* "Ageing and Leisure" (R. W. Kleemeier, ed.). Oxford University Press, New York.

Klopfer, W. G. (1946). Personality patterns of old age. *Rorschach Res. Exch.* **10**, 145–166.

Kobrynski, B. (1968). A new look at geriatric care. *J. Amer. Geriatrics Soc.* **16**, 1114–1125.

Kornetsky, C. (1963). Minnesota Multiphasic Personality Inventory: results obtained from a population of aged men. *In* "Human Ageing: a Biological and Behavioural Study" (J. E. Birren, *et al.* eds.). Chapter 13. U.S. Department of Health, Education and Welfare, Bethesda, Md.

Kraepelin, E. (1909–13). "Psychiatry", 8th edn. G. Thieme, Leipzig.

Kral, V. A. (1962). Senescent forgetfulness: benign and malignant. *Canad. Med. Assoc. J.* **86**, 257–260.

Kubo, Y. (1938). Mental and physical changes in old age. *J. Genet. Psychol.* **53**, 101–108.

Kuhlen, R. G. (1945). Age differences in personality during adult years. *Psychol. Bull.* **42**, 333–358.

Kuhlen, R. G. (1948). Age trends in adjustment during the adult years as reflected in happiness ratings. Paper read at a meeting of the American Psychological Association, Boston.

Kutner, B., Fanshel, D., Togo, A. and Langner, T. (1956). "Five Hundred Over Sixty". Russell Sage Foundation, New York.

Kuypers, J. A. (1972). Internal-external locus of control, ego functioning and personality characteristics in the old. *Gerontologist,* **12**, 168–173.

Lakin, M. and Eisdorfer, C. (1960). Affective expression among the aged. *J. Proj. Tech.* **24**, 403–408.

Landis, J. T. (1942). Social psychological factors of ageing. *Social Forces,* **20**, 468–470.

Larsson, T. and Sjogren, T. (1954). A methodological, psychiatric and statistical study of a large Swedish rural population. *Acta Psychiat. Scand.* **39**, Suppl. 79.

Larsson, T., Sjogren, T. and Jacobson, G. (1963). Senile dementia. *Acta Psychiat. Scand.* **39**, Suppl. 167.

Lawton, G. (1943). "New Goals for Old Age". Columbia Press, New York.

Lebo, D. (1953). Some factors said to make for happiness in old age. *J. Clin. Psychol.* **9**, 385–387.

Lecky, P. (1945). "Self Consistency: a Theory of Personality". Island Press, New York.

Lehner, G. and Silver, H. (1948). Age relationships on the Draw a Person Test. *J. Personality*, 22.

Lehner, G. and Gunderson, E. (1953). Height relationships on the Draw a Person Test. *J. Personality*, 22.

Lemon, B. W., Bengston, V. L. and Peterson, J. A. (1972). An exploration of the activity theory of ageing. *J. Gerontol.* 27, 511–523.

Lewis, A. (1946). Ageing and senility: a major problem of psychiatry. *J. Ment. Sci.* 92, 150–170.

Light, B. H. and Amick, J. H. (1956). Rorschach responses of the normal aged. *J. Proj. Tech.* 20, 185–195.

Lipscomb, C. F. (1971). The care of the psychiatrically disturbed elderly patient in the community. *Amer. J. Psychiat.* 127, 1067–1070.

Lorge, I. (1941). Intellectual changes during maturity and old age. *Rev. Educ. Res.* 11, 553–561.

Lorge, I. (1944). Intellectual changes during maturity and old age. *Rev. Educ. Res.* 14, 438–445.

Lorge, I. (1956). Gerontology (later maturity). *Ann. Rev. Psychol.* 7, 349–364.

Lowenthal, M. F. (1964). Social isolation and mental illness in old age. *Amer. Sociol. Rev.* 29, 54–70.

Lowenthal, M. F. (1968). The relationship between social factors and mental health in the aged. *Psychiat. Res. Rep.* 23, 187–197.

Lynn, R. (1964). Personality changes with ageing. *Behav. Res. Therapy.* 1, 343–349.

McDonald, C. (1965). Psychoneurosis in the elderly. *Postgrad. Med. J.* 38, 432.

McDonald, C. (1968). Treatment of the mentally disturbed geriatric patient. *Geriatrics*, 23, 168–176.

McGuire, R. J., Mowbray, R. M. and Vallance, R. C. (1963). The Maudsley Personality Inventory used with psychiatric patients. *Brit. J. Psychol.* 54, 157–166.

Mack, M. J. (1953). Personal adjustment of chronically ill old people under home care. *Geriatrics*, 8, 407–416.

Macmillan, D. (1969). Features of the senile breakdown. *Geriatrics*, 24, 109–118.

Macmillan, D. and Shaw, P. (1966). Senile breakdown in standards of personal and environmental cleanliness. *Brit. Med. J.* ii, 1032.

Markson, E., Kwoh, A., Cumming, J. and Cumming, E. (1971). Alternatives to hospitalisation for psychiatrically ill geriatric patients. *Amer. J. Psychiat.* 127, 1055–1062.

Mason, E. P. (1954). Some correlates of self-adjustments of the aged. Unpublished Ph.D Thesis, Washington University, St. Louis.

Mayer-Gross, W. (1945). Electric convulsive treatment in patients over sixty. *J. Ment. Sci.* 91, 101–103.

Mayer-Gross, W. (1969). "Clinical Psychiatry" (E. Slater and M. Roth, eds.). 3rd edn. Bailliere Tindall, London.

Medawar, P. B. (1955). Presidential address to CIBA Foundation Colloquia on ageing.

Meggendorfer, F. (1926). Uber die hereditare Disposition zur Dementia senilis. *Z. Ges. Neurol. Psychiat.* 101, 604.

Menotti, A. A. (1967). Ageing: illness and disengagement: are they similar? *Dissertn. Abs.* **283b**, 1170.

Messer, M. (1967). The possibility of age-concentrated environment becoming a normative system. *Gerontologist*, **7**, 247–251.

Miles, W. R. (1942). Psychological aspects of ageing. *In* "Problems of Ageing" (E. V. Cowdry, ed.) 2nd edn. pp. 756–784. Williams and Wilkins, Baltimore.

Millard, D. W. (1968). The clinician in the community. *Brit. J. Psychiat. Soc. Work*, **9**, 124–129.

Miller, H. C. (1963). "The Ageing Countryman". National Corporation for the Care of Old People, London.

Moberg, D. O. (1953). Leadership in the church and personal adjustment in old age. *Sociol. Social Res.* **37**, 499–509.

Morgan, M. (1937). The attitudes and adjustments of recipients of old age assistance in upstate and metropolitan New York. *Arch. Psychol.* **30**, No. 214, 131.

Mueller, C. (1967). "Alterspsychiatrie". G. Thieme, Stuttgart.

Murray, H. A. (1943). "Thematic Apperception Test" (3rd revision). Harvard University Press, Cambridge, Mass.

Neugarten, B. L. (1963). *In* "Processes of Ageing", vol. 1 (R. H. Williams, C. Tibbits and W. Donahue, eds.). Atherton Press, New York.

Neugarten, B. L. (1964). Summary and implications. *In* "Personality in Middle and Late Life" (B. L. Neugarten, ed.). Atherton Press, New York.

Neugarten, B. L. (1965). Personality and patterns of ageing. *Gawein*, **13**, 249–256.

Neugarten, Bernice, Havighurst, R. J. and Tobin, S. (1961). The measurement of life satisfaction. *Gerontology*, **16**, 134–143.

Nielson, J. (1963). Geronto-psychiatric period prevalence investigation in a geographically delimited population. *Acta Psychiat. Scand.* **38**, 307–328.

Norman, R. D. (1949). Concealment of age among psychologists: evidence for a popular stereotype. *J. Soc. Psychol.* **30**, 127–135.

O'Neal, P., Robins, E. and Schmidt, E. H. (1956). A psychiatric study of attempted suicide in persons over 60 years of age. *Arch. Neurol. Psychiat.* **75**, 275–284.

Oberleder, M. (1969). Emotional breakdowns in elderly people. *Hospital and Community Psychiatry*, **20**, 191–196.

Oberleder, M. (1970). Crisis therapy in mental breakdown of the ageing. *Gerontologist*, **10**, 111–114.

Pan, J. S. (1950). Personal adjustment of old people in Church homes for the aged. *Geriatrics*, **5**, 166–170.

Pappas, W. and Silver, R. J. (1958). Developmental differences between the successful and unsuccessful aged. *J. Amer. Geriat. Soc.* **6**, 360–367.

Parsons, P. L. (1965). Mental health of Swansea's old folk. *Brit. J. Prev. Soc. Med.* **19**, 43.

Payne, R., Gibson, F. E. and Pittard, B. B. (1969). Social influences in senile psychosis. *Sociol. Symp.* **2**, 137–140.

Peck, R. F. (1956). Psychological developments in the second half of life. *In* "Psychological Aspects of Ageing" (J. E. Anderson, ed.) pp. 44–49. A.P.A., Washington.

Peck, R. F. and Berkowitz, H. (1959). Personality and adjustments in middle age.

Unpublished manuscript on file with Committee on Human Development, University of Chicago.

Pidwell, D. (1971). Personality and life satisfaction in the aged. Unpublished M.Sc. Dissertation, University Newcastle upon Tyne.

Phillips, B. S. (1957). A role theory approach to adjustment in old age. *Amer. Soc. Rev.* **22**, 212–217.

Pollock, H. M. (1945). A statistical review of mental disorders in later life. *In* "Mental Disorders in Later Life" (O. J. Kaplan, ed.) pp. 7–22. Stanford University Press, Stanford, California.

Post, F. (1951). The outcome of mental breakdown in old age. *Brit. Med. J.* **1**, 436–440.

Post, F. (1962a). "The Significance of Affective Symptoms in Old Age". Maudsley Monograph No. 10. Oxford University Press, London.

Post, F. (1962b). The impact of modern drug treatment on old age schizophrenia. *Geront. Clin.* **4**, 137–146.

Post, F. (1965). "The Clinical Psychiatry of Later Life". Pergamon Press, Oxford.

Post, F. (1966a). Somatic and psychic factors in the treatment of elderly psychiatric patients. *J. Psychomat. Res.* **10**, 13.

Post, F. (1966b). "Persistent Persecutory States of the Elderly". Pergamon Press, Oxford.

Post, F. (1967). Aspects of psychiatry in the elderly. *Proc. Roy. Soc. Med.* **60**, 249–260.

Post, F. (1968). The factors of ageing in affective disorders. *In* "Recent Developments in Affective Disorders" (A. J. Coppen, ed.). Royal Medico-Psychological Association, London.

Postema, L. J. and Schell, R. E. (1967). Ageing and psychopathology: some MMPI evidence for seemingly greater neurotic behaviour among older people. *J. Clin. Psychol.* **23**, 140–143.

Prados, M. and Fried, E. G. (1947). Personality structure in older age groups. *J. Clin. Psychol.* **3**, 113–120.

Primrose, E. J. R. (1962). "Psychological Illness: a Community Study". Tavistock Publications, London.

Raimy, V. C. (1943). The self concept as a factor in counseling and personality organization. Unpublished Ph.D Dissertation, Ohio State University, Ohio.

Rao, C. R. (1952). "Advanced Statistical Methods in Biometric Research". Wiley, New York.

Registrar-General (1964). "Statistical Review of England and Wales for the Year 1960" (Suppl. on Mental Health). H.M.S.O., London.

Reichard, Suzanne, Livson, Florence and Peterson, P. G. (1962). "Ageing and Personality: a Study of Eighty-Seven Older Men". Wiley, New York and London.

Rentz, R. and White, W. (1967). Congruence of the dimension of self as object and self as process. *J. Psychol.* **67**(2), 277–285.

Rogers, C. R. (1950). The significance of self-regarding attitudes and perception. *In* "Feeling and Emotion: The Mooseheart Symposium" (E. L. Reymert, ed.) pp. 374–382. McGraw-Hill, New York.

Rogers, C. R. (1951). "Client-Centered Therapy". Houghton-Mifflin, Boston.

Rogers, C. R. and Dymond, R. (1954). "Psychotherapy and Personality Change". University of Chicago Press, Chicago.

Rorschach, H. (1942). "Psychodiagnostics". Grune and Stratton, New York.

Rosen, J. L. and Neugarten, B. L. (1960). Ego functions in the middle and later years: a thematic apperception study of normal adults. *J. Gerontol.* **15**, 62–67.

Roth, M. (1955). The natural history of mental disorder in old age. *J. Ment. Sci.* **102**, 281–301.

Roth, M. (1963). Neurosis, psychosis and the concept of disease in psychiatry. *Acta Psychiat. Scand.* **89**, 128–145.

Roth, M. and Hopkins, B. (1953). Test performance of patients over 60. *J. Ment. Sci.* **99**, 439–450.

Roth, M. and Morrissey, J. D. (1952). Problems in the diagnosis and classification of mental disorder in old age. *J. Ment. Sci.* **98**, 66–80.

Roth, M., Tomlinson, B. E. and Blessed, G. (1967). The relationship between quantitative measures of dementia and of degenerative changes in the cerebral grey matter of elderly subjects. *Proc. Roy. Soc. Med.* **60**, 254–260.

Rothschild, D. (1937). Pathologic changes in senile psychoses and their psychobiologic significance. *Amer. J. Psychiat.* **93**, 757–758.

Rothschild, D. (1942). Neuropathological changes in arteriosclerotic psychoses and their psychiatric significance. *Arch. Neurol. Psychiat.* **48**, 414–436.

Rubenstein, E. and Lorr, M. (1956). A comparison of terminators and remainers in out-patient psychotherapy. *J. Clin. Psychol.* **12**, 345–349.

Rybak, W. S., Sadnavitch, J. M. and Mason, B. J. (1968). Psycho-social changes in personality during foster grandparents program. *J. Amer. Geriat. Soc.* **16**, 956–959.

Sainsbury, P. (1960). Psychosomatic disorders and neurosis in out-patients attending a general hospital. *J. Psychosom. Res.* **4**, 261–273.

Sainsbury, P. (1962). Suicide in later age. *Geront. Clin.* **4**, 161–170.

Sarbin, T. G. and Rosenberg, B. (1955). Contributions to tole-taking theory: a method for obtaining a qualitative estimate of self. *J. Soc. Psychol.* **42**, 71–81.

Savage, R. D. (1962). Personality factors and academic performance. *Brit. J. Educ. Psychol.* **32**, 251–253.

Savage, R. D. (1970a). Intellectual assessment. *In* "The Psychological Assessment of Mental and Physical Handicaps" (P. Mittler, ed.) pp. 29–81. Methuen, London.

Savage, R. D. (1970b). Psychometric assessment and clinical diagnosis in the aged. *In* "Recent Advances in Old Age" (D. W. K. Kay and A. Walk, eds.). Royal Medico-Psychological Association, London.

Savage, R. D. (1972). Old age. *In* "Handbook of Abnormal Psychology" (H. J. Eysenck, ed.) 2nd edn. Pitman's Medical Publications, London.

Savage, R. D., Britton, P. G., Bolton, N. and Hall, E. H. (1973). "Intellectual Functioning in the Aged". Methuen, London.

Savage, R. D. and Hall, E. H. (1973). A performance learning measure for the aged. *Brit. J. Psychiat.* **122**, 721–723.

Savage, R. D. and McCawley, J. (1966). The questionnaire measurement of emotionality. *In* "Readings in Clinical Psychology" (R. D. Savage, ed.). Pergamon Press, Oxford.

Saville, P. (1972). The British standardisation of the 16PF supplement of norms. NFER, Windsor.

Schaie, K. W. and Strother, C. R. (1968). The effect of time and cohort differences on the interpretation of age changes in cognitive behaviour. *Multivariate Behav. Res.* **3**, 259–294.

Sealy, A. P. E. L. (1965). Age trends in adult personality as measured by the 16PF test. *Bull. Brit. Psychol. Soc.* **18**, 59.

Sealy, A. P. E. L. and Cattell, R. B. (1965). Standard trends in personality development in men and women of 16 to 70 years determined by the 16PF measurement. Paper presented at the British Social Psychology Conference.

Semrad, E. V. and McKeon, C. C. (1941). Social factors in old age psychosis. *Dis. Nerv. System*, **2**, 58–62.

Shapiro, M. B. (1956). An experimental investigation of an anomaly in the performance of the block design test. Unpublished Ph.D., London.

Sheldon, J. H. (1948). "The Social Medicine of Old Age". Nuffield Foundation, London.

Shepard, W. P. (1955). Does the modern pace really kill? *J. Amer. Geriat. Soc.* **3**, 139–145.

Shepherd, M., Cooper, B., Brown, A. C. and Kalton, G. W. (1966). "Psychiatric Illness in General Practice". Oxford University Press, London.

Shock, N. W. (1951). Gerontology (later maturity). *Ann. Rev. Psychol.* **2**, 353–370.

Shock, N. W. (1968). Age with a future. *Gerontologist*, **8**, 147–162.

Sigal, J. J., Star, K. H. and Franks, C. M. (1958). Hysterics and dysthymics as criterion groups in the study of introversion–extraversion. *J. Abnorm. Soc. Psychol.* **57**, 143–148.

Simchowicz, I. (1910). Histologische Studien über die Senile Demenz. *Histol. Histopath. Arb.* **4**, 267–444.

Slater, E. and Roth, M. (1969). *See* Mayer-Gross, W. (1969).

Slater, P. E. and Scarr, M. A. (1964). Personality in old age. *Genet. Psychol. Monogr.* **70**, 229–269.

Star, K. H. (1957). An experimental study of "reactive-inhibition" and its relations to certain personality traits. Unpublished thesis, Univ. of London.

Stengel, E. and Cook, Nancy G. (1961). Contrasting suicide rates in industrial communities. *J. Ment. Sci.* **107**, 1011–1019.

Stenstedt, A. (1959). Involutional melancholia: an aetiological, clinical and social study of endogenous depression in later life with special reference to genetic factors. *Acta Psychiat. Neurol. Scand.* **34**, Suppl. 127.

Strong, E. K. J. (1943). "Vocational Interests of Men and Women". Stanford University Press, Stanford, California.

Sward, K. (1945). Age and mental ability in superior men. *Amer. J. Psychol.* **58**, 443–470.

Swenson, W. M. (1961). Structured personality testing in the aged: an MMPI study of the geriatric population. *J. Clin. Psychol.* **17**, 302–304.

Thomas, H. (1970). Theory of ageing and cognitive theory of personality. *Human Develop.* **13**, 1–16.

Thompson, W. (1972). "Correlates of the Self Concept". Dede Wallace Center Monograph, No. VI. Nashville, Tennessee.

Thompson, W. E., Streils, G. F. and Kosa, J. (1960). The effect of retirement on personal adjustment: a panel analysis. *J. Gerontol.* **15**, 165–169.

Tissue, M. A. (1971). Disengagement potential: replication and use as an exploratory variable. *J. Gerontol.* **26**, 76–80.

Tomlinson, B. E., Blessed, G. and Roth, M. (1968). Observations on the brain in non-demented old people. *J. Neurol. Sci.* **7**, 331–356.

Turner, B. F., Tobin, S. S. and Lieberman, M. A. (1972). Personality traits as predictors of institutional adaptation among the aged. *J. Gerontol.* **27**, 61–68.

Uecker, A. E. (1969). Comparability of two methods of administering the MMPI to brain-damaged geriatric patients. *J. Clin. Psychol.* **25**, 196–198.

Vinson, D. (1961). Objectivity in the assessment of psychobiologic decline. *Vita Humana*, **4**, 134–142.

Vispo, R. H. (1962). Pre-morbid personality in the functional psychoses of the senium. A comparison of ex-patients with healthy controls. *J. Ment. Sci.* **108**, 790–800.

Ward, J. H. (1963). Hierarchical grouping to optimize an objective function. *J. Amer. Stat. Assoc.* **58**, 344–366.

Watson, R. I. (1954). The personality of the aged: a review. *J. Gerontol.* **9**, 307–315.

Watts, C. A. H. and Watts, B. M. (1952). "Psychiatry in General Practice". Churchill, London.

Wechsler, D. (1944). "The Measurement of Adult Intelligence". 3rd edn. Williams and Wilkins, Baltimore.

Wechsler, D. (1958). "The Measurement and Appraisal of Adult Intelligence". 4th edn. Williams and Wilkins, Baltimore.

Welford, A. T. (1958). "Ageing and Human Skill". Oxford University Press, London (for Nuffield Foundation).

Welford, A. T. (1964). The study of ageing. *In* "Experimental Psychology" (A. Summerfield, ed.). *Brit. Med. Bull.* **20**, 65–69.

Welford, A. T. (1968). "Fundamentals of Skill". Methuen, London.

Welsh, G. S. (1952). An anxiety index and internalisation ratio for the MMPI. *J. Consult. Psychol.* **16**, 65–72.

Welsh, G. S. (1956). Factor dimensions A and R. *In* "Basic Readings on the MMPI in Psychology and Medicine" (G. S. Welsh and W. G. Dahlstrom, eds.). University of Minnesota Press, Minneapolis.

Williams, H. L., Quesnel, E., Fish, V. W. and Goodman, L. (1942). Studies in senile and arteriosclerotic psychoses. *Amer. J. Psychiat.* **98**, 712–715.

Williamson, J., Stokoe, I. H., Gray, S., Fisher, M., Smith, A., McGhee, A. and Stephenson, E. (1964). Old people at home: their unreported needs. *Lancet*, **i**, 1117–1120.

Willoughby, R. R. (1938). The relationship to emotionality of age, sex and conjugal condition. *Amer. J. Sociol.* **43**, 920–931.

Witkin, H. A., Lewis, H. B., Hertzman, M., Machover, K., Meissner, P. B. and Wapner, S. (1954). "Personality through Perception: an Experimental and Clinical Study". Harper and Row, New York.

Wood, V., Whylie, M. and Sheafor, B. (1969). An analysis of a short self report measure of life satisfaction: correlation with rater judgements. *J. Gerontol.* **24**, 465–469.

World Health Organisation (1959). Mental health problems of ageing and the aged. *WHO Techn. Rep. Ser.*, 171.

Zimmer, M. (1954). Self-acceptance and its relation to conflict. *J. Consult. Psychol.* **18**, 447–449.

Author Index

179

Subject Index